MASS INCARCERATION NATION

The United States imprisons a higher proportion of its population than any other nation. Mass Incarceration Nation offers a novel, in-the-trenches perspective to explain the factors – historical, political, and institutional – that led to the current system of mass imprisonment. The book examines the causes and impacts of mass incarceration on both the political and criminal justice systems. With accessible language and straightforward statistical analysis, former prosecutor turned law professor Jeffrey Bellin provides a formula for reform to return to the low incarceration rates that characterized the United States prior to the 1970s.

JEFFREY BELLIN is the Mills E. Godwin, Jr., Professor at William & Mary Law School.

Mass Incarceration Nation

HOW THE UNITED STATES BECAME ADDICTED TO PRISONS AND JAILS AND HOW IT CAN RECOVER

Jeffrey Bellin
William & Mary Law School

CAMBRIDGE
UNIVERSITY PRESS

Shaftesbury Road, Cambridge CB2 8EA, United Kingdom

One Liberty Plaza, 20th Floor, New York, NY 10006, USA

477 Williamstown Road, Port Melbourne, VIC 3207, Australia

314–321, 3rd Floor, Plot 3, Splendor Forum, Jasola District Centre, New Delhi – 110025, India

103 Penang Road, #05–06/07, Visioncrest Commercial, Singapore 238467

Cambridge University Press is part of Cambridge University Press & Assessment, a department of the University of Cambridge.

We share the University's mission to contribute to society through the pursuit of education, learning and research at the highest international levels of excellence.

www.cambridge.org
Information on this title: www.cambridge.org/9781009267540

DOI: 10.1017/9781009267595

First published 2023

A catalogue record for this publication is available from the British Library.

Library of Congress Cataloging-in-Publication Data
Names: Bellin, Jeffrey, author.
Title: Mass incarceration nation : how the United States became addicted to prisons and jails and how it can recover / Jeffrey Bellin, William & Mary Law School.
Description: First edition. | Cambridge, United Kingdom ; New York, NY : Cambridge University Press, 2023. | Includes bibliographical references and index.
Identifiers: LCCN 2022025431 (print) | LCCN 2022025432 (ebook) | ISBN 9781009267540 (hardback) | ISBN 9781009267557 (paperback) | ISBN 9781009267595 (epub)
Subjects: LCSH: Criminal justice, Administration of–United States. | Imprisonment–United States. | Sentences (Criminal procedure)–United States. | Law reform–United States.
Classification: LCC KF9223 .B45 2023 (print) | LCC KF9223 (ebook) | DDC 345.73/05–dc23/eng/20220830
LC record available at https://lccn.loc.gov/2022025431
LC ebook record available at https://lccn.loc.gov/2022025432

ISBN 978-1-009-26754-0 Hardback
ISBN 978-1-009-26755-7 Paperback

CONTENTS

FIGURES

TABLES

ACKNOWLEDGMENTS

Thanks to the numerous scholars who offered feedback on either the entire manuscript or specific chapters, including Rachel Barkow, Shima Baughman, Bennett Capers, Andrew Ferguson, Brandon Garrett, Adam Gershowitz, Ryken Grattet, Ben Grunwald, Carissa Hessick, Laura Heymann, Shon Hopwood, Darrell Jackson, Ben Levin, Sandy Mason, Rebecca Roiphe, David Sklansky, and Chris Slobogin. Alexa Deutsch and Fred Dingledy provided invaluable research assistance. Thanks as well to the faculties at William & Mary and Vanderbilt Law School, who helped me fine-tune my ideas in workshops. And thanks to the researchers at the Bureau of Justice Statistics, the Pew Research Center, and elsewhere, who collected and compiled some of the data described in this book. Finally, this book would not be possible without the support of my institution, William & Mary Law School, Dean Ben Spencer, and, more than anything else, my family.

INTRODUCTION

In 2019, the United States locked up almost 2 million people. And there is no simple explanation for what is going on. There were 196,300 people imprisoned for homicides and another 176,300 people in prison for drug offenses. Each of those numbers is close to three times the entire prison population of countries like France (75,000) or Germany (60,000), and each number rivals the United States' total prison population in the early 1970s (200,000). Add in all the people incarcerated for other crimes, and those awaiting trial in jail, and you get 2 million – a number that would have been incomprehensible fifty years ago.[1]

In 2020, America's prison population declined 15 percent in the wake of a global pandemic that slowed court operations and pushed officials to ease the crowding of correctional facilities. But with law enforcement operations returning to normal and a growing perception of rising crime, this welcome decline is already showing signs of reversal.[2]

This book answers the increasingly important and surprisingly complex questions of how we got here – and what needs to change. These are questions that I have thought about for decades both as an academic researcher who studies Mass Incarceration and also as a participant in the phenomenon. In the early 2000s, as Mass Incarceration took hold across America, I worked in one of the country's largest law enforcement offices, the US Attorney's Office for the District of Columbia. I was "Jeffrey Bellin for the United States," prosecuting crimes ranging from drug sales to murder.

When I joined the US Attorney's Office, D.C. was trying to shed its reputation as the nation's "murder capital." Viewed through one lens, my office could have been the backdrop for any of the crime dramas that saturate American television, *Law and Order: District of Columbia*. In 1991, D.C. hosted almost 500 murders – a record high. By 2000, the number was down to 239, but that's still a lot for a small city. Overwhelmed D.C. police solved only about a third of murders, and our office tried to obtain convictions in those cases.[3]

Barely a year out of law school, I found my caseload included seven murder appeals. Each case told a different terrible story. Here's one of the worst. There had been a triple murder at a Starbucks. A civic-minded drug user thought the folks in a local drug house knew who did it. He contacted the police and offered to go undercover. The undercover operation was a complete failure. As police handlers waited outside in a squad car, a group of people stomped the informant to death in an alley behind the house. Under intense media scrutiny and facing a lawsuit from the informant's family, the police tracked down a guy nicknamed "Bruiser" who, witnesses claimed, was responsible for the worst of the stomping. A jury convicted and the judge sentenced him to the "maximum sentence," twenty years to life in prison. As I worked on the appeal in my windowless office, I got a surprise visit from *the* United States attorney – "don't screw this up kid." I didn't. Bruiser is one of the 2 million people that make up Mass Incarceration.[4]

That's one sliver of American criminal law enforcement, and the part that best fits the traditional label, "the criminal justice system." People are accused of grave offenses and the government seeks to hold them accountable. And increasingly over the past decades that meant that people who committed serious violent crimes served long prison terms. But there are lots of other parts of the criminal law landscape that look very different.

After the Appeals section, I moved to the first of my trial rotations: Misdemeanors. Here, most of the cases were small. Formal intervention seemed pointless: a packet of drugs in the console of a car; minor assaults; soliciting prostitution. There was a police officer who would leave a convertible filled with stereo equipment in busy areas of the city. When someone grabbed the stuff, the officer swooped in to make an arrest.

Few misdemeanor cases could be framed as quests for justice. That didn't change as much as you'd think when I graduated to felonies. The Felony Trial section included some cases where justice played a role. But most of the cases concerned car thefts, gun possession, and lots and lots of drug sales. In college, I had written a column for the student paper arguing that drugs should be decriminalized. A few years later, I was prosecuting drug cases. I rationalized that the legislature had the power to pass criminal laws (even ones I didn't like) and prosecutors (or at least line prosecutors like me) had to apply them. Still, these weren't cases that anyone in the office got excited about. We told ourselves we were just enforcing the law.

Years later, I was teaching a class about a 2009 Supreme Court case on car searches. Buried in the case is testimony from a Tucson (Arizona) police officer about why he searched a car leading to the discovery of a bag of cocaine and a gun. You'd expect the answer to focus on the reasons he expected to find this contraband. Instead, the officer said he searched the car "because the law says we can do it."[5] That answer struck me as expressing a larger truth about what the system had become. As Mass Incarceration spread across the nation, government officials increasingly locked people up because the law said they could. This wasn't about justice. Criminal laws had become, at best, a policy tool that politicians used to discourage behaviors, like drug use or drunk driving or possessing weapons. At worst, these laws were toxic vectors for bias and discrimination. Whichever characterization you prefer, the criminal **justice** system was becoming a criminal **legal** system. Criminal courts were moving away from their core purpose: as a forum where citizens went to obtain justice. Courts were increasingly a place where the government went to enforce the law.

As I worked on this book, I began to see that a lot of the disagreements about American criminal law stem from conflating two distinct systems: (1) a criminal justice system where the public seeks justice in response to crimes like murder and rape and (2) a criminal legal system where the government enforces a variety of laws ostensibly to achieve certain policy goals, like reducing drug abuse or gun violence or illegal immigration. As I will explain in the pages that follow, both of these systems became more punitive during the rise of Mass Incarceration, but it is necessary to analyze them separately for the overall phenomenon to make sense.

★★★

It all starts, counterintuitively, with a police force that catches only a fraction of the people who commit even serious crimes. The crime most likely to be solved in this country is murder, with about 60 percent of homicides leading to an arrest. The arrest rate plummets for other crimes. About 35 percent of reported rapes lead to an arrest; 30 percent of robberies; 20 percent of arsons; 13 percent of burglaries; 13 percent of car thefts. That's *reported* crimes. Only about a third of rapes are ever reported to police.[6] The probability of getting arrested for crimes like drug dealing or tax cheating or theft is probably less than 1 percent.

Things don't improve much after an arrest. For example, in 2000, my office filed almost 23,000 criminal cases. We resolved about 15,000 over the course of the year. The most common resolution? Dismissed. There were 811 guilty verdicts after trial, 381 acquittals, 6,505 guilty pleas, and almost **8,000 dismissals**.[7]

Hard to believe? Here's a chart for the D.C. Office that I found buried deep in the Department of Justice's 2000 annual report (Tables I.1 and I.2).

Table I.1 *Washington, D.C., case outcomes: Dispositions*

Case Dispositions		
	Number of Guilty Pleas	Number of Dismissals
Felony	2,723	1,931
Misdemeanor	3,782	5,864
Total	6,505	7,795

Table I.2 *Washington, D.C., case outcomes: Convictions*

Convictions		
	Number of Convictions	Conviction Rate (%)
Felony	2,951	58.7
Misdemeanor	4,365	41.6
Total	7,316	47.1

Note the 41.6 percent conviction rate for misdemeanors. Things improved for felonies, but not much (convictions in 58.7 percent of filed felony cases). This isn't the kind of thing prosecutors advertise. Dismissals rarely make the news. I wouldn't have believed it if I hadn't experienced it myself.

When my friends asked me what I did as a prosecutor, I'd joke that I dismissed cases. The police thought the same thing. If the D.C. police wrote the introductory segment to *Law and Order*, the show's famous slogan would be very different: "In the criminal justice system, the people are represented by two separate yet equally important groups. The police who investigate crime and the district attorneys who dismiss their cases."

But this was only part of a larger truth. With thousands of cases pouring into the system, the stars frequently aligned. The officers showed up, the drug analysis came back on time, the witnesses and the defendant came to court, the jury convicted or the defendant pled guilty, and the conviction held up on appeal. Even with all those dismissals, there were thousands of convictions: thousands of people in D.C. and across the country rotating in and out of jails and prisons.

Low arrest rates and frequent dismissals seem out of place in a discussion of Mass Incarceration. But they are critical to understanding the phenomenon. American penal severity expanded through a series of policy choices, like longer sentences and a war on drugs. But the government officials across the political spectrum who made those choices weren't trying to fill prisons. At least, that's not how they sold these policies to the public. Politicians claimed to be trying to solve the problem of crime. The critical flaw in the last fifty years of "tough on crime" policies is that this never works.

Deterrence – preventing crime through punishment – works when people expect to be caught. That's not the system we've built. In a free society with large, sprawling cities and some semblance of individual rights, it is hard to detect crimes and even harder to convict those we suspect are guilty. Increasing criminal punishments is like increasing a lottery prize from $1 million to $50 million. It's a big deal for the winner, but for most people nothing changes. Increasing the penalties for crime in this country didn't end crime. Crime continued to ebb and flow as it had for centuries. Our "tough on crime" policies filled prisons with a small percentage but growing number of unlucky "criminals." And once they got locked up, tougher laws and tougher officials made sure they stayed locked up. In D.C., I saw this all firsthand. We were punishing a handful of serious crimes severely, a smaller percentage of moderate crimes moderately, and throwing a tiny fraction of minor offenders in jail. This system may seem sensible when you look at an individual case. But when you step back and take in the big picture, it becomes clear that, as a country, we lost our way.

What went wrong? In the early 1970s, the US incarceration rate was low and unremarkable. Then, spurred by a temporary spike in crime, everyone discovered something they wanted to punish more severely. From liberal Senator Ted Kennedy to conservative evangelist Pat Robertson, the details (and motives) differed, but the broad themes were consistent: Americans wanted tougher laws, tougher cops, tougher prosecutors, and tougher judges. We got our wish. The changes spread through the system in two distinct but overlapping waves. In the 1970s and 1980s, additional police and harsher laws targeted the crimes that were spiking: homicides, robberies, rapes, burglaries. When those crimes fell in the 1990s, however, arrest numbers continued at around the same level, and convictions actually increased. These numbers stayed high even as crime dropped because the system pivoted to commonly occurring, easily detected, and readily provable offenses where arrests were driven by law enforcement resource allocations (like drugs) or whose characterization often hinged on subjective assessments (like assault). And because this second wave of aggressive law enforcement had more to do with policy choices than crime, it predictably fell on the easiest targets – which in this country often means the poor and minorities.

Now it seems like the punitive consensus is crumbling, but the new consensus may not be that different from the old. When crime goes down, as it has now for decades, prison populations decrease. But, for the reasons explored in the pages that follow, that will only push on the margins. And those gains are easily reversed with increases in crime and the shiny new laws that follow in the wake of each new tragedy. It may be comforting to think of Mass Incarceration as a temporary problem created by a few familiar villains – and that's how typical treatments of the topic are framed. But the villains in this story aren't (only) racist Southerners or Richard Nixon or the drafters of the Thirteenth Amendment. The villains aren't just police or prosecutors or politicians. The villains include us, the American public, and we are the ones who need to turn things around.

A precise diagnosis of the causes of Mass Incarceration is vital because it highlights a promising pathway to the phenomenon's demise. Simply put, we can look at what changed between the 1970s and today and, with respect to incarceration, change things back to the way they were. The country has made great progress in the past fifty years, but one area where we went backward is criminal law enforcement. Invoking the rhetoric of justice, we ratcheted up severity and then, with little thought, applied the increased severity to an expanding catalog of crimes that had little to do with justice. For the offenses where it played a role, "justice" increasingly meant more prison time. For the vast bulk of offenses, however, justice played no role at all; the criminal courts became just another local bureaucracy processing an endless flow of cases in what could, at best, be characterized as a myopic effort to "enforce the law."

This book fills out the sketch offered above, laying out, step by step, what changed after the 1970s and how those changes led to Mass Incarceration. It begins with an explanation of why this matters. Part I offers a snapshot of where we are today, stuck on a plateau of historically unprecedented incarceration rates, exceeding those of any country in the world. These rates can be found across the nation, not just in one region or a handful of States. And while there has been some progress in recent years, the big picture has not changed. It is the scope and persistence of American Mass Incarceration that makes the phenomenon so important, so difficult to understand, and so remarkable.

Part II travels fifty years into the past to explore how we went from long-standing, unremarkable incarceration rates to Mass Incarceration. It highlights a crime surge that increased the popular appeal of new criminal laws and spawned "tough on crime" rhetoric and attitudes that continue to haunt our public discourse. These laws and attitudes emerged as a response to violent crimes but steadily expanded to encompass all forms of criminal law enforcement, from drug offenses to drunk driving to violations of conditions of release (parole and probation).

Part III turns to the mechanics of Mass Incarceration, the police, prosecutors, judges, and parole-probation officers who enforce the criminal laws. This part presents an essential supplement to the standard narrative about the "tough on crime" laws that gave rise to Mass Incarceration. Increased severity always requires two components: harsher laws and harsher enforcement. After the 1970s, a new consensus emerged with all of the law enforcement actors gravitating toward the same punitive methods. With everyone on the same page, the system's expanding focus and increased severity collided with ongoing crime to fill prisons and jails. Finally, Part IV lays out the long road to recovery. This Part reframes the preceding discussion as a road map for reform. The clearest solution to the problem of Mass Incarceration is to identify the things that changed since the 1970s with respect to incarceration and change them back.

A note on methodology. Wherever possible in the pages that follow, I test my arguments against the historical data and lay out that data for readers to draw their own conclusions. To enhance the transparency of the presentation and allow skeptics to check my claims, I rely as much as possible on the most widely accepted, official, public data sources.

I often highlight 2019 data even when more recent data is available because the most recent data is skewed by the impact of Covid-19. For example, the Bureau of Justice Statistics flags the "40% decrease in admissions to state and federal prison from 2019" to 2020 as a temporary anomaly, stating: "The COVID-19 pandemic was largely responsible for the decline in prisoners under state and federal correctional authority" because "[c]ourts significantly altered operations for part or all of 2020, leading to delays in trials and/or sentencing of persons."[8] That said, Covid-19's impact may mask the results of budding reforms and could spur policy makers to turn temporary reductions into permanent ones. This book offers support for doing just that.

PART I

What Is Mass Incarceration?

Any book about "Mass Incarceration" should begin with an explanation of that phrase. Clarity about the phenomenon adds precision to explanations of how it came about and the transformative changes needed to reverse it.

1 DEFINITION

In 1970, the United States locked up approximately 200,000 people in state and federal prisons, with another 161,000 in local jails. The country's incarceration rate – the number of people incarcerated as a percentage of the overall population – had been remarkably steady for decades and not that different from other Western nations, like England, France, or Germany.

Since then, incarceration shot up rapidly until it plateaued in the 2000s at previously unimagined levels. In recent years, the United States has averaged around 1.5 million people confined in state and federal prisons, with another 700,000 held in local jails. In addition to the stark human toll represented by those numbers, there is also a financial cost. Between 1982 and 2010, the total amount spent by the States on incarceration (including parole and probation) rose from $15 billion a year to $48.5 billion. Between 1980 and 2013, annual federal corrections spending grew from under $1 billion to almost $7 billion.[1]

There is some cause for optimism. The most recent incarceration numbers reflect modest decreases. The public appears to be waking to the problem of overbearing law enforcement. In addition, Covid-19 forced government officials to confront the public health consequences of crowded correctional institutions, leading to a reduction in jail populations. But jail populations are rebounding, and prison populations remain stubbornly high. Despite recent progress, we are closer to landing an astronaut on Mars than we are to returning to 1970s incarceration levels.

It is impossible to pinpoint one moment as the point when America reached Mass Incarceration. Despite that imprecision, it is easy to explain experts' confidence in using the label. That's because Mass

Incarceration isn't a number; it is a matter of degree. There are three ways to look at it.

1. **Historical.** We have simply never experienced anything like the current number of people incarcerated or rate of incarceration. Until the 1970s, America had roughly the same, low incarceration rate. In fact, in 1973, two prominent scholars published an article titled "A Theory of the Stability of Punishment." The article stressed the consistency of incarceration in the United States, highlighting that between 1930 and 1970, "the imprisonment rate was reasonably constant, having an average value of 110.2 prisoners per 100,000 population." The authors argued that this demonstrated that "there are a variety of processes in the society which operate to maintain a constant level of punishment, and this level adapts to changing levels of actual crimes."[2] Shortly after the article was published, the incarceration rate began its steady climb, disproving the authors' thesis. The American incarceration rate increased to more than 700 per 100,000 in the 1990s, before dipping to 629 per 100,000 in 2019 and 551 per 100,000 in 2020.[3] The 1973 article is famous, but it is famous for being incredibly wrong.

2. **Comparative.** Another way to think about incarceration is to compare the United States to other countries. Again, we stand alone. No other country incarcerates as high a proportion of its population as we do.

   Table 1.1 uses the most recent data from the World Prison Brief to compare each nation's incarcerated populations. The second column is the country's incarceration rate (per 100,000 population); the third column is the number of people incarcerated. The first five countries in the chart are the world's top incarcerators by rate. The next entries represent notable examples from around the world and include the top five incarcerators in terms of absolute numbers.[4]

   This is not a list that any country wants to top. But there we are. When it comes to throwing our own people in prison, we are #1.

Table 1.1 *Worldwide incarceration*

Country	Rate	Number
United States	629	2,068,800
Rwanda	580	76,099
Turkmenistan	576	35,000
El Salvador	564	36,663
Cuba	510	57,337
Brazil	381	811,707
Russia	322	465,896
Mexico	171	223,416
U.K.	132	79,412
China	119	1,690,000
France	103	69,812
Japan	37	47,064
India	35	488,511

With any criminal justice data, caveats are in order – and comparing across countries is especially tricky. Data is easier to obtain for the United States than for many of the other countries on this list. And the fine print in the World Prison Brief data actually suggests that China, not the United States, locks up the most people. The numbers provided by the Chinese government do not include pretrial detainees and persons held in "administrative detention" – a group that is estimated to include as many as 650,000 people. Adding in that number would push China's incarcerated population above that of the United States. In addition, China carries out executions estimated in the thousands per year and reportedly holds a large number of Uyghurs in some form of detention. But China's population is much higher. The fairest way to assess incarceration is rate. And in terms of incarceration rate, the United States is the world's unquestioned leader.

3. **Excess.** A final way to think about Mass Incarceration is that we are incarcerating more than we need to. The most frequent justification for incarceration is that it reduces crime. And, in fact, some studies find that a 10 percent increase in incarceration reduces the crime rate by about 2–4 percent.[5] But these studies offer little support for the degree of incarceration in America. As to whether the levels of incarceration maintained for decades in this country are necessary

to fight crime, the National Research Council offered this conclusion: "The increase in incarceration may have caused a decrease in crime, but the magnitude of the reduction is highly uncertain and the results of most studies suggest it was unlikely to have been large."[6]

That is because the same evidence that suggests that incarceration reduces crime also warns of a diminishing rate of return. In jurisdictions with high crime and few people incarcerated, an increase could meaningfully affect crime rates by taking the worst, most frequent offenders off the streets. When a system already imprisons hundreds of thousands, that effect disappears. As a result, the expert consensus is that whatever benefits come from penal severity, we are way overdoing it.

We are also incarcerating some groups much more than others. At times during the era of Mass Incarceration, African Americans, who make up about 12 percent of the American population, accounted for almost half of the prison population.[7] As Chapter 9 discusses in more detail, that disparity raises important questions about the legitimacy of the law enforcement enterprise and, combined with this country's history of racial subordination, hints that there is more going on than crime and punishment.

1.1 OBJECTIONS AND ALTERNATIVE DEFINITIONS

Some people object to the term "Mass Incarceration." Former FBI director James Comey wrote in his memoir that he found President Barack Obama's use of the term "insulting": "It was inaccurate in the sense that there was nothing 'mass' about the incarceration: every defendant was charged individually, represented individually by counsel, convicted by a court individually, sentenced individually, reviewed on appeal individually, and incarcerated. That added up to a lot of people in jail, but there was nothing 'mass' about it."[8]

This kind of objection misses the point. It is true that every incarcerated person went through a process. Every one of those individuals has an important story to tell. But what is of primary importance to researchers, government officials, citizens, and presidents is the large number of these stories. Every society responds when people break its rules. What differentiates the United States at this moment both from every other country and from every other period in our own history is the extent to which we rely on incarceration. It's the "mass" of it that demands the nation's collective attention.

And contrary to Comey's objection, we use "mass" like this all the time. The phrase "mass production" doesn't mean every widget is created instantly with a push of a button. When "mass hysteria" strikes, each person freaks out individually, but *all* the people freaking out is what gets our attention. Scientists refer to the passing of the dinosaurs as a "mass extinction." Each dinosaur died in its own way and at different moments, but what matters if you are researching dinosaurs, or living among them, is that so many of them died.

That's the phenomenon we are talking about, and that's why we call it **Mass** Incarceration. It's not an insult to the people like Comey (or me) who worked in the criminal justice system. It doesn't ignore the individuals who serve time in prison or jail. It's a way to bring attention to the scale of all those individuals locked up through individualized processes. It's a way to say that even though there are lots of other important things that demand our attention, like climate change or pandemics, this is something we need to understand and try to fix.

There are also different perspectives on the **incarceration** part of the phrase. When this book discusses incarceration, it is referring to locking people up in prisons and jails. Other scholars, such as Michelle Alexander, use a broader definition of the term. In her groundbreaking book *The New Jim Crow*, Alexander writes, "The term *mass incarceration* refers not only to the criminal justice system but also to the web of laws, rules, policies, and customs that control those labeled criminals both in and outside of prison."[9] To my mind, noncustodial punishments and stigmas, like restrictions on voting and difficulties obtaining housing or employment, stretch the term "incarceration" too far. Using the term "incarceration" in its conventional sense allows me to narrow the discussion, making an almost impossibly complex topic manageable. This focus admittedly leaves out some important aspects of the system, but the benefits of this focus outweigh the costs. While there are a wide variety of negative consequences that flow from a criminal conviction, incarceration is invariably the most serious (apart from rare executions). Also, virtually every solution to Mass

Incarceration referenced in the pages that follow will reduce collateral consequences like voting restrictions that accompany incarceration, even if those consequences are not directly addressed.

Finally, because this is a book about the criminal law and its enforcement, it will not address the tens of thousands of people locked up in America's civil immigration detention facilities or the approximately 30,000 people held involuntarily in mental institutions through civil commitment proceedings.[10] These are both important topics and fit conceptually under the term "incarceration." But they represent specialized applications of a different body of laws and processes, and so require separate treatment.

2 THE DEPRIVATION OF INCARCERATION

While this book seeks to move past anecdotes and rhetoric by relying, whenever possible, on data and large-scale statistical analysis, it is important not to lose sight of the awesome deprivation of liberty suffered by the people reflected in that data. People incarcerated in prisons and jails are subject to a host of harms, including physical injuries inflicted by guards and other inmates. Many facilities offer poor access to medical care, and the cramped setting creates fertile ground for the spread of illness. One study of the health impacts of New York prisons found "a 2-year decline in life expectancy for each year served in prison."[1]

The deprivations suffered by people imprisoned by the government begin at the threshold of the process. In 2012, the US Supreme Court considered the case of Albert Florence, who was arrested in New Jersey because the State's records (mistakenly) reflected that he had failed to pay a fine imposed in an earlier criminal case. Florence was held for seven days before the charge was dismissed. Once released, he brought a lawsuit challenging jail policies that required him to undergo multiple strip searches during his short detention. The Supreme Court related Florence's description of one of the searches as follows:

> When they left the holding cell, they were instructed to remove their clothing while an officer looked for body markings, wounds, and contraband. [A]n officer looked at their ears, nose, mouth, hair, scalp, fingers, hands, arms, armpits, and other body openings. This policy applied regardless of the circumstances of the arrest, the suspected offense, or the detainee's behavior, demeanor, or criminal history. Petitioner alleges he was required to lift his genitals, turn around, and cough in a squatting position as part of the process. After a mandatory shower, during which his clothes were inspected, petitioner was admitted to the facility.[2]

Reflecting a judicial tradition of "deference ... to the officials in charge," the Supreme Court dismissed Florence's lawsuit. Writing for the Court, Justice Anthony Kennedy explained that: "Maintaining safety and order at these institutions requires the expertise of correctional officials, who must have substantial discretion to devise reasonable solutions to the problems they face."

Few experts were surprised that the Supreme Court signed off on jail strip searches. Strip searches are far from the worst aspect of incarceration. But this legally sanctioned intrusion, broadly applied at the threshold of the detention process, symbolizes the awesome deprivations that await when the State imprisons its citizens. Anyone locked up is at the mercy of local government officials. It takes only slight imagination to appreciate the risks of placing hundreds of thousands of people in this situation every year for decades.

One of the gravest dangers of incarceration is physical harm. A federal judge writing in 1980 highlighted this danger in a ruling commanding Texas to reduce overcrowding in the State's prisons: "[V]irtually all inmates are exposed to, and many are victimized by, the concomitants of unguarded, overcrowded cells and dormitories, the ever-present risk of assaults, rapes and other violence for every day of their incarceration."[3]

Even without active victimization at the hands of guards or other inmates, prisoners face grave danger from neglect. A 2011 Supreme Court opinion in another case where the courts confronted prison overcrowding, this time in California, illustrates this stark reality. Justice Kennedy, again writing for the Court, explained:

> Prisoners are crammed into spaces neither designed nor intended to house inmates. As many as 200 prisoners may live in a gymnasium, monitored by as few as two or three correctional officers. As many as 54 prisoners may share a single toilet.
>
> Prisoners in California with serious mental illness do not receive minimal, adequate care. Because of a shortage of treatment beds, suicidal inmates may be held for prolonged periods in telephone-booth-sized cages without toilets. A psychiatric expert reported observing an inmate who had been held in such a cage for nearly 24 hours, standing in a pool of his own urine, unresponsive and nearly catatonic. Prison officials explained they had "no place

to put him.".... Wait times for mental health care range as high as 12 months. ...

Prisoners suffering from physical illness also receive severely deficient care. ... A correctional officer testified that, in one prison, up to 50 sick inmates may be held together in a 12-by-20-foot cage for up to five hours awaiting treatment. The number of staff is inadequate, and prisoners face significant delays in access to care. A prisoner with severe abdominal pain died after a 5-week delay in referral to a specialist; a prisoner with "constant and extreme" chest pain died after an 8-hour delay in evaluation by a doctor; and a prisoner died of testicular cancer after a "failure of MDs to [treat] a young man with 17 months of testicular pain."[4]

It is no small thing to lock up a human being. When the government imprisons over 2 million people, harms like those described above are inevitable. Improving prison conditions is one solution. But unless we decrease the scale of incarceration, there will always be stories like these, and countless other instances of human misery that never find their way into the pages of books.

3 WHERE IS MASS INCARCERATION?

The key to understanding the "American criminal justice system" is that there is no such thing. There are, instead, thousands of local systems, each functioning in different ways.

At the most basic level, each of the fifty States has its own distinct system. If you rob a store in Texas, you've violated section 29.02 of the Texas Penal Code. You can get arrested by a Texas sheriff, prosecuted by a Texas district attorney, convicted by a Texas jury, and sent to a Texas prison (for up to twenty years) by a judge elected by Texas voters. A Texas parole board will refuse to let you out, and the Texas governor will decline to grant you a pardon. You will become a part of Mass Incarceration: the Texas part.

As far as States go, Texas is the biggest contributor to Mass Incarceration. Texans like to say, "Everything is bigger in Texas." Incarceration is no exception. But it's not just Texas. It's a fifty-one-part problem: fifty States and the federal government. The best way to predict which States have the most people locked up is to look at the States with the most people. Some States (like Texas) and some regions (like the South) lock up more Americans than others, but it's not just one place or one region.

Table 3.1 shows the count of prisoners by jurisdiction in descending order for the seven jurisdictions that combine to lock up about half of the prisoners in the United States. It also shows the prisoner counts in 1972 and the percentage change since that time.[1]

Over a period when the nation's population increased about 55 percent, federal and State prison populations increased more than ten times that. That's Mass Incarceration. And in America, it's everywhere.

Table 3.1 *Incarceration by jurisdiction*

	2019	1972	% change
Federal	175,116	21,713	+707
Texas	158,429	15,709	+909
California	122,687	16,970	+623
Florida	96,009	10,382	+825
Georgia	54,816	8,225	+566
Ohio	50,338	8,276	+508
New York	43,500	11,693	+272
All Others	729,910	103,124	+608

Within each State, there is further variation, with distinct local systems of law enforcement, driven by sheriffs, police chiefs, district attorneys (prosecutors), and judges. Mass Incarceration isn't just an outcome of fifty State processes; it's the result of local processes in over 3,000 counties. This decentralization is what makes Mass Incarceration so complex – and so remarkable.

The splintered nature of American criminal justice invites oversimplification. For example, the media often exaggerates the importance of the federal government in causing (and undoing) Mass Incarceration. Most law enforcement is handled by local authorities. That means Mass Incarceration is primarily a State phenomenon. In 2019, for example, there were 163,653 people locked up in federal prisons and 1,249,717 people in State prisons (see Figure 3.1).

But labeling Mass Incarceration a State phenomenon is also a simplification, since there is not one "State" jurisdiction. Each of the fifty States has its own distinct approach to criminal justice, and each contributes to Mass Incarceration in its own way.

The federal government filled its prisons by targeting a handful of crimes, primarily involving drugs, guns, and immigration. As detailed in Chapter 19, the formula was straightforward. Congress increased funding for law enforcement agencies like the Drug Enforcement Agency and the Federal Bureau of Investigation and increased the penalties for federal crimes through mandatory minimum sentences, strict sentencing guidelines, and the elimination of federal parole.

States followed different trajectories to a similar outcome. Texas topped the Mass Incarceration chart without any of the federal

Prisoners 2019

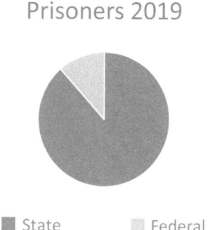

State   Federal

Figure 3.1 State versus federal

ingredients. Texas police and prosecutors focused on a different mix of crimes. The State didn't need mandatory minimums to promote severe sentencing. Texas judges (and juries) were willing to hand down long sentences without legislative mandates. Texas did not abolish its parole system. Instead, it took steps to ensure that the parole board granted fewer early releases. Texas and the federal system took different paths to Mass Incarceration, but they ended up at the same place. The other States fell somewhere in between. Each has its own wrinkles, combining tougher laws with tougher officials to lock more people up and keep them locked up longer.

To unpack this paradox of variation and consistency, legal scholar Franklin Zimring applied a statistical lens to the growth in incarceration rates of all fifty States. He concluded that the distinctions between the States' post-1970s prison growth rates fit neatly into a normal statistical distribution. Thus, while different States incarcerate at meaningfully different rates, that is largely a function of distinctions that predated Mass Incarceration. Zimring concludes that the spike in incarceration across the country – every State's remarkable upward trajectory starting in the 1970s – is best viewed as "50 different outcomes of a uniform process."[2]

Just as no one jurisdiction can be blamed for Mass Incarceration, no one law is at fault either. This comes up when people try to blame specific politicians for Mass Incarceration. For example, during the 2020 presidential campaign, a reporter for PolitiFact asked me to "fact-check" a statement by then-presidential candidate Joe Biden, one of the sponsors of the Violent Crime Control and Law Enforcement Act of 1994 ("the 1994 Crime Bill"). At a campaign event, Biden said, "This idea that the ('94) crime bill generated mass incarceration – it *did not generate mass incarceration.*"

Here's my response: "The 1994 bill did not cause Mass Incarceration, but it is a little misleading to frame the issue as whether the bill 'generate[d]' mass incarceration. No one piece of legislation or policy decision caused mass incarceration. It was a series of many laws and policy changes over time. The 1994 bill was one of those changes." The reporter thanked me for the answer but didn't print it. Nobody likes nuance anymore. But in this context it is unavoidable. The key to understanding Mass Incarceration is that lots of different government officials were doing lots of different things over long periods of time. Most of these actions either increased the number of folks sent to prison, lengthened prison stays, or both. Parts II and III turn to the precise laws and mechanisms that filled our prisons and jails. For now, it is enough to see that there was no single pathway to Mass Incarceration. Instead, there were countless local variations on a common theme.

4 DISTINGUISHING THE CRIMINAL JUSTICE AND CRIMINAL LEGAL SYSTEMS

As we will see in the chapters to come, there is wide variety among and across different American jurisdictions in the causes and motives of the march toward increased penal severity. Generalization is possible but requires separating the system into two components: the "criminal justice system" and the "criminal legal system."

I borrow the latter term from a debate among criminal scholars. In the past few years, many scholars stopped using the phrase "criminal justice system." To these scholars, the system is undeserving of the "justice" label. Instead, they describe it as the "criminal legal system" or even the "criminal punishment system." I continue to use the label "criminal justice system," in part because that is the phrase most people recognize. I also think there is value in holding on to the word *justice* to emphasize that, whatever its faults, the system's primary focus *should* be "justice." That said, I think there is an important message in the critiques of those who switched to using "criminal legal system" and adopt their insight to describe the large and growing portions of the system that have little to do with justice.

There are always two types of cases pouring into criminal courts. The first set of cases, epitomized by homicides, are cases that the system has little choice but to forcefully address. A person is accused of a serious crime. The public demands justice. Rather than leaving justice to informal resolution among civilians, government officials funnel widespread concern and outrage into a formal judicial process for determining guilt and imposing punishment. That process is fairly characterized as "the criminal justice system."

The second set of cases, epitomized by drug offenses, is different. In this category of cases, the government makes a policy decision to discourage certain behavior through the criminal law. If the behavior continues undeterred, that policy decision generates a new flow of cases into the courts. The number of those cases and the intensity of enforcement depend on additional policy choices, not merely the prevalence of the underlying crimes. And while these cases go through the same adjudicative process as homicides, prosecution and punishment is about enforcing the law, not justice. This process can fairly be described as "the criminal legal system."

As I refer to this dichotomy in the pages that follow, readers will likely wonder where various offenses belong. I suggest answers throughout the book but never offer a comprehensive catalog. There are two reasons for this omission. First, the details matter. A typical theft does not strongly implicate justice concerns, but Bernard Madoff's decades-long pyramid scheme that deprived numerous individuals of their life savings does. Second, I do not purport to be an expert on "justice" and, even if I were, my answers are not essential to the Mass Incarceration narrative. My argument throughout the book is that the mix of cases that led to incarceration changed throughout the era of Mass Incarceration, with an especially notable shift toward drug crimes, weapons possession offenses, and other analogous crimes. That argument does not depend on readers agreeing with the "criminal legal system" label I attach to these cases or my view of their severity.

That said, while I readily concede that some offenses fall into a gray area and others present questions of degree, the dichotomy is clearer than may be facially apparent. For the most part, Americans – and people generally – share intuitions about the relative severity of crimes. The social-science literature points to "the existence of wide general agreement and stability across different social sectors and population groups with regard to the relative seriousness of behaviors considered to be criminal."[1] These relative severity intuitions map neatly on to the distinction I am drawing between crimes that strongly implicate justice concerns and those that do not.

To illustrate, the National Crime Severity Survey conducted by the Bureau of Justice Statistics (BJS) in 1985 asked Americans to assess the relative severity of a broad list of abbreviated fact patterns.

The offenses that fell in the top range (scores above 35) of the survey responses follow, along with the relative severity scores:

72.1 A person plants a bomb in a public building. The bomb explodes and twenty people are killed.

52.8 A man forcibly rapes a woman. As a result of physical injuries, she dies.

47.8 A parent beats his young child with his fists. As a result, the child dies.

43.9 A person plants a bomb in a public building. The bomb explodes and one person is killed.

43.2 A person robs a victim at gunpoint. The victim struggles and is shot to death.

39.2 A man stabs his wife. As a result, she dies.

39.1 A factory knowingly gets rid of its waste in a way that pollutes the water supply of a city. As a result, twenty people die.

35.7 A person stabs a victim to death.

35.6 A person intentionally injures a victim. As a result, the victim dies.[2]

These offenses share a variety of attributes, but the most obvious is grave harm to an identifiable victim. This fits the traditional conception of criminal justice – the system acts on behalf of an identifiable victim, seeking accountability from the person who caused them harm. These cases offer the strongest justification for a formal government response, including punishment of the perpetrator. This is as much a function of the inherent gravity of the offenses as the societal perception of that gravity. People in all strata of American society fear these offenses and expect the government to mount a formal response to those who would commit them. If the government does not respond, others will. These types of cases led to incarceration in the 1970s and, of course, do so today.

I also see justice implicated in offenses further down the survey's severity scale, such as the following:

24.5 A person kidnaps a victim. A ransom of $1,000 is paid and the victim is returned unharmed.

21.0 A person robs a victim of $1,000 at gunpoint. The victim is wounded and requires hospitalization.

20.1 A man forcibly rapes a woman. Her physical injuries require treatment by a doctor but not hospitalization.

But some serious offenses do not implicate justice-related concerns in nearly the same way, such as the following:

20.6 A person sells heroin to others for resale.
15.5 A person breaks into a bank at night and steals $100,000.
10.8 A person steals a locked car and sells it.
10.5 A person smuggles marijuana into the country for resale.
7.6 A person steals $1,000 worth of merchandise from the counter of a department store.
7.4 A person illegally gets monthly welfare checks.
6.5 A person uses heroin.
3.6 A person knowingly passes a bad check.

That does not mean these activities are not harmful, merely different. I would classify these latter offenses as criminal legal system cases: offenses that either do not cause grave harm to a discernable individual or are harmful only indirectly. Criminal legal system offenses (e.g., drug offenses, weapons possession, theft, illegal immigration) are prosecuted to discourage behaviors and prevent potential harms, rather than to obtain justice on behalf of an identifiable victim. As we will see, the criminal legal system label also comfortably attaches to procedural shortcuts to incarceration like pretrial detention, parole and probation revocations, and repeat-offending laws.

Again, one does not need to accept my view of the relative severity of offenses listed above or agree about whether these crimes implicate "justice" or should lead to incarceration. The key point is that there are two systems operating in parallel in America's criminal courts. And the story of Mass Incarceration is a story of the expansion of both systems through the 1970s and beyond. For crimes like rape and homicide that had always led to incarceration, politicians and voters sought harsher punishments, and law enforcement officials delivered. As we will see, the core criminal justice system became more punitive. But the changes didn't stop there. The same energy that increased the severity of the criminal justice system rushed into the parallel criminal legal system. Perhaps to address serious societal problems, or perhaps for less noble

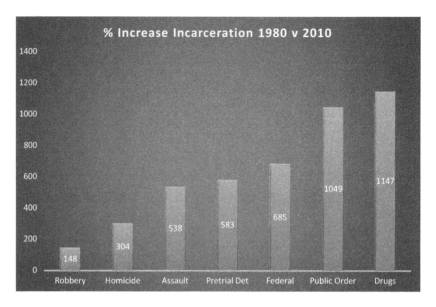

Figure 4.1 Incarceration increases

reasons, politicians and voters supported an unprecedented expansion of incarceration as a policy tool, transforming broad swaths of the law enforcement architecture into a legal system, not a justice system.

These changes, discussed throughout the book, are illustrated in Figure 4.1 which shows the percentage increase between 1980 and 2010 in State prisoners for selected offenses as well as the percentage increase in pretrial detention (people jailed prior to trial) and federal prison inmates.

As the left side of the chart reflects, imprisonment for core criminal justice offenses increased substantially over the period.[3] The number of people incarcerated in State prison for homicide, for example, increased by more than 300 percent between 1980 and 2010, reflecting both a temporary spike in homicides and longer sentences for those convicted of that offense. But as the right side of the chart illustrates, the scale of the increases for criminal legal system offenses is even larger. ("Public order" offenses include weapons possession, drunk driving, and offenses that interfere with court administration.) Federal prisoners, the vast majority of whom are serving time for drug, immigration, and weapons offenses (see Chapter 19), illustrate the same trend, as does the sharp increase in people incarcerated while awaiting trial (Chapter 17), and probation and parole revocations (Chapter 15).

Importantly, Figure 4.1 should not be read to suggest that the system's horizontal expansion (sending more people to prison for "criminal legal system" offenses like drug and weapons offenses) is more important than its vertical expansion (increasing sentence lengths across the board, especially for violent crimes like homicide). In terms of overall incarceration numbers, the percentage increase in homicide incarceration is more impactful, and the change in public order and drug incarceration less impactful, than the chart suggests. That's because in 1980, the system incarcerated most people convicted of homicides and few of those convicted of drug or public order offenses. That means the base number (from which the percentage growth shown in the chart is measured) is much higher for homicides and robberies than for criminal legal system offenses. But both changes mattered, as the raw numbers reflect. People in prison for homicide shot up from 46,600 in 1980 to 188,200 in 2010; for drugs, from 19,000 in 1980 to 237,000 in 2010.

The key insight here is that there are two important and distinct things changing simultaneously. As the chart reflects, and the rest of the book will explain in greater detail, it is both a vertical increase in sentence severity (for all crimes, including criminal *justice* offenses) and a horizontal expansion of the criminal law's footprint (reaching out to more criminal *legal* system offenses) that combine to fuel American Mass Incarceration.

PART II

The Building Blocks of Mass Incarceration

Mass Incarceration resulted from a uniform process that unfolded in different ways in different jurisdictions. But what triggered that process? The next chapters summarize the changes in public attitudes that transformed American criminal law enforcement, emphasizing the widespread consensus for the need both to replace the "revolving door" of the 1970s criminal justice system and to use criminal law to achieve broad policy goals, like reducing drug abuse and weapons possession.

5 A CRIME SURGE

The many ingredients that fed Mass Incarceration, including racism, populism, media sensationalism, and political opportunism, are long-standing features of the American landscape. What changed that made these factors particularly salient and channeled them into a transformation of the criminal justice (and legal) system? The best answer is a crime surge.

In the 1960s, crime shot up. The crime spike continued well into the 1980s. In the 1990s crime started going down. No one really knows why crime went up or down, but most experts agree on the pattern. For example, Michelle Alexander, author of *The New Jim Crow*, acknowledges the crime spike at the outset of Mass Incarceration, noting that "sociologists and criminologists agree that crime did rise, in some categories quite sharply." The National Research Council similarly concludes that: "The country experienced a large increase in crime from the early 1960s until the 1980s. From the early 1990s, crime rates began to fall broadly for the following two decades."[1] Rising crime was the spark that lit the fire that became Mass Incarceration. Changing laws, policies, and attitudes that arose in the wake of that spark explain the rest.

Experts are always skeptical of claims about crime rising (or dropping). Measuring crime is tricky. Lots of crime is unreported. And it can be difficult to distinguish changes in crime from changes in reporting. Inconsistent reporting of crime by civilians is not the only challenge. We get most of our data about crime from police. But police departments have both an incentive and opportunity to fudge crime statistics. To make things even more complicated, not everyone agrees about what should count as "crime."

Figure 5.1 Homicides

Researchers have a work-around for the long-recognized problem of detecting changes in crime. There is one crime that civilians pretty much always report, police almost always record, and everyone agrees is really a crime: homicide (aka killing people). This is true for virtually every US jurisdiction and time period. In addition, studies show that homicide rates track crime generally, or at least the violent crimes that most people care a lot about. As legal scholar John Donohue explains: "While homicide data may not be perfectly reflective of the time trend in all crimes, it does seem to follow the pattern of most other street crimes fairly well during the recent periods when more accurate data is available for these other crimes."[2] When questions about crime data arise, researchers can look at trends in "the one crime – murder – that is well measured" and extrapolate from those trends to conclusions about crime generally. (See Figure 5.1.)

A sharp increase in homicides starting in the mid-1960s is the best evidence of the crime surge that appeared at the dawn of Mass Incarceration. Prior to the 1960s, American homicides averaged well under 10,000 per year, usually close to 5,000. Between 1950 and 1977, however, homicides steadily climbed. The trend continued into the 1990s, resulting in an "all-time high of 24,703 homicides in 1991." That was a dramatic change. In the 1950s, the homicide rate was around 4 per 100,000 persons. From about 1970 and well into the 1990s, the rate more than doubled. At times in the 1980s, the homicide rate was 10 per 100,000.[3] (These rates calculated from homicides reported by the police match up almost perfectly with data tabulated from death certificates over the same period by the Centers for Disease Control.)[4]

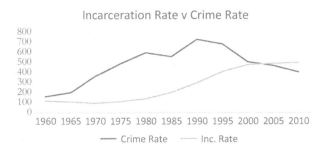

Figure 5.2 Incarceration versus crime rate

If, as appears to be the case, crime rose in the 1960s through the 1990s, a connection between rising crime and rising incarceration seems undeniable. The trend takes shape in Figure 5.2, when the reported crime rate (top line) is plotted on the same graph as incarceration rate (bottom line).[5] But as we will see in subsequent chapters, the connection is much more complicated than it first appears.

Perhaps no place illustrates the ebb and flow of violent crime better than New York City. Recent headlines suggest that the city is suffering from a crime wave because homicides increased from 314 in 2019 to 437 in 2020. But in 1990, New York City hosted 2,245 homicides – a record high. In the 1990s, increasing crime plus constant media coverage hung like a cloud over New Yorkers – leading to the election of Rudolph Giuliani, a former prosecutor, as the city's mayor in 1993. Giuliani's "tough on crime" message resonated with voters for a reason. As Giuliani ran for election, a survey of New York City residents found that nearly half had been victimized by crime that year.[6]

New York City's experience is representative both in terms of its sharp crime surge and a distinctive feature of that surge. The primary problem the city faced was gun violence. The New York City Police Department expressed its frustration with gun crimes in a 1994 internal bulletin, stating: "Whatever we are doing to reduce violent – especially handgun related – crime is not working."[7] The bulletin emphasized that between 1960 and 1992, the number of murders committed in New York City with a handgun increased by almost 2000 percent, growing from one-quarter to three-quarters of all murders.

As New York City's experience illustrates, high incarceration rates are not the only way that the United States stands out. A recent study published in the *American Journal of Medicine* examined the causes of death in high-income countries.[8] Its key finding: "In 2010, the US homicide rate was 7.0 times higher than the other high-income countries, driven by a gun homicide rate that was 25.2 times higher." The study goes on to say: "The United States has a serious homicide problem . . .. The homicide rate is fueled by the firearm homicide rate in the United States. More than two thirds of the homicides in the United States are firearm homicides; by contrast, firearm homicide accounts for less than 20% of homicides in the other high-income countries."

Other comparative scholars concur, concluding that: "the United States experiences a distinctively higher level of serious violence compared with other relatively similar countries."[9] So just as the crime spike is critical to understanding the rise of Mass Incarceration, gun violence is critical to understanding America's unique problem with crime. In fact, the ongoing problem of gun violence may be the biggest obstacle to reform. But as we will see, crime and violence are only parts of a long and complex story. In fact, New York City and much of the rest of the country has seen a dramatic decrease in violence since the 1990s – even as the phenomenon of Mass Incarceration persists. And, most importantly, large swaths of Mass Incarceration have nothing to do with violence or guns.

6 REPEATING PATTERNS
Crime, Outrage, and Harsher Laws

Prisons in this country did not fill simply because crime went up, police arrested more people, and judges sent them to prison. The crime surge's primary contribution was that it fostered an environment where politicians and the public became attracted to harsh criminal laws. The steady ratcheting up of the severity of American criminal law played a larger role in Mass Incarceration than the transitory crime rise. This chapter introduces the critical punitive pattern: crime leads to public outrage, and outrage leads to harsher laws.

In a democracy, voters influence policy and crime influences voters. In 2001, the Pew Research Center surveyed city residents about their communities' most important problems: crime was first, drugs second.[1] It is important to note that what people think about crime can be different from how much crime is actually occurring. Since 1989, the Gallup Poll has asked, "Is there more crime in the U.S. than there was a year ago, or less?"[2] There is a consistent pattern. Falling crime causes perceptions of crime to fall, but not by much. Crime has decreased steadily since the 1990s, but most Americans continue to perceive crime as rising. As John Donohue puts it: "Rivaling the astonishing crime drop is the level of ignorance Americans have about this good news."[3] Nevertheless, for understanding criminal justice policy, what people think about crime and punishment matters as much as the underlying reality. This is especially true when everybody is saying the same thing. In the 1970s and 1980s, with crime actually rising and the public feeling its effects, the nation reached a consensus – new measures were needed to fight crime.

The problem Americans perceived in the 1970s was not just increasing crime. They viewed the government's response as a "revolving door." A 1977 poll asked Texas residents how they thought courts were "dealing with convicted criminals." Only 1 percent of respondents thought courts were "too harsh"; 20 percent said courts did a "good job"; 73 percent said courts were "too easy."[4] In the public's imagination, not only was crime rising, but the government did not care. People committed serious crime, walked into the courthouse, said they were "sorry," and spun through a revolving door back out onto the street.

6.1 "TOUGH ON CRIME" DEMOCRATS

For a sampling of how the debate sounded in the 1970s, we can start with voices that you would least expect to find at the origin of an incarceration boom, like Ted Kennedy, the "liberal lion of the Senate."[5] In 1975, Senator Kennedy published an op-ed in the *New York Times*, titled "Punishing the Offenders." It began: "Violent crime is spreading like a national plague."[6] Kennedy mentioned the need for broad policy measures to increase opportunities for all Americans. But his theme was that, first, politicians needed to "punish the offenders."

In the op-ed, Kennedy homed in on "the Achilles' heel of our criminal justice system," "overloaded" courts, whose plight, he labeled "a national disgrace." In America's courts, Kennedy proclaimed, "crime does pay" and "'[r]evolving door' justice convinces the criminal that his chances of actually being caught, tried, convicted and jailed are too slim to be taken seriously." Kennedy closed with a proposal for tough solutions: "promoting certainty of punishment and imprisonment" through "mandatory minimum sentence[s]" for violent offenders, and people "using a handgun or other dangerous weapon in committing a crime" or "trafficking in heroin."

The most jarring aspect of the op-ed for modern ears is Kennedy's attack on prosecutors, who, he asserted, "ease the pressures and reduce the bottlenecks by bargains that allow violent offenders to 'cop a plea' and return to circulation." In America, almost 95 percent of convictions result from guilty pleas, typically via plea bargains – where defendants agree to plead guilty in return for concessions from the prosecution. Today, most experts argue that prosecutors use plea bargaining to coerce defendants to admit guilt and accept "punishment without trial."[7] But that's not how things looked in the 1970s. At the dawn of Mass Incarceration, politicians like Kennedy viewed plea bargains as the engine that turned the revolving door. Some jurisdictions even tried to ban plea bargains. New York's infamous Rockefeller Drug Laws enacted in the 1970s paired severe mandatory sentences with strict limits on plea bargains.[8] Alaska banned plea bargaining in 1975 in an effort to "bring about longer sentences."[9] The 1982 Victim's Bill of Rights enacted by California voters prohibited prosecutors from "[p]lea bargaining in any case in which the indictment or information charges any serious felony."[10] These efforts were largely unsuccessful because it is difficult to stop defendants and prosecutors from cutting deals. But it speaks to the strength of the emerging "tough on crime" consensus that, at the dawn of Mass Incarceration, liberals were attacking the excessive lenience of prosecutors and plea bargains.

The most important aspect of Kennedy's op-ed is the vacuum it reflects. American politics is dominated by two parties: Republicans and Democrats. The parties' limited ability to agree stymies most policy changes and dilutes the impact of laws that are enacted. But on the crime issue, there was little division. Republicans consistently called for harsher criminal laws. Democrats agreed. No one with sufficient political power remained to get in the way. Many of the laws discussed below passed with little opposition. That's why liberal California is as responsible for Mass Incarceration as conservative Texas, and severe penalties for crime are as common in rural Oklahoma as they are in New York City.

Experts debate whether the public drove politicians to embrace tougher criminal laws (bottom up), or politicians and other government officials cynically solicited votes with "tough on crime" rhetoric (top down). Surely there were elements of both, sometimes even in the politicians themselves. Ted Kennedy undoubtedly recognized that "tough on crime" was good politics. But he was also personally affected by violent crime: two of his brothers had been gunned down in the decade before he penned the op-ed.

Above all, "tough on crime" was good politics *because* it resonated with voters. A powerful illustration of this point can be found in one of the laws that epitomizes Mass Incarceration, California's "three strikes" law. The law was first championed by Mike Reynolds, whose 18-year-old daughter was shot to death in 1992 by Douglas Walker, a frequent drug user with a long criminal record.[11] After the tragedy, Reynolds sketched out the harsh law and lobbied California's legislators to adopt it. When the legislators declined, Reynolds turned to California's voter initiative process. In California, if a citizen gathers enough signatures, a proposed law goes on the ballot, where the voters can directly enact it. Reynolds's lonely campaign received a boost of support after the high-profile 1993 murder of 12-year-old Polly Klaas in Northern California by a repeat offender who, at the time of the murder, was out on parole.

In 1993, the *Los Angeles Times* noted the growing momentum behind Reynolds's proposal: "Sponsored by a father whose daughter was murdered by a parolee, and favored by an electorate angry about crime, the 'three strikes and you're out' initiative is winning political support up and down California."[12] As Reynolds's voter initiative gathered steam, the legislators who rejected it the year before now climbed onboard. Trying to preempt the ballot measure, California legislators swiftly enacted an almost word-for-word version of Reynolds's proposal.[13] Reynolds continued with his initiative campaign, hoping to send a message to the legislators. He succeeded: the initiative was enacted by California voters with 72 percent of the vote.

An artifact of this history is that California has two separate but identical three strikes laws, one enacted by the legislature and the other through the initiative process. Perhaps the most notable application of those laws occurred in 2018, when a California judge sentenced Douglas Walker, the man whose crime inspired the three strikes law, to life in prison based on a new domestic violence offense, which constituted Walker's third strike.[14]

The successful political career of Bill Clinton best exemplifies modern Democrats' embrace of "tough on crime." Clinton lost his first re-election bid as Arkansas governor amid criticism that he was "soft on crime" – an accusation that drew on Clinton's grant of clemency to seventy prisoners during his first two-year term.[15] Reelected in 1983, Clinton's clemency practices changed dramatically. Over his next five terms as Arkansas governor, Clinton granted clemency only seven times.

While campaigning for president in 1992, Clinton presided over Arkansas's execution of Rickey Ray Rector. Suffering from a gunshot wound to the head received during his offense, Rector was described by his lawyers as "a zombie," with no comprehension of his impending execution. Clinton's pro-execution stance was widely viewed as calculated, with the *New York Times* explaining that "many political experts feel a record of favoring the death penalty is a major plus for a Democratic Presidential candidate." It worked. As political scientist David Holian would later explain: "The 'soft-on-crime liberal' taunt, so effective [for Republican presidential candidate] Bush in 1988 – and Reagan before him – rang hollow against an opponent who dramatically underscored his position on the death penalty by allowing the execution of a brain-damaged convict."[16] After the execution, Clinton observed that "no one can say that I'm soft on crime."[17]

It wasn't just the political spectrum that exhibited unusual consensus. As legal scholar James Forman Jr. chronicles in his book, *Locking Up Our Own*, arguments for harsher criminal laws found support among African Americans, a group that would be disproportionately impacted. Why? Forman explains:

> [I]n the years preceding and during our punishment binge, black communities were devastated by historically unprecedented levels of crime and violence. Spurred by a heroin epidemic, homicides doubled and tripled in D.C. and many other American cities throughout the 1960s. Two decades later, heroin would be eclipsed by crack, a terrifying drug whose addictive qualities and violent marketplace caused some contemporaries to label it "the worst thing to hit us since slavery."[18]

Not surprisingly, members of hard-hit communities sought a response from their political leaders. Those leaders, including politicians who made their names in the Civil Rights movement, recognized the severity of the crime problem. The prominent African American politician Jesse Jackson Jr., for example, voiced a "tough on crime" message throughout his career, famously stating in 1975 that: "A black man selling dope hurts communities more than a white man dangling a rope."[19]

Attacked from the left during her 2016 presidential campaign for her husband's 1994 Crime Bill, Hillary Clinton emphasized the era's "great demand, not just from America writ large, but from the black community, to get tougher on crime." In fact, the Congressional Black Caucus supplied the critical votes President Clinton needed to pass the 1994 law.[20] Black politicians were searching for an answer to the crime faced by their constituents. And like other Democrats, they typically favored nonpunitive solutions and an improved social safety net. But while waiting for those responses to materialize, they also often backed the one tool that everyone else supported: ratcheting up the severity of American criminal law.

6.2 "TOUGH ON CRIME" REPUBLICANS

The debate surrounding the 1994 Crime Bill is notable for the comments of another prominent Democrat, Joe Biden, one of the bill's sponsors. In a speech on the Senate floor, Biden highlighted the Democrats' changing approach, mocking earlier efforts to introduce nuance into the "tough on crime" consensus. Biden stated, "Every time Richard Nixon, when he was running in 1972, would say, 'Law and order,' the Democratic match or response was, 'Law and order with justice' – whatever that meant. And I would say, 'Lock the S.O.B.s up.'"[21]

As Biden's comments suggest, as tough as the Democrats got, they were always playing catch-up to Republicans. Richard Nixon famously brought the local issue of crime and punishment into national politics, making "Law and Order" a theme of his campaign. In 1982, President Reagan appointed a high-profile Task Force on Victims of Crime. The task force's report, hailed as "an historic milestone in the victims' rights movement," was a blueprint for Mass Incarceration. Here is how the Report begins:

> Something insidious has happened in America: crime has made victims of us all. . . . Rather than alter a system that has proven itself incapable of dealing with crime, society has altered itself. Every 23 minutes, someone is murdered. Every six minutes a woman is raped. While you read this Statement, two people will be robbed in this country and two more will be shot, stabbed, or seriously beaten. Yet to truly grasp the enormity of the problem those figures must be doubled, because more than 50 percent of violent crime goes unreported.

The bulk of the Report consists of heartbreaking stories of crime, placing the reader in the victim's shoes and highlighting the speedy return of offenders to the streets: "The judge sentences your attacker to three years in prison. . . . [H]e'll probably serve less than half of his actual sentence. The man who broke into your home, threatened to slit your throat with a knife, and raped, beat, and robbed you will be out of custody in less than 18 months." The Report offers a list of recommendations, including many that would be adopted across the country, such as (1) restricting pretrial release, (2) longer sentences, and (3) the abolition of parole.[22]

> The Task Force on Victims of Crime included influential televangelist Pat Robertson. Robertson had previously predicted that the world would end in 1982. The Task Force released its report just prior to the end of that year.

In 1988, Republican presidential nominee George H. W. Bush ran a television advertisement, titled "Revolving Door." The ad shows a stream of prisoners exiting a prison yard thorough a revolving door. The narrator states that Democratic presidential nominee Michael Dukakis "vetoed mandatory sentences for drug dealers" and allowed "first degree murderers" to leave prison on furloughs. The narrator adds that some of the furloughed prisoners escaped and committed additional crimes. The ad closes with: "Now Michael Dukakis says he wants to do for America what he's done for Massachusetts. America can't afford that risk." Bush supporters created another, more famous version of the ad that featured a Black furlough recipient, William Horton. While furloughed under the Massachusetts program, Horton, who had previously been convicted of murder, committed further serious crimes. According to the *New York Times*, the Horton version, "was shown only briefly on cable television, but its impact was magnified by repeated coverage on television newscasts." The ultimate influence of the Horton ad on the election is disputed, but no one doubts the lesson politicians learned. Bush trounced Dukakis in the election, and politicians have feared looking "soft on crime" ever since.

Criticized for failing to respond to the attacks, the Dukakis campaign ran an ad two weeks before the end of the campaign called, "George Bush's False Advertising," which attempted to "fight fire with fire." The ad's narrator states that Bush "won't talk about the thousands of drug kingpins furloughed from Federal prison while he led the war on drugs," and "[o]ne of his furloughed heroin dealers [who] raped and murdered [a] pregnant mother of two."[23]

Republicans' embrace of incarceration may seem natural now, but it was not inevitable. At the dawn of Mass Incarceration, Republicans' defining issues were small government and fiscal conservatism. Yet their traditional skepticism of government overreach and open-ended spending gave way to the powerful appeal of a war on crime. Perhaps nowhere is this more apparent than Texas where, sociologist Michael Campbell explains, these competing principles clashed, but "[u]ltimately, Texans were more committed to harsh punishment than they were to fiscal conservatism"; "Democratic and Republican legislators joined the 'law and order' tide and embarked on one of the most remarkable and expensive public spending sprees in Texas history."[24]

6.3 BIPARTISAN SEVERITY

With Republican and Democratic support, similar stories played out across the country. In 1977, under a Democratic governor and a split legislature, Arizona ratcheted up the severity of its criminal justice system. Projections accompanying the tough-on-crime bills made clear that the new laws would almost double the State's prison population in just four years. The predictions came true. Years later, financially strapped Arizona legislators crafted legislation that would reduce the cost of the State's punishment binge by reducing prison populations. Republican Governor Fife Symington vetoed the bill in 1992. Here is a portion of the veto message where Symington rejects the argument that the existing laws were "not fair" and "too hard" on defendants:

The public seems to perceive, and I agree with them, that criminal defendants as a class are faring pretty well in the justice system. . . .

And most of the public is not even aware that about 70 percent of all convicted felons in Arizona are already on the street, through probation, parole, early release programs.... [L]egions of burglars ... run through the system two or three times before ever seeing the inside of a prison cell. If the justice system becomes any more "fair" to criminals, soon they will be leaving the courtroom with parting gifts, citizens' vacation schedules and passkeys to high-rise apartment buildings."

Republicans took back the Arizona legislature that year.[25]

Governor Symington's time in office ended when he was criminally charged with seven counts of bank fraud. In one of his last acts in office, President Clinton, an old college friend, pardoned Symington. Media accounts of the pardon noted that decades earlier, Symington saved Clinton from drowning at a beach party in Massachusetts.

These stories played out even in States that remained comfortably Democratic, like California. This is one of the key points for understanding Mass Incarceration. Its ingredients appealed to voters and politicians across the political spectrum. In 1994, for example, the *Los Angeles Times* highlighted an effort by Democrats "to turn the tables on Republican Gov. Pete Wilson, who has spent most of his political career building an image as a tough crime fighter." Wilson had backed an earlier reform that reduced the number of parolees returned to prison, a policy that critics blamed for a series of high-profile crimes. Democrats tried to exploit this perceived political weakness when Wilson ran for reelection in 1994. As reported by the *Times*:

"Arlo Smith, a Democratic candidate for attorney general, said it was hypocritical for Wilson to call for stricter sentencing laws while also seeking to reduce the number of prisoners returned to custody for violating parole. 'They talk tough at the front door but they let them out the back door,' Smith said."[26]

The Democrats failed to unseat Wilson, but the power was in the message, not the messenger. Responding to the Democrats' unsuccessful political attack, California changed its parole rules causing parole violations to once again become a key contributor to the State's ballooning prison population (see Chapter 15).

This pattern repeated across the country and across time periods. Politicians and media outlets spotlighted the tragedies that inevitably arise in a country of more than 300 million people, and those tragedies left enduring marks on the political landscape. The resulting fallout generally included replacing one politician or official with another who promised to be "tougher" and new laws that ensured increased severity no matter who was in office.

One of the clearest examples of this political feedback loop involved Mark Singel. Singel held a comfortable lead over his Republican opponent in the 1994 Pennsylvania governor's race. That lead evaporated after Reginald McFadden, whose murder sentence Singel had voted to commute as a member of the State Parole Board, went on a violent crime spree. Singel would later write that the "political fallout was immediate and brutal": "My opponent went into full attack mode and overnight had a political ad on every television station in the state all but charging me with Mr. McFadden's crimes." Singel's 8 percent lead in the polls evaporated, and he lost the election.

These stories are important not only because they influenced the behavior of individual politicians, but also because they changed the law. For example, at the time of McFadden's clemency vote, a majority of the parole board could release a life prisoner. In McFadden's case one member of the board (the then–attorney general) voted "no." After McFadden's crimes and Singel's defeat, Pennsylvania voters approved a constitutional amendment requiring a unanimous vote to release prisoners serving life sentences. Pennsylvania's then-Lieutenant Governor John Fetterman later explained that this "effectively ended the process." A recent analysis revealed that, in Pennsylvania, commutations for prisoners serving life sentences dropped from about thirty per year in the 1970s to fewer than one per year after 1994. Similarly, after Horton's crimes and their role in the 1988 presidential campaign, Massachusetts cut back its furlough program.[27]

Politicians didn't just receive negative feedback for leniency. They received positive feedback for severity. As noted in Chapter 4, crime did, in fact, decline through the 1990s. And while the connection between particular laws and a crime decrease is always speculative, that is not what legislators are told. For example, a 1999 report by a

Texas government agency to the Texas legislature contained this headline "Your Reforms, Along with the Impact of Local Initiatives and Other General Trends, Have Impacted a Decline in Crime." No doubt reflecting the agency's expertise, the headline is almost comically nuanced. But it is unlikely that the legislators noticed.[28]

The most prominent recent example of the broad bipartisan consensus for increased severity arose in California in 2015. That year, a jury convicted Brock Turner of sexual assault. Judge Aaron Persky sentenced Turner to six months in jail and ordered him to register as a sex offender for life. Outraged at a sentence viewed as too light, and the perceived preferential treatment of Turner, a white Stanford University student, voters ousted Persky in an almost unprecedented recall of a sitting judge. They selected Cindy Hendrickson, then a prosecutor, to take Persky's place. California's legislature responded as well, strengthening its sexual violence laws and enacting a new three-year mandatory minimum prison sentence for sexual assault of an unconscious person.[29]

7 LEGISLATING MORE PUNISHMENT AND LESS REHABILITATION

The previous chapter discussed the wave of political energy introduced into American politics by a desire to fight crime. The message resonated beyond the "street crimes" Senator Kennedy singled out in 1975, like rape and murder. Politicians also turned to the criminal justice architecture to solve society's most vexing problems, like drug addiction, gun violence, child pornography, drunk driving, and intrafamily abuse. This approach required two components: new laws and increased enforcement. Legislators changed the laws, and they funded a hiring spree of police officers to catch people who broke those laws, prosecutors and judges to put them in jail, and correctional officers to keep them there. Perhaps the most dramatic example of these funding increases came in the 1994 Crime Bill. A fact sheet distributed by the Department of Justice, explained:

> The Violent Crime Control and Law Enforcement Act of 1994 ... is the largest crime bill in the history of the country and will provide for 100,000 new police officers [and] $9.7 billion in funding for prisons.... The Crime Bill provides $2.6 billion in additional funding for the FBI, DEA, INS, United States Attorneys, and other Justice Department components, as well as the Federal courts and the Treasury Department.[1]

Part III will discuss how the beefed-up law enforcement apparatus (police, prosecutors, judges) performed their individual roles. This chapter focuses on the legal changes. It shows how legislators channeled public outcry for increased enforcement and harsher punishments into law. The discussion is broken down into parts, with the first discussing the dramatic transformation of criminal sentencing laws and the second highlighting crime-specific legislation.

7.1 FROM INDETERMINATE TO DETERMINATE SENTENCING

When it comes to prison populations, legislators' most important contribution to Mass Incarceration was not the creation of new offenses. It was remaking the system so that people who were convicted of existing crimes served more prison time. This effort resonated with a remark in the 1982 Task Force on Victims of Crime Report that the time had come to "alter a system that has proven itself incapable of dealing with crime." Legislators sought transformation. And that is how they talked about the changes that would follow. For example, the US Senate's 1983 report on proposed new federal sentencing laws explained: "These provisions introduce a totally new and comprehensive sentencing system," intended to replace the "outmoded rehabilitation model."[2]

Transforming a system is not easy. Legislators' ultimate success in increasing criminal punishments reflected a concerted, long-term effort and close attention to detail. Legislators were not looking for symbolic victories. They wanted to close the revolving door.

Prior to the 1970s, the buzzword of the American correctional system was rehabilitation, not punishment. The revolving door was a function of that purpose. Unless you are going to imprison everyone for life, prisons will always have revolving doors. Even today, almost all of the people sent to prison eventually return.[3]

The American criminal justice system used to believe strongly in rehabilitation – or at least it claimed to. Here is an excerpt from a 1954 judicial opinion from the Court of Appeals of New York that mercilessly scolds a trial judge. What did the judge do wrong? He tried to impose a specific sentence (three years), rather than an "indeterminate" sentence. An indeterminate sentence is like sending someone to prison, and when they ask how long they'll be in, saying "we'll see." The appeals court explained why "we'll see" was the only permissible approach:

> Under the Correction Law the function of the sentencing court is to determine, at the time of sentence, whether or not the defendant is capable of receiving substantial benefit by commitment to a correctional and reformatory institution. If the court concludes, as it did here, that the defendant is so capable, then it must impose

an indeterminate term of imprisonment. Nowhere in the statute is authority given to courts to recommend the length of imprisonment at the time of such sentencing and it was improper for the court to have done so here.[4]

In language that sounds foreign today, the opinion assumes that prison offers a "benefit," namely rehabilitation, in a "correctional and reformatory institution." The appeals court further explained that it "is the function of the Parole Commission to determine, in the first instance, when the prisoner is sufficiently rehabilitated or reformed to be fit for return to society."

The model of punishment invoked by the New York court was echoed in the federal system, as discussed in the US Senate's 1983 report on the need for change to federal sentencing laws:

> The sentencing provisions of current law were originally based on a rehabilitation model in which the sentencing judge was expected to sentence a defendant to a fairly long term of imprisonment. The defendant was eligible for release on parole after serving one-third of his term. The parole commission was charged with setting his release date if it concluded that he was sufficiently rehabilitated. At present, the concepts of indeterminate sentencing and parole release depend for their justification exclusively upon this model of "coercive" rehabilitation – the theory of correction that ties prison release dates to the successful completion of certain vocational, educational, and counseling programs within the prisons.[5]

Reflecting a long-standing tradition, indeterminate sentences were a central component of 1970s criminal justice. After a trial or a guilty plea, when everyone is paying attention, judges want to look tough. We may even need them to look tough in that moment, to repair the tear in the fabric of society – and send a message to others contemplating similar crimes. But the past decades have shown why looking tough is preferable to being tough. In the 1970s, the judge could send someone "to the penitentiary." That's tough. Then later, when the excitement died down, professionals would evaluate the incarcerated person and decide how long keeping that person in prison made sense. This approach worked for decades. And it hinges on a recognition that, as bad as it sounds, a revolving door beats the alternative.

Indeterminate sentences do have a negative side. While they generate hope for even the most serious offenders of eventual release, they also permit lengthy stays based on less serious crimes, especially for the unrepentant (or innocent). And indeterminate sentences leave room for officials to discriminate. The perception of improper discrimination made indeterminate sentences unpopular even for those who favored lenience. As historian James Whitman explains: "The movement for determinate sentencing can partly be traced back to a widespread sense among liberals ... that rich, white defendants did better under the system of indeterminate sentencing than poor, dark-skinned ones."[6] And, again, Senator Ted Kennedy channeled the spirit of this movement, writing in another *New York Times* op-ed in 1977 that "[c]riminal sentencing today is a national scandal." Kennedy blasted indeterminate sentencing and parole for its arbitrariness and inequality. He acknowledged that the system had been created "in the name of benevolence"; "But this approach – noble in purpose and based on-the best-of intentions – has dramatically backfired."[7]

Criticized from the left for being discriminatory and from the right for being too lenient, indeterminate sentencing also had another problem. It wasn't clear that rehabilitation – the whole point of the exercise – was occurring. In theory, the rehabilitation that prisoners received in prison prior to their expertly determined release date reduced recidivism – the likelihood that the prisoner would commit new crimes upon release. But experts struggled to marshal evidence that prisoners were being rehabilitated. One of the most prominent voices in this academic consensus was sociologist Robert Martinson.[8] In an influential 1974 article, Martinson explained: "Rehabilitation, tested empirically, is a failure; 'nothing works' as a prison reform program to reduce recidivism."[9] Martinson's influence went beyond academic journals. In 1975, he delivered his somber message to everyday America in an interview with Mike Wallace on the era's most popular television show, "60 Minutes":

MARTINSON: I looked at all the methods that we could find – vocational, educational – and a variety of other methods. These methods simply have no fundamental effect on the recidivism rate of people who go through ... the system.

WALLACE: No effect at all?

MARTINSON: No effect, no basic effect.

Martinson put it even more bluntly in a 1976 interview published in *People Magazine*: "Primarily, our correctional system is not working because of this focus on rehabilitation. Present methods simply have no effect whatever on recidivism – the tendency of criminals to return to jail."[10] That was bad news for the indeterminate sentencing system and the rehabilitative premise on which it was based. And it couldn't have come at a worse time. America and its politicians were mobilizing to fight rising crime. The perceived failure of rehabilitation reduced their options.

When Congress abandoned indeterminate sentencing in 1983, it cited Martinson's article, along with other research, to support the proposition that "recent studies suggest that [the rehabilitative] approach has failed."[11] The expert consensus that "nothing works" pushed policy makers in the opposite direction. If there was no point in rehabilitation, all that was left, to borrow Joe Biden's words, was to "Lock the S.O.B.s up."

To the extent any theory supported the transformation of American criminal sentencing, it was that harsh punishments could reduce crime in a different manner. Long prisons terms would deter offenders and incapacitate those who were not deterred. Martinson again appeared in a 1977 CBS Evening News segment offering advice on what needed to be done: offenders need "certainty in being caught and certainty in being punished."[12] The politicians tried to make it so.

> Martinson later renounced his claim that "nothing works," writing in a 1979 law review article that, "contrary to my previous position, some treatment programs do have an appreciable effect on recidivism."
> A university professor reported asking Martinson, "What will I now tell my students?" Martinson responded: "Tell them I was full of crap."[13]

In the late 1970s, determinate sentencing schemes began to replace indeterminate sentencing across the country. California provides a powerful example. Prior to 1977, California trial judges sentenced convicted defendants to very broad ranges prescribed by law. For example, in 1974, after robbing an avocado orchard with a sawed-off shotgun, Joseph Rozzo was sentenced to one year-to-life in prison, the time specified in California's robbery statute as a kind of placeholder punishment. This meant the real sentence would be decided by the "Adult Authority" who could make that determination at "any time after the actual commencement of ... imprisonment."[14] The Adult Authority – essentially a parole board – was made up of political appointees with "a varied and sympathetic interest in corrections work including persons widely experienced in fields of corrections, sociology, law, law enforcement, and education."[15] In the case just described, the parole board released Rozzo, who had a lengthy criminal record, after two years.

In 1977, California enacted the Determinate Sentencing Act, which abolished indeterminate sentencing and designated three possible terms of imprisonment for most felony offenses: a low, middle, and high term. For example, after 1977, the statutory punishment for second-degree robbery (Rozzo's offense) was "imprisonment in the state prison for two, three, or five years."[16] These statutes directed California trial judges to select a precise term of imprisonment from the three choices prescribed for each offense. And, most importantly, since the Act eliminated early release on parole for most offenses, the sentence set by the judge now determined the actual time the defendant would spend in prison.[17]

Washington State passed its own Sentencing Reform Act in 1981, a law often credited as the first "Truth in Sentencing" law. The Washington law created a sentencing grid that judges would use to calculate a precise sentence for the wide variety of crimes that come before State judges. The Act also eliminated early parole release.[18] This meant that the sentences imposed by Washington State judges would now closely reflect the actual time served.

The federal system followed the pattern pioneered by Washington State. As explained in a publication from the Department of Justice:

> During the 1980's Federal sentencing policy and practice underwent a series of changes. The Sentencing Reform Act of 1984 (SRA) ... established sentencing guidelines that abolished parole, required a determinate prison term, reduced the amount of good conduct time that Federal offenders could earn, and required Federal offenders to serve the entire sentence imposed, less up to 54 days of any good conduct time earned per year served.
>
> Before implementation of the SRA, Federal offenders served about 58% of the sentence imposed, on average, in prison. ... Following implementation of the SRA, Federal offenders could

expect to serve approximately 87% of the sentence imposed, assuming they earned all available good conduct time.[19]

Under the new determinate sentencing schemes, judges would no longer sentence offenders "to the penitentiary," or with broad ranges, like "six months to life" – the sentence for an aggravated assault under pre-1977 California law.[20] Instead, judges imposed precise terms, often calculated in months. This increased the transparency of criminal sentences. Under an indeterminate system, judges could appear tough by imposing a sentence with a high sticker price. A judge could even omit the low part of the range, sentencing the defendant to "twenty years" or "life" in prison, knowing that the real sentence would ultimately be determined by a parole board and would, in all likelihood be much lower, perhaps a third or less. The shift to determinate sentencing eliminated this sleight of hand.

Determinate sentencing also created a scoreboard to judge the judges. Since judges had to issue precise, meaningful sentences, it became easy to identify and replace judges who were "soft on crime." Conversely, judges who handed down harsh sentences could do so with great fanfare and be rewarded through re-election and promotion.

In addition to creating determinate sentencing schemes, legislatures enacted mandatory sentences for some offenses (described in more detail in the next section), taking away judges' discretion entirely. As in Washington State and the federal system, some jurisdictions created broadly applicable, formulaic guidelines that pointed judges to the "correct" sentence for most crimes, often limiting judges' ability to deviate from the narrow ranges dictated by the formula. For example, Minnesota's 1980 sentencing guidelines allowed judges to depart from the recommended sentences only in "substantial and compelling circumstances."[21]

Precise sentencing regimes made it easier for legislatures and other government officials to influence sentences to score political points. In an era when severity was popular, this meant a gradual ratcheting up of sentence lengths. Legislatures could signal toughness by increasing sentencing ranges or mandatory minimum sentences. And in systems with sentencing guidelines, legislatures could tinker with sentence lengths by increasing the variables for the sentencing formulas. For example, after creating strict federal sentencing guidelines, Congress developed a habit of directly intervening in the guideline for child pornography offenses, increasing the severity of these punishments every few years.[22] An official history of Washington State's switch to determinate sentencing notes that "[t]he Legislature has amended the Sentencing Reform Act in almost every legislative session, requiring longer periods of confinement for violent offenders, sex offenders and drug offenders."[23]

The move to determinate sentences worked hand in hand with reforms to back-end release systems, like parole. This ensured that the sentence announced by the judge matched the time the defendant served. This distinction between the sentence imposed and the time actually served is critical to understanding the American penal system and its evolution over time. Even today, people convicted of crimes can expect, with "good behavior," to leave prison in advance, and sometimes well in advance, of the expiration of their formal sentence. Most commonly this is because a parole board lets them out early. This had become a particularly frequent occurrence in the 1970s. In 1977, the Department of Justice reported that 72 percent of offenders who exited State prison that year had been released early by a parole board, having served only about a third of their sentence.[24] This pattern continued, although at lower levels, in the following years as legislative restrictions on parole eligibility – which applied only to sentences imposed after their enactment – gradually kicked in.[25] One study found that only 13 percent of defendants released in 1990 served the full sentence imposed and defendants released that year had served on average 38 percent of their sentences.[26]

Legislatures seeking to increase the severity of punishments recognized the distinction between the formal sentences imposed and the time actually served, and worked to close the gap. The variety of tools in this effort came to be known by the moniker Truth in Sentencing.

> The federal Truth in Lending Act passed by Congress in 1968 appears to have inspired the parallel Truth in Sentencing label.

Truth in Sentencing could most directly be achieved by abolishing parole. The rhetoric supporting parole abolition fits neatly into the political dynamic described in Chapter 6. For example, in the early 1990s, George Allen made parole abolition a centerpiece of his Virginia gubernatorial campaign. After a landslide victory and implementation of the reforms he sought, Allen explained why his State had needed a "complete overhaul" in a column in *Corrections Today*:

> Convicted felons were serving about one-third of their sentences, and many were serving only one-sixth . . . . First degree murderers were given average sentences of 35 years, but spent an average of only 10 years behind bars. Rapists were being sentenced to nine years and serving four. Armed robbers were receiving sentences averaging 14 years and serving only about four. . . . On Oct. 13, 1994, I signed . . . legislation that . . . restores trust in the criminal justice system . . . eliminated discretionary parole . . . and established truth in sentencing.[27]

As suggested in the previous chapter, these changes to the criminal laws made a difference not only to people serving prison time but also to politicians like Allen. A local newspaper summed up Allen's career as follows: "George Allen went from political oblivion to an easy gubernatorial victory last year largely by crystallizing fears about violent crime into a pair of seemingly simple, appealing ideas: Get violent criminals off the street and keep them behind bars longer."[28]

By 2000, at least half the States had either abolished or severely restricted parole release, with fourteen States and the federal government eliminating parole entirely.[29] Even this description masks the degree of change since States were constantly tinkering with their parole systems to reduce early releases. For example, Michigan increased the time between parole hearings for prisoners from two to five years. Texas's parole system is established by the State's constitution, but that did not stop legislators from increasing the percentage of the sentences that prisoners had to serve before becoming eligible for release.[30] Georgia and Missouri made similar changes, requiring those serving life sentences (in some jurisdictions the only prisoners still eligible for parole) to wait substantially longer for their first parole hearings. Georgia increased the wait from seven to thirty years; Missouri increased it from thirteen to twenty-three years.[31] These efforts had a profound impact. Criminal justice researchers Jeremy

Travis and Sarah Lawrence reported that, nationwide, the percentage of prisoners released early by parole boards dropped to 24 percent by 1999.[32]

Truth in Sentencing laws also targeted "good time" credits – a long-standing tool used by prison officials to incentivize good behavior while in custody. Good time credits allow prisoners to reduce their time served by avoiding disciplinary infractions. Depending on the formula for calculating these credits, they can be substantial. Reflecting the attention to detail that marked the legislative efforts to increase severity, Governor Allen explained that in addition to abolishing parole, "We eliminated 'good time.'"[33]

Congress added momentum to the Truth in Sentencing movement with the 1994 Crime Bill. The bill authorized federal grants to States that met certain conditions, including that violent offenders would serve 85 percent of the sentences judges imposed. In 1996, thirty States applied for grants, and twenty-five received them – a total of $196 million. Grant amounts were tied to the number of prisoners, and so led to the biggest windfalls for the highest incarcerating states: ranging from $76,322 for North Dakota to $46 million for California.

Although commentators often highlight the 1994 Crime Bill's truth-in-sentencing incentives as a milestone on the road to Mass Incarceration, the bill is more illustrative than causal. By 1994, States were already embracing penal severity. Thus, these federal incentives did not cause States to change course, but instead reinforced the path they were already on. Still, a review performed for Congress concluded that the grants were a partial factor for adopting Truth in Sentencing Laws in eleven States and a "key factor" in four. For example, the report noted that Oklahoma had been considering a law that would require offenders to serve 75 percent of their sentences and increased that percentage to 85 percent to qualify for the grants.[34]

Not every State followed the same formula, but they all moved in a similar direction. Texas did not formally adopt "truth in sentencing," but it reduced the amount of "good time" credits prisoners could receive. It also tinkered with its parole laws and carefully selected the personnel who made release decisions, publishing statistical break-downs of the voting records of each parole board member. These measures had the desired effect. In a 2001 report, a state agency presented a chart to the Texas Legislature, congratulating that body on closing the "Prison Revolving Door" (see Figure 7.1).

The chart reflects the dramatic increase in the percentage of sentences served by certain offenders from 38 percent in 1992 to 75 percent in 1998 to a projected 90 percent for future years. Two years later, the same agency's report included another chart showing the dramatic changes in parole releases, dropping from 54,759 in 1990 to 15,246 in 2002 – while the State's prison population expanded (see Figure 7.2).

Each State's story is unique. Texas, in fact, faced decarcerative pressure from a federal court ruling (referenced in Chapter 2) directing the State to reduce prison overcrowding. The initial reaction to this pressure – a temporary reduction in imprisonment spurred by a high number of parole releases in 1990 – was followed by media outcry, building of new prisons, and harsher laws.

Similar stories played out across the country. California retained parole release only for prisoners serving life sentences, and parole grants for these so-called lifers became increasingly rare, mirroring the politics of the State. Between 1991 and 2000, as California's prison population exploded, the highest number of parole releases in any year was fifty-two, with a low of eight in 1995 – 0.3 percent of those eligible for parole that year.[35] This illustrates an important point. The ratcheting up of American penal severity typically married two components: law and discretion. In some jurisdictions, dramatic changes to the laws drove increased severity. In other jurisdictions, the people who acted under those laws, like members of the parole board, dispensed less lenience. Most commonly – as in California – both things were happening simultaneously. That's because the same energy that was leading to changes in the laws was changing the membership in key criminal justice positions and altering the attitudes of the people who retained discretion to choose between lenience and severity. Thus, as new California laws removed the possibility of release for most offenders, California parole board members consistently voted to deny release to those who remained eligible.

You Have Met the Goal of Increasing Punishment for Incarcerated Violent Offenders and Closing the Prison Revolving Door

Percentage of Prison Sentence Served

Year of Release (First Time Releasees)	Non-Aggravated Violent Offenders	Aggravated Violent Offenders (Most Severe)
1992	23.8%	38.2%
1998	64.4%	75.6%
Projected	66.5%	89.1%

Projected Percentage of Prison Sentence to Be Served - Specific Aggravated Offenses

Homicide	94.1%
Kidnapping	92.1%
Sexual Assault	99.6%
Robbery	88.3%
Assault	85.6%
Other Aggravated	83.3%

Parole Approval Rate by Year

You Have Closed the Prison Revolving Door

FY	90	91	92	93	94	95	96	97	98	99	00
Parole Approval Rate	78.1%	74.3%	58.1%	39.1%	28.0%	21.0%	21.2%	16.7%	20.2%	18.2%	22.5%

Page 5

Criminal Justice Policy Council, Biennial Report to the 77th Texas Legislature, January 2001

Figure 7.1 Report to Texas legislature I

59

60

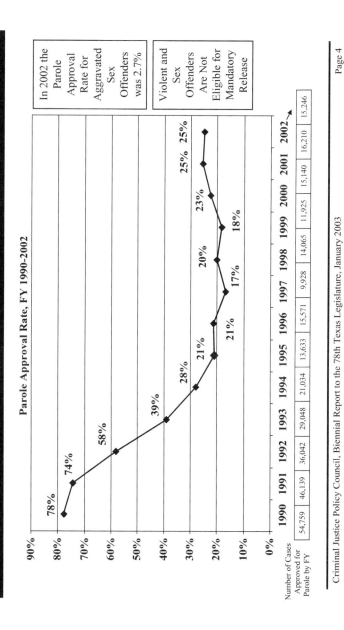

Parole Approval Rate, FY 1990–2002

In 2002 the Parole Approval Rate for Aggravated Sex Offenders was 2.7%

Violent and Sex Offenders Are Not Eligible for Mandatory Release

78%

74%

58%

39%

28%

21%

21%

17%

20%

23%

25% 25%

18%

Number of Cases Approved for Parole by FY	1990	1991	1992	1993	1994	1995	1996	1997	1998	1999	2000	2001	2002
	54,759	46,139	36,042	29,048	21,034	13,633	15,571	9,928	14,065	11,925	15,140	16,210	15,246

Criminal Justice Policy Council, Biennial Report to the 78th Texas Legislature, January 2003

Page 4

Figure 7.2 Report to Texas legislature II

7.2 ENCOURAGING ARRESTS, PROSECUTIONS, AND LONGER SENTENCES

Legislatures also sought to increase the likelihood that people who committed crimes would be caught and punished. Most generically, they paid for more police officers (Chapter 10), prosecutors (Chapter 11), and judges (Chapter 12) to process all the cases that their "tough on crime" policies created. Legislators also sought to micromanage this crime fighting by paying special attention to specific crimes.

America's legislators are always enacting new criminal laws. In April 1983, the Presidential Commission on Drunk Driving noted that States enacted 38 new drunk-driving laws during the 1982 legislative session.[36] Between 2008 and 2013, Congress created 400 new federal offenses.[37] Michigan added "more than 45 new criminal offenses to the books annually, on average, from 2008 through 2013," with almost half of the new additions constituting felonies. Between 2009 and 2014, North Carolina's legislature enacted an average of 34 crimes per year, jumping to 83 new criminal offenses in 2016. Many of these crimes have a small footprint, like a 2016 North Carolina provision criminalizing the removal of labels affixed to bedding, and a 2012 Michigan law commanding that barge owners prominently display their name, address, and telephone number on the hull. But others are more impactful, such as a 1968 federal law prohibiting anyone with a felony conviction from possessing a firearm (an offense that would go on to generate almost 10 percent of federal convictions), and the first federal law prohibiting the possession of child pornography enacted in 1990.[38]

New laws also increase the incarcerated population in indirect ways. In 1970, Congress mandated that banks report transactions over $10,000 and then in 1986 enacted a new criminal offense – "structuring" – as part of a broad money-laundering bill that, among other things, made it a felony to deposit money in a way that evaded the reporting requirement.[39] Other laws made prosecutions easier by, for example, adopting evidence rules that permitted damaging evidence to be introduced against repeat sex offenders and limiting the admissibility of defense evidence in sexual assault cases. Relatedly, States

Table 7.1 *Incarceration by crime*

% State Prisoners	1980	1999	2019
Homicide	16	13	15
Robbery	25	14	12
Sexual Assault	7	9	14
Other Assault	8	10	14
Burglary	17	10	8
Drugs	6	21	14
Total of Above	79%	77%	76%

enacted "gang enhancements" that permitted prosecutors to introduce evidence of defendants' membership in criminal street gangs in prosecutions for offenses like robbery or murder.[40]

Yet for the most part, Mass Incarceration did not require the creation of new offenses (or evidence rules). Few people are locked up for mattress tag violations or structuring. Instead, most people are incarcerated in the United States for familiar crimes. Table 7.1 lists the most common offenses that people in State prison had been convicted of in the past few decades alongside the percentage of the State prison population convicted of that offense.

The offenses listed in the Table account for the vast bulk of the entire State prison population. Other crimes that contribute substantial but lower numbers to prison populations are also familiar offenses: (2019 figures) Weapons Offenses (4 percent), Theft (4 percent), Fraud (2 percent), DWI (2 percent).[41]

Legislatures increased prison populations by facilitating and enhancing prosecutions of these existing crimes. Most obviously they did this by increasing the punishments for traditional crimes, including those listed above as described in the previous section. But legislatures did more than that. For example, New York was the first state to criminalize drunk driving, doing so in 1910. But the law was difficult to apply, arrests infrequent, and convictions rare. In one 1966 case, a New York appeals court threw out a jury conviction due to insufficient evidence despite the "admission by defendant to a police officer that he had been drinking, and the opinion of four witnesses that, based on their observations of defendant after the accident, they thought he was drunk."[42] A report to the New York State legislature, from its subcommittee on drunk driving, explained that in 1979, "the chances of being arrested were estimated as low as one in 2,000 drunk driving events." Further,

> If caught, he or she could likely plead guilty to a non-alcohol related charge, such as reckless driving, and receive a penalty not likely to include loss of license. Even if convicted of drunk driving, the average fine imposed amounted to only $11. With little chance of being either apprehended or adequately punished, it is not surprising that few motorists were deterred from drunk driving by New York State's laws or their enforcement.[43]

The report was part of a series of efforts over the years by the New York State legislature to combat drunk driving through criminal law. The legislature repeatedly revamped the State's drunk driving laws, establishing a series of graduated offenses that could be applied depending on the nature of the proof available to police and prosecutors. The legislature also increased the penalties, at one point enacting a mandatory sixty-day jail sentence, and barring prosecutors from plea bargaining around drunk driving charges.[44] These legal changes sparked and complemented increasingly aggressive enforcement. The State's drunk driving arrests rose from around 6,000 in 1970, to 60,000 in 1984, remaining at this elevated level for subsequent years – and convictions went up accordingly.[45]

The New York State experience reflects a national trend. Drunk driving arrests became the most common type of arrest in the country until passed by assault and drug arrests in the mid-1990s. And while DWI is not as severely punished as other offenses, all these arrests made an impact. In a study on the topic, the Bureau of Justice Statistics reported that: "In 1997 an estimated 513,200 offenders were on probation or in jail or prison for driving while intoxicated by alcohol (DWI).... DWI offenders accounted for nearly 14% of probationers, 7% of jail inmates, and 2% of State prisoners." This was a substantial change from a decade earlier: "The number [of DWI offenders] in jail increased from 18,600 to 41,100, and the number in prison increased from 3,300 to 17,600."[46] Drunk-driving enforcement is only one of many contributors to Mass Incarceration, but it is emblematic. The pattern of legislative efforts to address societal problems – like drunk driving – by removing obstacles to criminal prosecution and encouraging aggressive enforcement played out across offenses and across the country with similar results.

Domestic violence presents another important example. Assault is a long-standing offense. But prior to the 1970s, spousal assaults were rarely prosecuted. Oregon was one of the earliest States to try to change this, enacting legislation in 1977 that would become a national model. The Oregon law directed that if a police officer suspected domestic violence, "he shall arrest and take into custody the alleged assailant or potential assailant."[47] Virginia's legislature enacted a law commanding police responding to a domestic violence call to either make an arrest or compile a report explaining the "special circumstances which would dictate a course of action other than an arrest." For every arrest, the statute also required the officer to "petition for an emergency protective order."

> Protective orders are a common tool in criminal cases and can be obtained with minimal process. They typically require those suspected of violence to refrain from contact with the alleged victim pending the case's resolution, often barring even remote communication, like phone calls. Domestic violence can sometimes be difficult to prove. By contrast, a protective order violation can be conclusively established when police respond to a 911 call and find the defendant at the victim's residence or through a recording of a defendant's call to the alleged victim from jail. This essentially irrefutable evidence can support an arrest and also be offered in court to prove the protective order violation (a separate criminal offense) with or without the victim's cooperation. In 1991, Texas enacted a mandatory arrest statute for violations of domestic violence protective orders.[48]

Legislators packaged laws targeting specific offenses with other measures, including funding, designed to increase the number of criminal prosecutions. Utah enacted legislation that limited the dismissal of domestic violence cases "[b]ecause of the serious nature of domestic violence."[49] Florida declared that "[i]t is the intent of the Legislature that domestic violence be treated as a criminal act rather than a private matter" and backed up its desire by directing the development of new units that would "specialize in the prosecution of domestic violence cases."[50] Connecticut created a reporting requirement, directing each police officer responding to a domestic violence call to complete an offense report, and directing the State police "to compile and report annually to the Governor, the Legislature and the Advisory Council on Domestic Violence on the tabulated data from the domestic violence offense reports."[51] The 1994 Crime Bill similarly supported domestic violence prosecution offering large financial grants to States to "support police and prosecutor efforts and victims services in cases involving sexual violence or domestic abuse, and for other programs which strengthen enforcement and provide services to victims in such cases."[52] As Chapter 10 explains, these laws and the attitudes behind them proved effective in transforming the legal response to domestic violence.

Legislators also tried to enhance the punishments for existing crimes through mandatory sentences and sentencing enhancements. The most prominent illustration of this phenomenon occurred in the federal system, where political scientist Naomi Murakawa documented a "staggering increase" in the number of mandatory minimum sentencing laws enacted over the era of Mass Incarceration. And while mandatory minimum sentences had once been reserved for "crimes that were infrequent, minor, and decisively federal in nature," over time mandatory minimum sentences increasingly targeted "common crimes with high chances of ... apprehension."[53] For example, in 1968, Congress enacted 18 U.S.C. § 924(c), which created a mandatory one-year sentence enhancement for anyone who "used" or "carried" a firearm during a federal offense. Over the years, Congress broadened the statutory language and increased the length of the enhancement. Section 924(c) enhancements became powerful determinants of sentences, leading to infamous examples, like that of Weldon Angeles who received a fifty-five-year sentence for selling marijuana. The sentence was almost entirely a function of the application of three 924(c) enhancements for carrying a gun during the sales.[54] As with the examples in the previous paragraph, federal 924(c) gun enhancements were just one of a suite of legislative and policy changes, often including additional funding and other incentives, designed to crack down on a particular problem, like gun crime.

More familiar examples include Congress's efforts to ramp up the sentences for drug offenses. Perhaps the most notorious of all is the Anti–Drug Abuse Act of 1986, which established, among other things, a five-year mandatory prison sentence for selling 5 grams of cocaine base (crack cocaine) or 500 grams of powder cocaine.[55] For context, a nickel weighs five grams. States enacted similar weapons and drug laws and pursued other avenues as well. In 1988, California enacted a new law that made it unlawful to promote or assist criminal conduct by members of a criminal street gang, along with a sentencing enhancement that added years to a prison sentence for anyone who committed a crime for the benefit of a gang.[56] Other States followed suit, with one tally finding eighteen States that followed California in adopting gang sentencing enhancements.[57] These legislative efforts to increase punishments for specific crimes complemented and strengthened the broader efforts to increase time served for all offenses through the Truth in Sentencing provisions described in the previous section.

It would be impossible to catalog all the legislative changes that contributed to Mass Incarceration. But the discussion set out above provides an outline of the kinds of changes that mattered most. As Part III will detail, some of the changes were more impactful than others. But the momentum was always in the same direction. Legislatures looked for lenience in traditional criminal justice contexts (e.g., low sentences for violent offenses) and in new areas as well (drugs, weapons possession, drunk driving, domestic assault). When they found it, they pushed police, prosecutors, and judges to be more aggressive and more punitive through new funding and laws.

8   THE FUTILITY OF FIGHTING CRIME WITH CRIMINAL LAW

There is a paradox in the American narrative of Mass Incarceration. In theory, making criminal laws more severe should not lead to large prison populations in the long term. That's because as laws become more severe, crime becomes increasingly unattractive. That should lead, over time, to less crime and shrinking prison populations. No crime is worth the punishments currently on the books. And by now, decades into "tough on crime" policies, everyone should know that crime doesn't pay. There should be no drug dealing, no unlawful weapons possession, no violence, no repeat offenders. It may sound silly, but if you look at the claims politicians made about why they were increasing criminal severity, this was the idea.

Legal scholar Franklin Zimring observes that the basic flaw in America's response to societal problems over the past decades was a knee-jerk default to incarceration: "[W]hatever the question of the day, the answer was always prison."[1] But prison wasn't really what the politicians were promising. When New York governor Nelson Rockefeller proposed severe new drug laws in 1973, he proclaimed that harsh mandatory sentences would make drug dealing "totally unattractive."[2] The *New York Daily News* editorialized that the laws "would cause hordes of drug pushers to go out of business rather than chance a lifetime in the clink." Senator Kennedy called for tougher sentences because "our existing criminal justice system is no deterrent at all to violent crime in our society." President Reagan's Task Force on Victims of Crime claimed that action was needed because "[t]he criminal knows that his risk of punishment is minuscule." The federal gun sentencing enhancement discussed in the preceding chapter was supposed to "persuade the man tempted to commit a Federal felony to leave his gun at home."[3] California's criminal street-gang sentencing enhancement sought "the eradication of criminal activity by street gangs."[4] Politicians didn't sell a war on crime as a way to fill prisons. They claimed that aggressive enforcement and severe penalties would make these crimes go away. But that didn't happen. This chapter explains why.

One reason that tough criminal laws don't deter crime is that people who commit crimes often aren't thinking rationally. They are angry, scared, or under the influence of drugs and alcohol. But another reason that is frequently overlooked is that the American criminal justice system isn't good at deterrence. The Department of Justice's publications recognize the key problem: "Research shows clearly that the chance of being caught is a vastly more effective deterrent than even draconian punishment."[5] All the penalties in the world have only a marginal impact on crime unless people expect to be caught.

That's a big problem. As Fyodor Dostoevsky hinted in 1866, there is a long and winding path from crime to punishment, and most crimes never make it the whole way. Some of the obstacles are legal, but most are practical. The biggest obstacle is that the odds of getting caught for most crimes are low. Police never hear about most offenses. And even when the authorities learn about a crime, they usually don't solve it. That means that even if we assume that everyone is a rational actor and aware of the severe penalties that await when they consider committing a crime (big assumptions), it is often rational to assume that you won't get caught.

Figure 8.1 is a chart published by the FBI with arrest rates for common crimes.[6] The chart shows the percentage of crimes reported to police that are solved either by arrest or "exceptional means." "Exceptional means" is an unusual event that makes an arrest unnecessary, like the suspect dies or the police figure out that the reported crime never happened.

> Clearance rates vary by jurisdiction and year. In 2012, Detroit police reported a homicide clearance rate of 9 percent.[7]

Keep in mind that the chart is just for *reported* crimes. Most crime is never reported. This is especially true for hard-to-detect crimes like

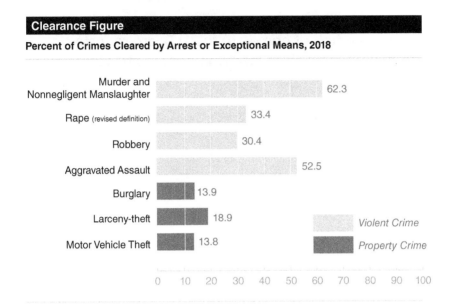

Figure 8.1 Crime clearance

wage theft, embezzlement, tax cheating, drugs, corruption, insider trading, and on and on. The arrest rates for those crimes are so tiny no one has even thought of a way to estimate them. One 2009 study that compared the prevalence of drunk driving in New York State to the frequency of arrests, estimated the likelihood of arrest for any particular incident of drunk driving at 1 in 481, or approximately 0.2 percent.[8]

Figure 8.2, from the PEW Research Center illustrates the two points together.[9] The Figure shows both the low reporting and low arrest rates and the lack of change over time. Even as the country ramped up penalties and poured more and more resources into a war on crime, a stubborn fact remained. Most crimes weren't reported, and for those crimes that were reported, the police usually didn't catch the responsible party. For example, in California, the clearance rate for major crimes reported to police – homicide, forcible rape, robbery, aggravated assault, burglary, and motor vehicle theft – hovered just over 20 percent in the 1990s, with California reporting a relatively high

Fewer than half of crimes in the U.S. are reported, and fewer than half of reported crimes are solved

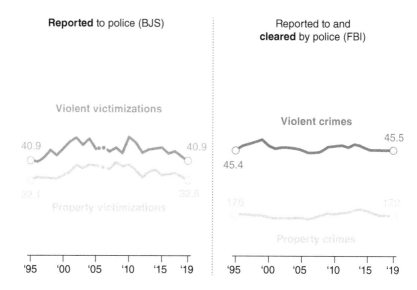

% of crimes ...

Reported to police (BJS)   Reported to and **cleared** by police (FBI)

Violent victimizations

40.9 ...... 40.9

Violent crimes

45.5

45.4

32.1 ...... 32.5

Property victimizations

17.6 ...... 17.1

Property crimes

'95 '00 '05 '10 '15 '19   '95 '00 '05 '10 '15 '19

Note: BJS and FBI crime definitions differ for some offenses. 2006 BJS estimates are not comparable with other years due to methodological changes. FBI figures reflect percentage of crimes cleared through arrest or "exceptional means," including cases in which a suspect dies or a victim declines to cooperate with a prosecution.
Source: U.S. Bureau of Justice Statistics (BJS), Federal Bureau of Investigation (FBI).

PEW RESEARCH CENTER

Figure 8.2 Reporting + clearances

26 percent solve rate for these crimes in 1999 before dipping back down again for subsequent years.[10]

This isn't the kind of thing that law enforcement officials brag about. But the general theme presented above is no secret. In fact, the people who regularly commit crimes are as well informed about the low likelihood of arrest and punishment as anyone. For example, the authors of the 2009 study referenced above interviewed a focus group of people who had been arrested for driving drunk. Despite having been arrested, the participants continued to perceive the risk of arrest as low: "quite negligible," "slim to none," "not a chance." "None of the participants thought they would ever get stopped." Why? Because that was their experience:

- "It's astronomical as to how many times I was drinking and driving before I got caught."
- "I drank and drove thousands of times before being caught; could probably drink and drive that many times again before getting caught."

And so far, all we are talking about is the distance between a crime and *an arrest*. An arrest is just the beginning. The drunk driver focus group also expressed the opinion that even if they were caught, the punishment, if any, would be light. And again, there is more truth to this than government officials would like to admit.

Figure 8.3 portrays the chances that a typical robbery offense in an American city will be punished by incarceration (about 5 percent), by illustrating the wide variety of ways that even serious offenses veer off the pathway to prison.[11]

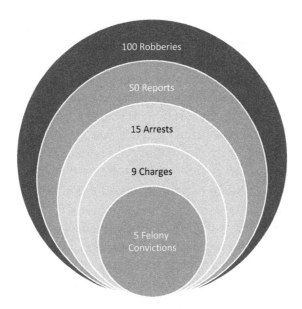

100 Robberies

50 Reports

15 Arrests

9 Charges

5 Felony Convictions

Figure 8.3 Case attrition: Robbery

As the chart reflects, a great deal of the fall-off comes from the lack of reporting and difficulty of arrest. But even after a case enters the system via arrest, it continues on a complex path, overseen by a bunch of independent actors who all must agree to get anything done. A police officer has to gather the evidence in a way that will hold up in court. The prosecutor has to charge the case and carry it to the finish line, while fighting off legal challenges from the defense attorney. The trial judge needs to allow the case to proceed. Either a jury of twelve strangers convicts or the defendant admits guilt as part of a plea deal. Then the judge has to sign off and hand down a sentence. Next, an appeals court gets a say. In many jurisdictions, a parole board still has the authority to release folks early and on top of all that, the governor (or, for federal crimes, the president) can issue a pardon. Sometimes prisons and jails get so overcrowded that wardens are forced to let people out to make space.

All of that is good. The government should face difficulties when it tries to lock people up. But these sensible hurdles – along with the bedrock principle that only the guilty should be punished – make it almost impossible in a large, heterogeneous nation of over 300 million people to use criminal laws to achieve policy goals. That didn't change when we started arresting, convicting, and sending more people to prison. The steadily increasing *number* of people getting locked up continued to represent only a tiny *fraction* of those committing crime.

The largest obstacle to enforcing the law is not the common complaint about defendants who get off on "technicalities." The biggest obstacle is the nontechnical problem of actually proving that a suspect committed the charged crime. That is why it is such a bad idea, tactically speaking, to confess. When you admit that you committed a crime, you sweep away most of the obstacles to conviction, the legal ones in the Constitution and the practical ones that keep police and prosecutors up at night.

For example, car theft is surprisingly difficult to go to prison for. Why? Because police rarely catch someone stealing a car. They catch people *driving* stolen cars. The cases unfold as follows. Step one: someone reports to the police that their car was stolen. Days, weeks, or months later (step two), police stop a car and find out from a computer search that the car was stolen. Then (step three), they arrest the driver. Case closed? No. Sure, somewhere out there is a person who is guilty of car theft, but how do we know it's the person the police caught driving the car?

> Auto theft is one of the most reported crimes, with almost 80 percent reported to the police.[12]

The problem is not the law. As in other contexts, legislators have bent over backward to try to make it easy to prosecute car theft. In fact, the typical car theft statute doesn't criminalize stealing a car, it criminalizes using a car without permission. Here is Washington, D.C.'s car theft law:

Unauthorized Use of a Motor Vehicle

A person commits the offense of unauthorized use of a motor vehicle under this subsection if, without the consent of the owner, the person takes, uses, or operates a motor vehicle, or causes a motor vehicle to be taken, used, or operated, for his or her own profit, use, or purpose.[13]

The offense is a felony, punished by up to five years in prison. Notice by prohibiting unauthorized "use," the statute makes it easier to prosecute the person that police typically catch – the driver. But there's still a hurdle for prosecutors. It is not enough to show that the driver of the stolen car used the vehicle without the consent of the owner. The driver has to *know* that they didn't have the owner's consent. It wouldn't be fair, for example, if you rented or borrowed a car from someone who claimed to own it and then got sent to prison for car theft because the car happened to be stolen.

And whenever there is a legal defense, people will invoke it. When people driving stolen cars get stopped, they don't tell the police, "Hi. I'm driving a stolen car." Often they don't say anything or just deny knowing that the car was stolen. When folks do say something, they say something like: "I borrowed the car from a close friend whose aunt left the car with him while she traveled overseas." That's from a real case. It may sound silly, but it doesn't have to be what really happened. All the driver needs the jury to (kind of) believe is that the driver didn't *know* the car was stolen.[14]

It is tempting to think that these stories are always made up. But they are not. A lot of cases involve stolen rental cars. Someone steals a rental car, and the rental company reports the theft to police. Later on, the police stop the car. The driver claims to have had no idea that the car was stolen – and the driver might be telling the truth. A police officer explained the problem in testimony in one D.C. case: "Rental cars are popular among car thieves, [the officer] said, because they often are not reported stolen until they have been missing for at least thirty days. That summer the Hertz Corporation in particular had been experiencing thefts of its cars in Virginia, which the thieves would then sell, he said, to 'unsuspecting' buyers in the District of Columbia."[15] All of this means that it is hard to convict someone of car theft. And it should be hard. In fact, in D.C. when I was a prosecutor, these cases were so hard to prove we frequently declined to prosecute them and failed to obtain convictions in many of the cases we tried.

Chapter 11 will highlight how the difficulty of proving some cases (car thefts) but not others (drug offenses) are a big part of the Mass Incarceration story. For now, the key point is the low odds of any particular crime traveling from offense to arrest to conviction to punishment. Most crimes are not reported, most reported crimes aren't solved, and most solved crimes don't result in incarceration. That doesn't mean police, prosecutors, and judges aren't trying. They are. It means that these efforts only touch a small fraction of America's "crime."

There's one more wrinkle. High case volume clogs up the system in predictable ways, hobbling its ability to perform efficiently and deter crime. But that's not all. Increasing severity, particularly inflexible severity, like a mandatory minimum sentence or an unfailingly harsh judge, also creates obstacles to efficient case processing. That's because the more that legislatures ramp up the penalties for criminal offenses, the more the people handling the cases try to find workarounds. Everybody wants to do the "right" thing, even prosecutors.

No case illustrates the way severe punishments create problematic distortions better than the prosecution of Joseph Tigano III.[16] I wrote about the case for *Slate*. The media was running with the story of an uncaring system that kept Tigano locked up seven years *before* trial. But neglect wasn't the right diagnosis. As I explained in 2018:

The problem in Tigano's case was not neglect, but a 20-year mandatory-minimum sentence that loomed over every decision in the case.

Tigano's case was no Agatha Christie mystery. Federal agents found 1,400 marijuana plants growing in Tigano's residence. What's more, three separate agents testified that Tigano confessed that he grew the marijuana. That's a tough case to fight. He was going to lose at trial, and he was going to lose big.

While many states are lining up to cash in on marijuana legalization, federal law still dictates that a person who grows "1,000 or more [marijuana] plants ... shall be sentenced to a term of imprisonment which may not be less than 10 years." That's a 10-year mandatory prison term for growing marijuana – doubled for anyone, like Tigano, with a prior felony drug conviction.

The attorneys and lower court judges in Tigano's case ... were not neglecting Tigano. They were, instead, repeatedly delaying his case – to the point of ordering three needless mental competency examinations – in the hope that Tigano would agree to a plea deal.

Tigano, however, insisted on his constitutional right to a trial. After seven years, he finally got it. There were no surprises. The jury convicted and the judge sentenced him to 20 years in federal prison. Of course, no one expected the final twist. On appeal, the lengthy pretrial delay set Tigano free.

The politicians who crafted the twenty-year mandatory minimum sentence thought they were getting tough on crime. But when punishments get so out of whack, the officials who are supposed to enforce those laws often blink. Or, as in Tigano's case, the system just crashes. Even worse, sometimes people actually do get the outrageous sentences politicians authorize.

If you asked Congress or a federal prosecutor about Tigano's case, they would explain that severe sentences are necessary "to put pressure on defendants to cooperate in exchange for a lower sentence so evidence against more responsible criminals can be attained."[17] That sometimes happens, although twenty years seems like overkill even for this purpose. And more importantly, severe punishments aren't surgical strikes. They are nuclear bombs. When cooperation becomes the goal, punishments get out of whack. People are punished most severely for loyalty or ignorance. The defendants in the most danger of severe sentences become the ones who know the least. Think of the "drug mules" hired by cartels to transport drugs across the border. When these folks are caught (a common arrest scenario), they have a lot of drugs, a tenuous legal defense, and little information to trade. Frequent disconnects like these between culpability and punishment further undermine the system's efforts to send clear messages and deter crime.

In sum, American criminal courts are not in a position to deter crime on a broad scale. And that remained true even as legislators, police, and prosecutors increased the volume of cases and the severity of the laws that applied. In light of the inherent difficulty of catching people who commit crimes in a free society, the many obstacles the government must overcome to impose formal punishment, and the neglect and mistakes that are inevitable in a complex, overburdened system, criminal courts cannot reduce crime efficiently through deterrence. Police, prosecutors and judges can send people to prison. And, as Chapters 10 through 12 will show, they did, in fact, substantially increase the number of imprisoned Americans. But even with those unprecedented increases, only a tiny percentage of crimes led to punishment. That's the stalemate that characterizes the last fifty years of American criminal law: increasingly severe enforcement in the face of stubbornly persistent crime. That's the recipe for Mass Incarceration.

9 THE ROLE OF RACE

The long reach of racism in American society is an important part of the Mass Incarceration story, but contrary to some recent accounts, the two phenomena are not the same. There are aspects of Mass Incarceration that can best be explained through a race lens and others that cannot. This chapter offers a way to distinguish between these aspects and explains why the distinction matters in understanding the rise of Mass Incarceration and the prospects for reform.

Mass Incarceration has widely different impacts on different racial groups. The Bureau of Justice Statistics reports that, nationwide, Hispanic people make up 16 percent of the population but 23 percent of the country's prison population; while white people, who account for 64 percent of the overall population, constitute only 30 percent of prison inmates.[1] The disparate impact is especially stark for Black Americans. Black people make up 12 percent of the American population, but 33 percent of the prison population. While this disproportion ultimately stems from the country's legacy of slavery and discrimination, the precise role that race plays is complex and varies based on context.

The Vera Institute of Criminal Justice offers online profiles of every State's prison populations. These profiles reveal the startling disproportionate percentage of Black people in the incarcerated population of many States. In Louisiana 66 percent of the prison population is Black: Mississippi (61 percent), Georgia (60 percent), North Carolina (51 percent), Florida (46 percent). Substantial disparities appear outside the South as well. Michigan's prisons are majority Black (55 percent) despite the State itself having only a 15 percent Black population; similar disproportions exist in States like New York (49–16 percent) and Pennsylvania (47–12 percent).

Racial and ethnic gaps shrink in U.S. prison population

Sentenced federal and state prisoners by race and Hispanic origin, 2007–2017

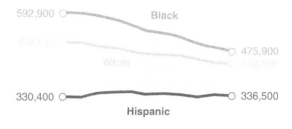

Note: Whites and blacks include those who report being only one race and are non-Hispanic. Hispanics are of any race. Prison population is defined as inmates sentenced to more than a year in federal or state prison.
Source: Bureau of Justice Statistics.

PEW RESEARCH CENTER

Figure 9.1 Incarceration and race

Alongside these dismal statistics, there are signs of improvement. The disparity has shrunk considerably in recent years. Black people made up 45 percent of American prison inmates in 1990, 46 percent in 2000, 37 percent in 2010, and 33 percent in 2019. The trend is reflected in Figure 9.1 from the Pew Research Center.[2]

Incarceration rates skew even more dramatically based on gender. Thus, it makes sense to focus on the demographic most disproportionately impacted by Mass Incarceration: Black males. Sociologists Steven Raphael and Michael Stoll calculated that at any point in time in 2007, 8 percent of Black males were incarcerated as compared to 2.7 percent of Hispanic males and 1 percent of white males.

And focusing in even more tightly, they found that the disparity is driven by a subset within that subset: young Black males with the least formal education. In 2007, Black men without a high school degree suffered far higher incarceration rates than any other group, about 25 percent for those aged 18–40.[3]

The simplest explanation for these disparities is the legacy of slavery and ongoing racism. That's the case legal scholar Michelle Alexander presented in her widely acclaimed 2010 book, *The New Jim Crow: Mass Incarceration in the Age of Colorblindness*. Alexander characterizes the criminal justice system as the third incarnation of American efforts to perpetuate a racial caste system, following slavery and Jim Crow. In Alexander's view, Mass Incarceration filled the void that opened when the Civil Rights Movement rooted out Jim Crow laws:

> Once again, in response to a major disruption in the prevailing social order – this time the civil rights gains of the 1960s – a new system of racialized social control was created by exploiting the vulnerabilities and racial resentments of poor and working-class whites. More than 2 million people found themselves behind bars at the turn of the twenty-first century, and millions more were relegated to the margins of mainstream society, banished to a political and social space not unlike Jim Crow, where discrimination in employment, housing, and access to educations was perfectly legal, and where they could be denied the right to vote. The system functioned relatively automatically.... Ninety percent of those admitted to prison for drug offenses in many states were black or Latino, yet the mass incarceration of communities of color was explained in race-neutral terms, an adaptation to the needs and demands of the current political climate. The New Jim Crow was born.[4]

Alexander's account is most convincing as a description of the impact of American law enforcement on certain communities of color, and least convincing as an account of the system's design. In part the difficulty in assigning motives is unavoidable. As explained in Chapter 3, the "system" is actually hundreds if not thousands of independent systems, all doing different things. Thus, its effects are easier to identify than its purpose. But even the effects are complicated.

Table 9.1 *Prison by race*

	1974	1991	2001
White	923,000	1,534,000	2,203,000
Black	646,000	1,290,000	2,167,000
Hispanic	102,000	422,000	997,000

One effect that tends to be overlooked in arguments like the one advanced by Alexander is Mass Incarceration's broad reach. For example, Alexander claims that the policies that fueled Mass Incarceration catered to "poor and working-class whites." But as of 2019, this country's incarcerated population included 757,000 whites, typically drawn from poor and working classes.[5] That's more than twice the entire incarcerated population in 1970. The Bureau of Justice Statistics' Census of State and Federal Adult Correctional Facilities reported that, as of 2019, 38.9 percent of adult prisoners in "confinement facilities" were white and 39.1 percent were Black; while 45.6 percent of prisoners in "community-based facilities" were white and 34.2 percent were Black.[6]

Table 9.1 shows the *number* of people living in America on the date indicated who had served time in an American prison, by race.[7]

The stunning disproportionate impact on Black people is the first thing that jumps out from the table. But it is also notable that in the same period that Alexander highlights ("the turn of the twenty-first century"), more white people had been sent to prison than any other group. This fact does not disprove Alexander's claim that Mass Incarceration is designed to appeal to the "racial resentments of poor and working class whites," but it complicates that thesis.

In addition, many American jurisdictions increased their prison populations in parallel with the broader Mass Incarceration trends without an apparent racial explanation. Idaho, for example, experienced an unusually high increase in incarceration between 1983 and 2015 – jumping by 505 percent. Yet 74 percent of the State's prison population is white and only 3 percent Black. States like Wyoming, Vermont, New Hampshire, Utah, Montana, and North and South Dakota all reflect the national trends of Mass Incarceration despite small minority populations.[8] One of the crimes for which enforcement and punishment increased most dramatically, child pornography, appears to be primarily committed by (and enforced against) white offenders.[9] A "new system of racialized social control" could have unintended "collateral damage" (Alexander's term),[10] but these facts suggest additional layers to the narrative.

None of this is to suggest that Alexander's account lacks force. In fact, a race-centered account fits neatly into one of this book's core themes: the distinction between the criminal **justice** and criminal **legal** system highlighted in Chapter 4. When we look at the entire landscape, we are viewing two intertwined, but distinct systems, one where racism likely plays a significant role and another where it is less salient. Distinguishing between those two systems helps to isolate the complex and varying role of race in American Mass Incarceration.

Officials enjoy the greatest discretion in the criminal legal system, and that is where we would expect unwarranted bias to appear. A race-centered account fits best with the war on drugs, the criminal legal system's defining component and the focus of *The New Jim Crow*. In 2009, for example, Black people made up over 50 percent of State inmates convicted of drug crimes.[11] Yet there is little evidence of any racial difference in drug offending. As the National Research Council explains,

> Although, according to both arrest and victimization data, blacks have higher rates of involvement than whites in violent crimes, the prevalence of drug use is only slightly higher among blacks than whites for some illicit drugs and slightly lower for others; the difference is not substantial. There is also little evidence, when all drug types are considered, that blacks sell drugs more often than whites.[12]

Thus, the disproportionate number of Black people incarcerated for drugs requires an explanation. One explanation commonly offered is a practical one: "The reason why so many more blacks than whites are arrested and imprisoned for drug crimes is well known and long recognized. They are much easier to arrest. Much white drug dealing occurs behind closed doors and in private. Much black drug dealing occurs in public or semipublic, on the streets and in open-air drug markets."[13]

But even if we accept this theory, ease of arrest – applying the law not where it is most needed but where it is easiest – is not a justification. When police recognize that they will face less resistance making drug arrests in poor urban neighborhoods, as opposed to college campuses or private high schools, they are bowing to the class and race biases that infect society generally.

As we will see in Part III, the process of enforcing criminal laws is filled with these kinds of inflection points, places where officials make decisions about who to target and with what degree of intensity. In some areas, like homicide investigations, this discretion is minimized, and in others, like drug arrests, it is maximized. Thus, if race is motivating official conduct, we would expect to see it more in some areas – like drugs – and less in others – like homicide. And that is what the data shows. Researchers attempting to isolate the degree to which different rates of offending might explain demographic incarceration disparities find little correlation between offending and incarceration for drug offenses, but greater correlation for homicide.[14]

The more discretionary an aspect of law enforcement, the more we can expect to find the influence of conscious and unconscious racial prejudice. Federal investigators uncovered an extreme illustration in Ferguson, Missouri. In 2014, after a police officer in Ferguson shot and killed a Black teenager, Michael Brown, the Department of Justice (DOJ) investigated the Ferguson Police Department (FPD). The DOJ's findings revealed how a small town's application of race-neutral criminal laws could, in fact, re-create Jim Crow.

Like many small towns, Ferguson struggled financially. In response, the town turned its criminal justice system into a piggy bank. The DOJ concluded, "Ferguson's law enforcement practices are shaped by the City's focus on revenue rather than by public safety needs."

> The City budgets for sizeable increases in municipal fines and fees each year, exhorts police and court staff to deliver those revenue increases, and closely monitors whether those increases are achieved. . . . The importance of focusing on revenue generation is communicated to FPD officers. Ferguson police officers from all ranks told us that revenue generation is stressed heavily within the police department, and that the message comes from City leadership. . . . Ferguson has allowed its focus on revenue gener-ation to fundamentally compromise the role of Ferguson's munici-pal court. The municipal court does not act as a neutral arbiter of the law or a check on unlawful police conduct. Instead, the court

primarily uses its judicial authority as the means to compel the payment of fines and fees that advance the City's financial interests.

The DOJ further explained that the FPD's improper use of law enforcement to generate revenue disproportionately impacted the city's African American population.

> Ferguson's law enforcement practices overwhelmingly impact African Americans. Data collected by the Ferguson Police Department from 2012 to 2014 shows that African Americans account for 85% of vehicle stops, 90% of citations, and 93% of arrests made by FPD officers, despite comprising only 67% of Ferguson's population. African Americans are more than twice as likely as white drivers to be searched during vehicle stops even after controlling for non-race based variables such as the reason the vehicle stop was initiated, but are found in possession of contraband 26% less often than white drivers, suggesting officers are impermissibly considering race as a factor when determining whether to search. African Americans are more likely to be cited and arrested following a stop regardless of why the stop was initiated and are more likely to receive multiple citations during a single incident. From 2012 to 2014, FPD issued four or more citations to African Americans on 73 occasions, but issued four or more citations to non-African Americans only twice. FPD appears to bring certain offenses almost exclusively against African Americans. For example, from 2011 to 2013, African Americans accounted for 95% of Manner of Walking in Roadway charges, and 94% of all Failure to Comply charges. Notably, with respect to speeding charges brought by FPD, the evidence shows not only that African Americans are represented at disproportionately high rates overall, but also that the disparate impact of FPD's enforcement practices on African Americans is 48% larger when citations are issued not on the basis of radar or laser, but by some other method, such as the officer's own visual assessment.

Policing in Ferguson looks a lot like the picture Michelle Alexander paints of the system generally. And it makes sense that racism is most likely to have an impact wherever government officials (police, prosecutors, and judges) have the most discretion. The most discretion of all arises with essentially made-up offenses like "Manner of Walking in

Roadway" as well as real offenses that can be found anywhere one looks, like drug sale and possession.

The flip side of the importance of discretion to racial discrimination is that race-focused explanations will not be as powerful in areas where officials (including lawmakers) possess less discretion. That's why a New Jim Crow narrative becomes less persuasive outside the criminal **legal** system – particularly with respect to serious violent crime. *The New Jim Crow* sidesteps this complexity by focusing on one important, but discrete, aspect of criminal law enforcement. Alexander singles out the war on drugs as the "vehicle" that propels Mass Incarceration, explaining that "the drug war is the system of control."[15] As Alexander's critics like to point out, however, only about 20 percent of the prison population is locked up for drug offenses.[16]

In response to criticism of her book on this point, Alexander later explained that she focused on drugs because "the time was overdue to move the conversation away from violence committed by individuals struggling to survive and direct public attention to organized violence perpetrated by our own government against black people. . . . This book was my chance, finally, to change the subject."[17] But by focusing on only one part of a broader system, Alexander limits the explanatory power of her account. And by declining to address violent crime, Alexander overlooks the most defensible aspects of the criminal **justice** system, such as its efforts to respond to instances of murder and rape. This partly explains the polarized reaction to *The New Jim Crow* even among criminal justice experts and practitioners, with many endorsing its message uncritically and others dismissing it out of hand. The truth lies somewhere in between.

By focusing on drugs, Alexander was able to tell an important story about American criminal law without being distracted by the familiar talking points of those who defend a racially disparate status quo. This move is understandable, since many references to disparities in offending and so-called Black-on-Black crime are little more than racist tropes. Still, a comprehensive explanation of the broader phenomenon of Mass Incarceration must address these points. And importantly, while doing so introduces additional complexity, it does not vindicate the status quo.

It is true that national data reflects demographic offending disparities for certain crimes. A recent Bureau of Justice Statistics publication compared data from the National Criminal Victimization Survey (NCVS), which records victims' perceptions of offender race, to arrest data reported by local police (UCR). With respect to violent crime, the data matches up fairly well. According to the BJS: "Based on the 2018 NCVS and UCR, black people accounted for 29 percent of violent-crime offenders and 35 percent of violent-crime offenders in incidents reported to police, compared to 33 percent of all persons arrested for violent crimes." Another government study of homicide data gathered between 1980 and 2008 finds disproportionate rates of offending that track the demographic disparities of people sent to prison for murder.[18]

Victim-reported data suggesting demographic differences in offending for some offenses complicates *The New Jim Crow* narrative. But the data only explains portions of the landscape and, even there, it is no exoneration of the status quo. Legal scholar Sandra Mayson explains:

> Differential crime rates do not signify a difference across racial groups in individuals' innate "propensity" to commit crime. They signify social and economic divides. Where the incidence of crimes of poverty and desperation varies by race, it is because society has segregated communities of color and starved them of resources and opportunity…. Crime rates are a manifestation of deeper forces; racial variance in crime rates, where it exists, manifests the enduring social and economic inequality produced by centuries of racial subordination.[19]

After surveying the academic literature, sociologist Michael Tonry similarly explains: "Race does not explain higher rates of violence by black people; social and economic handicaps associated with being black in twenty-first-century America do."[20]

Another complexity concerns the connection between the Civil Rights movement and the rise of Mass Incarceration. Alexander frames Mass Incarceration as a kind of "backlash" against the gains of the Civil Rights era. But the racial disparities in incarceration emerged much earlier. A Bureau of Justice Statistics publication notes this long-standing trend, explaining that: "Blacks represent a growing fraction of all admissions, composing about one-quarter of all admissions during 1926, about one-third of all [prison] admissions between 1941 and 1960, and 43.5% of all admissions estimated for 1981."[21]

Thus, while Alexander is right that incarceration rates increased in the wake of the Civil Rights movement, the system's disproportionate impact on Black people preceded that increase. Disparities worsened in the era of Mass Incarceration, but this was the product of two phenomena that should not be viewed through the same lens.

Thirteen years before Alexander published *The New Jim Crow*, legal scholar Randall Kennedy offered a more victim-focused account of the legacy of Jim Crow in American criminal justice. One aspect of the history Kennedy detailed was familiar: the long history of brutal victimization of Black people by whites, including the "unpunished raping of black women," routine lynching, and countless other forms of violence and theft – all encouraged or ignored by legal authorities. Kennedy notes that even "[m]idway through the twentieth century the American legal regime at both the state and federal levels displayed notable failings in terms of protecting blacks against racially motivated violence." But Kennedy also tells a less familiar story, tracing law enforcement's equally long-standing "fail[ure] ... often by design, to protect blacks from 'ordinary' criminality, much of it perpetrated by blacks."[22]

Contemporary studies of the Jim Crow South support Kennedy's account. Anthropologist Hortense Powdermaker, who studied Mississippi in the 1930s, found not only notable rates of violence, such as "wife beating," but also a striking indulgence of this violence when the victims were Black. Powdermaker explains: "The attitude of the Whites and the courts which they control is one of complaisance toward violence among the Negroes, and even toward intra-Negro homicide." Powdermaker situates this policy in a long history of Southern racism:

> The mildness of the courts where offenses of Negroes against Negroes are concerned is only part of the whole situation which places the Negro outside the law. It may be viewed as one result of the system which treats the Negro as sub-human and therefore places less value on his life than on that of a white person, and exacts less punishment for destroying it.[23]

A similar account comes from Swedish economist Gunnar Myrdal, who was commissioned to explore conditions in the American South in the 1940s. Myrdal's comprehensive report noted: "Everywhere in

Southern Negro communities I have met the complaint from law-abiding Negroes that they are left practically without police protection." With respect to the court system, Myrdal reported that: "It is part of the Southern tradition to assume that Negroes are disorderly ... and to show great indulgence toward Negro violence and disorderliness 'when they are among themselves.'... As long as only Negroes are concerned and no whites are disturbed, great leniency will be shown in most cases."[24]

These observations are consistent with sociologist Christopher Muller's contention that Black incarceration rates began to spike, in part, due to the Great Migration from the South to the North, when Black people "left a region with a comparatively low, and entered a region with a comparatively high, nonwhite incarceration rate."[25] But Muller adds a further nuance, consistent with Alexander's account. The nonwhite incarceration rate in Northern jurisdictions moved even higher with the arrival of Black migrants, a reaction, Muller argues, that reflected the threat they posed to the job security of Northern whites.

The problem of devaluing Black crime victims was not isolated to the South or the early part of the twentieth century. A comprehensive report by a commission established by President Johnson in the wake of "racial disorders [in] American cities" in the summer of 1967 (the Kerner Commission), included a section titled "The Problem of Police Protection." The section contends that, in predominantly Black neighborhoods, residents' hostility to police misconduct "may even be exceeded by the conviction that [their] neighborhoods are not given adequate police protection." The report communicated that these feelings were based on a belief "that the police maintain a much less rigorous standard of law enforcement" in segregated inner-city neighborhoods, "tolerating there illegal activities like drug addiction, prostitution, and street violence that they would not tolerate elsewhere." The report highlighted survey results from "Harlem and south central Los Angeles [that] mention inadequate protection more often than brutality or harassment as a reason for [the residents'] resentment toward the police." The report also quoted the following testimony that could have been pulled from the earlier-quoted reports of the 1930s South, "If a black man kills another black man, the law is generally enforced at its minimum."[26]

The Kerner Commission recommended that police provide greater protection to Black inner-city residents and "eliminate their high sense of insecurity and the belief in the existence of a dual standard of law enforcement."[27] This recommendation resonated with a Civil Rights movement that was, at that very moment, challenging double standards throughout American society, including in the courts. As America increasingly recognized the equality of Black citizens, it was inevitable that police, prosecutors, judges, and juries would become more receptive to applying formal criminal tools – "the criminal justice system" – to crimes involving Black victims. This change both added to incarceration totals and increased the risk of incarceration for Black defendants. That is because most crime, and especially violent crime, in this country is intraracial.[28] Drawing on victim reports, the Bureau of Justice Statistics explained in 2019 that "[t]he largest percentage of violent incidents committed against white, black, and Hispanic victims were committed by someone of the same race or ethnicity." Specifically, 70 percent of Black victims of violent crime reported that the offender was Black; 62 percent of white victims reported that the offender was white; and 42 percent of Hispanic victims reported that the offender was Hispanic. In a study of twelve cities in 1998, 84 percent of Black victims of violent crime described their attacker as Black.[29] The intraracial nature of American crime means that, as cases involving Black victims increasingly made their way into the criminal courts over the course of the twentieth century, the number of Black defendants increased as well. Of course, when the criminal justice system moved into Black neighborhoods, the criminal legal system followed, bringing drug stings and other aggressive policing tactics like those documented in Ferguson, all leading to the dismal statistics that led off this chapter. But it is important to distinguish the problematic expansion of the criminal legal system from the long overdue extension of the criminal justice system. Both developments increased Black incarceration numbers, but one was (arguably) an extension of Jim Crow and the other was a repudiation of it.

A nuanced understanding of the role race plays in American law enforcement highlights the importance of looking at the mix of cases flowing into the system, and distinguishing between those cases that are aspects of a criminal justice system and those that are aspects of a criminal legal system. It also illustrates the dangers of discretion, providing another reason to skeptically assess the bloated criminal legal system.

This account also offers guidance for evaluating potential reforms. For example, reforms focused on minor and nonviolent crimes will reduce discriminatory enforcement (as in Ferguson, Missouri) but may not eliminate racial disproportion in the remaining incarcerated population. An early sign of this dilemma can be seen in the many Northern states with relatively low incarceration rates but stark disparities in their prison populations. Legal scholar Richard Frase offers the general theory:

> A (more liberal, northern) state that uses its prisons mainly for violent offenders will have higher black incarceration rates, since blacks are more likely to be arrested and convicted of violent crimes. Other (more conservative, southern) states, where prison terms are frequently given to nonviolent offenders, will have higher white incarceration rates than the first group of states and, as a result, lower black/white prison ratios.[30]

This is particularly important since the most common reform proposals tend to exclude violent crime. As social scientist Marie Gottschalk notes, "[m]any of the most commonly talked about measures to reduce the detained population – such as diverting more low-level offenders from prison, ending the war on drugs, and reserving prison sentences for the most serious crimes – might actually result in greater, not smaller, racial disparities in imprisonment."[31]

A recent statistical analysis of potential decarceration strategies makes a similar point, noting that the most politically viable strategies "would likely exacerbate racial disparity among those left behind bars." The author, legal scholar Ben Grunwald, explains:

> This finding stems from the fact that, relative to white prisoners, Black prisoners are admitted at heightened and roughly constant rates across offense types, with the exception of violent offenses, for which they are admitted at even higher rates. It also stems from the fact that Black prisoners, on average, serve a similar length of time as other prisoners for non-violent offenses but more time for violent ones. The upshot is that decarcerating non-violent offenses alone likely increases racial disparities.... Out of all the

decarceration strategies tested, the only ones that reduce racial disparity are those that would decarcerate violent offenses far more than non-violent ones. And, even then, these strategies never reduce Black overrepresentation dramatically.[32]

These insights are reflected in a real-world reform in New Jersey. In 2017, New Jersey eliminated its cash bail system, dramatically reducing its jail population. But one thing that did not change was the disproportionate impact of jail on Black people. In October 2012, 54 percent of the people in New Jersey's jails were Black, and that percentage was unchanged, after reform, in October 2018 (see Figure 9.2).[33]

The persistence of racial disproportion in New Jersey's jail populations did not mean its landmark bail reforms failed minorities. The opposite is true. As of 2018, there were approximately 3,000 fewer Black, 1,500 fewer white, and 1,300 fewer Hispanic people locked up in jail in New Jersey. All these folks would have suffered if New Jersey's reforms had been rejected for failing to eliminate racial disparity, and Black people would have suffered most of all.

In sum, the pernicious influence of racism in American society is an important part of the Mass Incarceration story, but the two phenomena are not the same. Parts of American law enforcement that gave rise

NEW JERSEY JAIL POPULATION %

■ White ■ Black ■ Hispanic

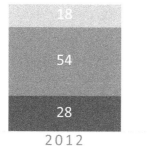 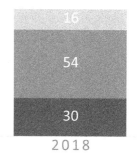

Figure 9.2 New Jersey jail population

to Mass Incarceration can fairly be characterized as a new Jim Crow. Other parts cannot. The good news is that the parts that seem to be the most infected by racism, like Ferguson's extortionate policing or the drug war, are also the parts that can most easily be dismantled. The bad news is that these efforts will not immediately eliminate racial disparities in incarcerated populations. Racial disparities – including those arising in the parts of the system that can properly claim a "justice" label – stem from a variety of sources and predate Mass Incarceration. Those disparities have already begun to decrease, and should continue to do so over time, particularly if sentence lengths can be reduced more generally. But racial disparities are likely to persist in some form as long as racism and the legacy of slavery and discrimination continue to infect American society.

PART III

The Mechanics of Mass Incarceration

The way that prisons fill can be depicted with an analogy. Imagine a road that leads to prison, the "prison road." The police divert people who are traveling on other roads onto the prison road. Between this police-controlled entry ramp and prison are a variety of off-ramps. The first off-ramp is controlled by prosecutors who can decline to prosecute, diverting people off the prison road. Another off-ramp is operated by grand juries who can decline to indict or trial juries who can vote to acquit. A large off-ramp is operated by judges who can dismiss cases or impose noncustodial sentences. On the other side of prison are additional ramps operated by parole boards, who can shrink the prison population by ordering early release (or expand it via parole revocations), and governors who can do the same through clemency. This whole enterprise – the road, the prison, and the on- and off-ramps – is designed and funded by legislators.

If someone asks why there are so many people in prison, one can point to any of the actors involved: legislators, police, prosecutors, judges, parole boards, and so on. After all, each actor could dramatically decrease the number of folks in prison. But in a system with numerous on- and off-ramps, it is misleading to highlight one ramp while ignoring the others. Keeping people moving down the prison road requires the cooperation of all the actors.

Mass Incarceration arose both through tougher new laws and more punitive choices made by those who implemented those laws. This Part focuses on this second part of the equation, cataloging the ways that the system's mechanics – primarily police, prosecutors, and judges but also probation and parole officials – worked together to increase the number of people flowing into the system and the punishments they received. Identifying these mechanisms serves two purposes. First, it presents an essential supplement to the standard narrative about the harsher laws that gave rise to Mass Incarceration. Second, precisely identifying the changes that brought us Mass Incarceration creates a blueprint for reform. The most basic solution to the problem described in Part I is to identify the laws (Part II) and practices (Part III) that changed after 1970 – and change them back (Part IV).

10 MORE POLICE, DIFFERENT ARRESTS

Police are the gatekeepers to the criminal justice system. Without police officers investigating offenses and bringing cases to prosecutors, criminal courts would have little to do. Thus, the decisions made by police are critical to understanding Mass Incarceration.

As Chapter 7 explained, America's politicians sought to increase the punishments for crimes. But punishment only matters if you get caught. That's why legislators didn't just increase the severity of the criminal law. They also funded the hiring of more police to catch people more often. And it worked, kind of. More police did mean more arrests. But arrest numbers went up and stayed high even after crime fell. That is a critical fact because it shows that many of the cases flooding the system, and perhaps a substantial majority of them, are not properly characterized as a reaction to rising crime. There is something else going on.

While historical data on police staffing is patchy, the data we have reflects a steadily increasing police presence throughout the era of Mass Incarceration. A national census conducted by the Department of Justice identified 496,143 sworn police officers (officers with arrest authority) in 1986. That number shot up to 765,246 by 2008. The largest police department in the country, the New York City Police Department, went from 22,170 sworn officers in 1981 to 31,236 in 1990 to 40,435 in 2000. Another federal study found that full-time employees in the nation's sixty-two largest police departments increased by 20 percent between 1990 and 2000, with a 17 percent increase in sworn officers.[1]

> The 1994 federal Crime Bill contributed to the hiring spree by offering large grants to local governments to hire police officers. A government report estimated that these grants led to the hiring of 88,000 additional local police officers between 1994 and 2001.[2]

The increasing number of police officers led to an increasing number of arrests. Table 10.1 presents annual arrest totals for the entire country for selected years between 1980 and 2010.[3]

This Table fits the Mass Incarceration story we have seen so far. In the 1970s and 1980s, crime went up, States hired more police, and the police made more arrests. The spike between 1980 and 1990 is the key change, with police making almost 4 million more arrests annually in 1990 than they had ten years earlier.

But after 1990, the picture clouds. Crime dropped dramatically between 1990 and 2000 and then kept dropping. That's why murder and rape arrests plummet. Yet even with crime falling, the total number of arrests remained high. There were almost the same number of arrests in 2000 as 1990, even though crime had fallen by almost a third.

If police arrested people only for crimes like murder, we could look to crime as the driver of arrest numbers. Serious violent crimes don't leave the police with much discretion. As a practical matter, police have to investigate murders, and when they find the guilty party, they make an arrest. This pattern holds to varying degrees for a variety of high-profile crimes, like forcible rape and robbery. But for other crimes, like drug offenses, policy judgments about where to focus police resources and which cases and people are worth pursuing explain arrest statistics better than actual crime.

Table 10.1 *Arrests over time*

Arrests	Total	Murder	Forcible Rape
1980	10,458,260	20,040	31,380
1990	14,217,170	22,990	39,160
2000	13,985,979	13,227	27,469
2010	13,122,113	11,201	20,088

Less crime after 1990 did mean fewer arrests for crimes like murder, rape, and robbery. But it didn't mean fewer arrests overall. That's because police shifted their efforts to combating other crimes like drug offenses and domestic violence, bringing a new set of problems into the system that officers once overlooked or handled informally. We can call this "arrest policy." The crime spike may have been the spark that ignited Mass Incarceration, but when that spark died out, a punitive response lingered in the form of lots more police and tough new laws and attitudes. Government officials pointed this law enforcement machinery at a variety of new targets, and that turned Mass Incarceration from a blip into a lasting phenomenon. The continued efforts by police, prosecutors, and judges superficially resembled "crime fighting" and "criminal justice" – and that's what officials said they were doing. But in important ways, this was no longer a crackdown on the murders and other crimes that generated the initial call for severity. It became a crackdown on crimes that were easiest to find and folks who were easiest to punish.

The most obvious example of the changing police focus over this period is the drug war. In 1980, drug arrests were the sixth most common type of arrest reported by American police departments, making up a total of 580,900 arrests. By 2000, drug arrests were the second most common type of arrest, totaling 1,579,566 arrests that year – an increase of 1 million annual drug arrests! But before we get into drugs, let's analyze the data for another crime that people rarely talk about: assault and, especially, aggravated assault. Aggravated assault is a felony offense that is best understood as a more serious version of its misdemeanor cousin, simple assault. Assaults – aggravated plus simple assault – were the most common type of arrest reported in 2000 (totaling 1,790,586 arrests), a change from 1980, when assault was the fifth most common type of arrest (and totaled 766,070).

Here's a typical aggravated assault definition:

> **Aggravated assault**: Aggravated assault is (1) intentionally and without legal justification causing serious bodily injury with or without a deadly weapon or (2) using a deadly or dangerous weapon to threaten, attempt, or cause bodily injury, regardless of the degree of injury. Aggravated assault includes attempted murder, aggravated battery, felonious assault, and assault with a deadly weapon.[4]

The legal boundary separating simple and aggravated assault is important because felony offenses are punished more severely than misdemeanors and are much more likely to lead to incarceration. Yet, as legal scholar David Sklansky notes, while the difference between the two offenses is of "very great consequence," the legal boundary that distinguishes them is "hazy."[5] What counts as "serious" bodily injury, a "threat," a "dangerous weapon" or an "attempt" to use it?

Baseball fans see aggravated assaults whenever an angry batter charges the pitcher's mound while holding the bat. But batters almost never get arrested, much less imprisoned for charging the mound. Why not? Because police let it go. Police encounter lots of gray areas like this. For example, sometimes a police officer on foot tries to stop a car from driving away, and the car keeps going. If the officer has to move out of the way to avoid injury that can be an "aggravated assault": using a dangerous weapon (the car) to threaten or attempt bodily injury. Or, imagine that police respond to a call about drunk college students fighting in a bar. Is it an aggravated assault if a student swings a beer bottle in a wide slow arc as the officers push him outside? The point is not that these things are likely to get charged as aggravated assaults (although they sometimes are). The point is that even when the facts are clear, the decision whether to arrest someone for a misdemeanor simple assault or a felony aggravated assault, or to do nothing at all, depends on a police officer's discretion.[6]

Assaults are also different from other violent crimes, like robberies, burglaries, rapes, or murders in terms of their solvability – that is, the ease of identifying the person who committed the crime. In many assaults, the victim can readily identify the assailant. This is most obvious when the victim is a police officer who is assaulted during an arrest. But it is also true when civilians are the victims. That means these cases can be solved quickly and easily. If the assailant is still on the scene, as is often the case with domestic violence or fights in bars or clubs, the responding officers can make an immediate arrest. The case is closed minutes after the first 911 call. Contrast that with a typical robbery, rape, car theft, or homicide, where the victims and police often have no idea whom to arrest and where to find them. For example, in the late 1990s, California reported that police solved 61 percent of assaults, a remarkably high figure as compared to the solve rate for robberies (30 percent), burglaries (14 percent), or car thefts (10 percent) – all numbers that correspond to the national clearance rates highlighted in Chapter 8.[7]

The ubiquity of assaults, the subjectivity inherent in the offense, and the ease of detecting and solving assault cases make police attitudes toward assaults a critical ingredient in determining the number and type of assault cases funneling into the system. And attitudes change. Nowhere is this more apparent than with the change in law enforcement's approach to domestic violence.

In the early part of the twentieth century, formal legal structures explicitly sought to distinguish domestic violence from "regular" crime. As legal scholar Reva Siegal explains,

> During this period, cities began to establish special domestic relations courts staffed by social workers to handle complaints of marital violence; by the 1920s, most major cities had such courts. The family court system sought to decriminalize marital violence . . . . Rather than punish those who assaulted their partners, the judges and social workers urged couples to reconcile, providing informal or formal counseling designed to preserve the relationship whenever possible. Battered wives were discouraged from filing criminal charges against their husbands, urged to accept responsibility for their role in provoking the violence, and encouraged to remain in the relationship and rebuild it.[8]

This mindset continued into the 1970s, as official guidance encouraged informal responses to domestic violence. Writing in 1967, legal scholar Raymond Parnas summarized Chicago police training as follows: "[T]he teaching outlines, lectures, and Training Bulletins dealing with domestic disturbances instruct the officer to cautiously attempt to settle the dispute through the exercise of common sense and discretion. He is also told to avoid arrest whenever possible." The Police Training Academy in Michigan similarly instructed cadets responding to domestic calls to "[a]void arrest if possible." Standards promulgated in 1973 by the American Bar Association to guide police officers encouraged methods "other than arrest and prosecution." Specifically, the Standards proposed that police "engage in the resolution of conflict such as that which occurs so frequently between husband and wife or neighbor and neighbor . . . without reliance upon criminal assault or disorderly conduct statutes."[9] A training manual used by the Oakland Police Department in 1975 counseled officers that their primary role was more of a "mediator and peacemaker than enforcer of the law"; that "[n]ormally, officers should adhere to the policy that arrests shall be avoided" and "encourage the parties to reason with each other."[10]

As legal scholar Aya Gruber explains, the explanation for the informal approach to domestic violence was not that police were "club-dragging cavemen who high-fived rather than arrested suspects." Instead, she explains, when asked about the less formal approach to domestic violence,

> Officers did not opine that abuse was legitimate, no big deal, or a private matter . . . . Rather, they articulated . . . why the "traditional" police functions . . . worked poorly in domestic violence situations. Police cautioned that the very intrusion into an emotional conflict could escalate the violence, pointing to evidence that DV calls were particularly lethal to first responders . . . . Relatedly, the police asserted that arrest could increase the severity of subsequent battering . . . . [T]hey [also] worried that arrest caused batterers to lose employment, thereby harming victims and putting greater strains on dysfunctional relationships. [And], the most straightforward and frequent explanation for nonarrest was that *victims* objected.[11]

The shift from treating domestic violence as a family matter to a criminal one illustrates the kinds of changes that characterized the rise of Mass Incarceration – and how these changes could have noble motives. In many jurisdictions, the change was dramatic with police guidance shifting from discouraging arrests to mandating them, as noted in Chapter 7. This shift was also impactful because police are frequently called to scenes of domestic violence and, when they are, the perpetrator is easy to identify, locate, and arrest.

Changing legislative guidance and policing attitudes led to more domestic violence arrests. In California, for example, domestic violence arrests doubled between 1988 and 1997, from 31,886 per year to 63,636.[12] In 1999, the *Los Angeles Times* reported that domestic violence arrests shot up throughout Southern California over the preceding decade, with a 431 percent increase in Orange County,

234 percent increase in San Diego, 226 percent increase in San Bernardino, 160 percent increase in Riverside, and 38 percent increase in Los Angeles. Emphasizing the comprehensive shift in attitudes, the *Times* quotes a police sergeant who stated, "We don't (make arrests) to slap their hand or to make a point. If we arrest someone, we fully intend to prosecute them." That meant lots of new cases flowing into the system. Importantly, there is little evidence that domestic assaults were actually increasing over this period, and the *Times* story helpfully reported that, statewide, 911 calls for domestic violence were falling through the period of increased arrests.[13]

The most impactful policing policy changes are not simply those where the police take more interest in a crime. The greatest impacts in terms of incarceration occur when police take more interest in a crime that arises frequently and is regularly detected and solved. Assaults fit that description perfectly. Assaults arise in a variety of common scenarios that police routinely encounter. Domestic violence is one example, but there are numerous others, such as attacks in bars and nightclubs. Judicial case reports are replete with repeating patterns of mundane violence that lead to felony assault convictions, from assaults with fists at a bar in Nueces County, Texas,[14] bottles at Bellisario's Lounge in Alleghany County, Pennsylvania,[15] a beer glass at Scorcher's Bar in Eastlake, Ohio,[16] chairs at the Back Street Lounge in Cleveland,[17] a pool cue at a bar in Helena, Montana,[18] and a bar stool in Park County, Wyoming.[19] The cases are as simple as they are ubiquitous. Police are called to a disturbance. They arrive to find someone engaged in, or just after, an assault; and they talk to witnesses who describe the offense and identify the perpetrator.

A critical decision point in cases like those described above is what happens next. As Mass Incarceration gathered steam, police increasingly invoked formal court processes – either because they were following new legislative directives, or because they agreed with the sentiments underlying those directives. Prosecutors, judges, and juries were also receptive to this new form of severity. Piece by piece, across jurisdictions and over time, subtle changes like these ratcheted up the number of cases entering the system. Crimes that might have been ignored decades earlier or handled informally were becoming criminal convictions.

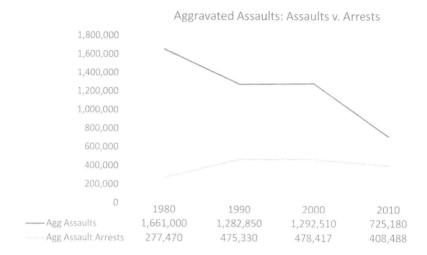

Figure 10.1 **Aggravated assaults**

Consider Figure 10.1, showing the trend in aggravated assault arrests over the past fifty years. Aggravated assault arrests (the lower line) rise dramatically between 1980 and 1990. That mirrors rising crime. But the jump in aggravated assault arrests (71 percent) is much higher than the jump in arrests for other violent crimes, like murder (15 percent) or forcible rape (25 percent). That is the first clue that this isn't a story of more crime leading to more arrests.[20]

To get a sense of what is going on, we need to know something about the number of assaults themselves. We can get at that number through the National Crime Victimization Survey (NCVS) – a widely respected tool for estimating actual crime. To conduct the NCVS, the government sends interviewers into the real world to ask people if they were victimized by crime.[21] It is a major undertaking: almost 250,000 persons were interviewed in 2019.[22] The BJS crunches the data and then uses statistical modeling to estimate totals for the entire country.

Things get interesting when we compare the NCVS data on actual aggravated assaults (top line of Figure 10.1 above) to the arrest data (bottom line). In 1980, over a million aggravated assaults resulted in no arrest. That's part of the story of Chapter 4 – the public feeling that their concerns about crime were being ignored. Next, notice how arrests trend up in the following years. Responding to the changing public mood, the police start taking this offense more seriously even as crime (including assaults) is falling. Then something remarkable happens. By 2010, the lines nearly converge. Aggravated assaults drop dramatically, but arrests remain elevated, meaning that a much higher percentage of aggravated assaults resulted in an arrest in 2010 than had been the case in 1980.

> The NCVS asks victims about reporting. In 1980 and 2010, about 60 percent of victims who say they were victimized by an aggravated assault say that they reported it to the police. This suggests that the difference over time is not a difference in reporting.

The best explanation of the two trends represented in Figure 10.1 is that a change in police attitudes ("arrest policy"), not an increase in assaults, caused the increase in arrests. Over time, police treated more things as aggravated assaults that they had treated as misdemeanors (simple assault) or let go in earlier years. Soaking in the perception that they needed to get "tougher" on crime, even as crime itself decreased, police started to see more "serious" injuries, "dangerous" weapons, and "threats" in circumstances where they hadn't seen them before. They started making felony arrests for aggravated assault – a crime that (as the next chapters will show) prosecutors and judges were taking more seriously too. A bar fight or domestic assault that generated an informal response years ago now meant a court case and prison time. This hypothesis that the increasing number of serious assault arrests stemmed from policing attitudes, not other factors, fits neatly with a finding by sociologist Richard Rosenfeld. Rosenfeld found that police-reported aggravated assaults during this period increased the most for non-gun related assaults – typically the assaults whose characterization involves the most subjectivity.[23]

One place to look for the impact of arrest policies is at crimes with a strong subjective component like "aggravated assault." Another is crimes that are constantly occurring but inconsistently policed. The best example in modern America is drug crimes.

It is hard to measure changes in drug offending, but both drug sales and possession can be inferred from use. The Monitoring the Future

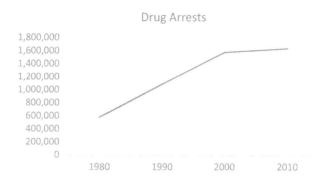

Figure 10.2 Drug arrests

Project has surveyed thousands of people about drug use since 1976. Its findings suggest ongoing, widespread illicit drug use by Americans since the surveys began. There is a decreasing trend in drug use between 1976 and the early 1990s and an increasing trend after that, but the changes are not substantial.[24] That means that the number of drug arrests in the United States tells us more about arrest policy than the frequency of drug use. As this graph (Figure 10.2) of American drug arrests (sales and possession) reveals, after 1980, police started looking harder for drugs. And they found what they were looking for.

Drugs aren't the only crime that offer endless opportunities for arrests. There are lots of things police can find if they look hard enough. But while police were looking harder for drugs, they were looking less hard for gambling, drunkenness, prostitution, and disorderly conduct – arrests that all dropped dramatically. This shift away from some kinds of vice to others is important because the police were shifting from crimes that didn't typically lead to court cases and incarceration (prostitution, drunkenness) to crimes that did (drugs, assaults). In 1980, drunkenness and disorderly conduct arrests were the second and third most common type of arrests reported nationally by police; by 2000 these crimes had fallen to sixth and seventh place (Figure 10.3).

National trends result from choices made by local decision makers, like police chiefs and sergeants. So it is helpful to look at the kinds of changes happening in a local jurisdiction. Table 10.2 reveals the changing mix of arrests for one large police department: the Los Angeles Police Department (LAPD).[25]

Table 10.2 *LAPD arrests*

LAPD	1980	1990	2000	2010
Burglary	12,107	9,927	3,232	2,479
Agg. Assault	8,391	18,569	14,071	9,048
Drugs	17,389	36,338	20,048	13,620
Gambling	4,408	1,322	211	309
Drunkenness	19,217	425	224	365

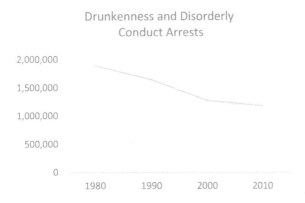

Figure 10.3 Drunkenness arrests

Overall LAPD arrest totals declined between 1980 and 2010, but that decline masks an important change in the mix of arrests, led by a dramatic midtrend spike in aggravated assault and drug arrests. LAPD arrests for crimes like burglaries plummeted along with arrests for certain vice crimes like drunkenness and gambling. Arrests for aggravated assaults and drugs took their place. The movement away from drunkenness arrests is the most dramatic. In the late 1970s, more than 25 percent of LAPD arrests were for "drunkenness." By 1982, that percentage dipped below 1 percent and stayed there.

Another place to look to get a sense of changing policing attitudes is the degree to which police let people off the hook after an arrest. This data is hard to find for obvious reasons, but California helpfully tracks the number of arrests that police decide not to bring to prosecutors. The data reflects the theme so far. In the early 1980s, California police released over 10 percent of the people they arrested for felonies,

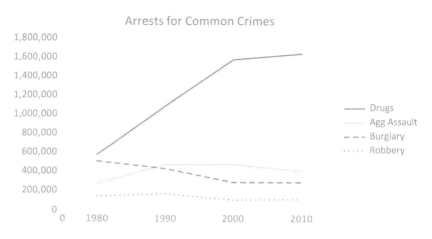

Figure 10.4 Common arrests

without pursuing formal charges. As time passed, that percentage steadily declined to around 3 or 4 percent in the 1990s and beyond.[26]

It is important to note that despite all the changes described above, including expanding police departments and increasing arrests, the one variable that is central to effective policing did not improve: the rate at which police solved the most serious crimes. While cities and towns hired thousands more police, and legislators, prosecutors, and judges ramped up the penalties for crime, homicide clearance rates fell, dropping from close to 80 percent in 1976 to just over 60 percent in 2019.[27] No one knows why police are solving fewer murder cases, but the data presented above suggests one possibility: police are too busy with other tasks.

Figure 10.4 brings together a variety of crimes to illustrate the theme of the chapter. The graph contrasts arrests for easy-to-find crimes, like drugs and aggravated assaults (the top two lines), with hard-to-solve, less-policy-driven arrests like burglary and robbery (the bottom two lines). Notice that arrests for crimes like robbery and burglary roughly track crime rates, going down as crime goes down or staying flat. But arrests for crimes like aggravated assault and drugs shoot up and stay high even while crime plummeted.

The graph suggests that over time, arrest totals increasingly tracked arrest policy choices, not crime. The explanation for all the drug arrests in the 2000s wasn't that more people were using drugs. And there weren't lots of aggravated assault arrests because there was a surge of aggravated assaults. Police were trying to get tougher on violence and fighting a war on drugs. But they weren't able to solve a higher percentage of crimes like robberies or murder, and those crimes were dropping. So police continued "fighting crime" through the path of least resistance, devoting more resources to the instances of law-breaking they could most easily detect and solve. And, as the next chapters show, these cases were tailor made for filling prisons and jails.

11 PROSECUTORS TURNING ARRESTS INTO CONVICTIONS

After making an arrest, a police officer typically refers the matter to the local prosecutor's office. Once presented with a case, that office decides whether to charge the defendant with a crime and, if so, which crime(s). Even if prosecutors initially file a charge, they can still dismiss the case later on. If prosecutors do not dismiss the case, they can seek an informal resolution (often called "diversion"), negotiate a plea bargain on behalf of the government, or take the case to trial. These decisions about which cases to prosecute, and how, are important contributors to the incarceration rate. As this chapter explains, over the era of Mass Incarceration, prosecutors' primary contribution was to follow the lead of police and legislators. Prosecutors applied the new tools enacted by legislators leading to more severe punishments for crimes generally. And, perhaps most importantly, they uncritically accepted the new mix of arrests forwarded to them by police, flooding the courts with a higher proportion of cases that were easy to prove and punish.

Many arrests never become criminal cases because prosecutors decline to prosecute. These are commonly referred to as "declinations." Legal scholars Ron Wright and Marc Miller studied prosecutor declinations in the New Orleans District Attorney's office over a ten-year period from 1988 to 1999. They found that the "office rejects for prosecution in state felony court 52% of all cases and 63% of all charges."[1] The study is notable because it occurred in a high-incarceration state (Louisiana) over a decade in which Mass Incarceration was reaching its peak. Yet it reveals a counterintuitive aspect of prosecution – much of what the local prosecutors in New Orleans did was reject cases brought to them by the police. While it is difficult to find precise statistics on declinations, New Orleans is both representative of busy urban prosecutor offices and indicative of the broad variation across American jurisdictions. The Bureau of Justice Statistics (BJS) reported data on prosecutorial charging between 1979 and 1988 using a sample of thirty urban jurisdictions. In 1979, prosecutors in those jurisdictions "carried forward," that is, prosecuted, 50 percent of felony arrests presented to them by police. This percentage increased modestly to 55 percent by 1988 (the last year of the series).[2] These percentages combine two distinct but related phenomena, declinations (rejections at the initial screening stage) and post-charging dismissals. As the BJS explains: "Data from this and previous reports in the series indicate that in most jurisdictions approximately half of all felony arrests are dropped at some point in the disposition process and about half will result in conviction. At what point cases are dropped and where convictions are obtained; however, vary considerably."

This variation arises from the rigor of the initial screening process with offices, like New Orleans, attempting to weed out weak cases early in the process, and other jurisdictions accepting more of those cases, but dismissing them (or suffering pre-adjudication judicial dismissals) later on. The percentage of case attrition at a particular stage depends both on the prosecutor office's charging philosophy and the characteristics of the cases presented to that office by police. Many jurisdictions, especially those outside crowded cities, report lower initial declination percentages. Drawing on a series of studies, criminologist Brian Forst estimated that prosecutors reject about a third of cases brought to them by police.[3] California reported that, statewide, prosecutors declined to prosecute about 15 percent of the felony arrests police referred to them over the last fifty years.[4]

The most common reason prosecutors decline a case is flawed evidence. The standard story of prosecutor declinations is that prosecutors measure the cases that police bring them against the applicable laws. If the prosecutor sees a problem that would eventually be exposed through court processes, it is easiest to decline the case at the outset. Thus, in the study described above, the New Orleans prosecutors' primary reasons for dismissing cases were the "quality of evidence," witness noncooperation, unlawful searches, and good defenses. Similarly, Forst's survey of the research revealed that "the vast majority of all felony cases dropped by the prosecutor are rejected because of insufficiency of evidence – the police fail to produce adequate physical evidence (such as stolen property or implements of the crime) or testimonial evidence from victims or eyewitnesses."[5]

Declining to prosecute based on lack of evidence is easy to justify. Prosecutors also decline cases for other reasons, such as that the crime is trivial or that prosecution is not a worthwhile use of limited resources. For example, in 2017, a fan threw a catfish onto the ice rink during a hockey game between the Pittsburgh Penguins and the Nashville Predators. Pittsburgh police arrested the fan and charged him with disorderly conduct, disrupting a meeting (!), and possession of an instrument of crime. Two days later, the local prosecutor dismissed the case, announcing that the conduct did "not rise to the level of criminal charges."[6] Every year, the Selective Service refers over a hundred thousand names and addresses to the Department of Justice (DOJ) of people it suspects of declining to register for the draft, a federal felony, but the DOJ has not brought a single prosecution for this offense since 1986.[7]

As crimes get more serious, prosecutors tend to focus on the strength of the evidence instead of other considerations. As a consequence, for the cases that typically lead to incarceration, the number and mix of arrests generally determines the number and mix of convictions. Police bring cases to prosecutors, and prosecutors charge some percentage of those cases based, largely, on their perception of the strength of the evidence. Of course, prosecutors do not get the final say in whether those charges become a conviction. In some jurisdictions, like in Washington, D.C., prosecutors obtain convictions in only about half of the cases they prosecute.[8] But even in jurisdictions with high case attrition, there will be a strong correlation between the number and type of charges prosecutors file and the number and type of convictions that result.

The strongest pattern that emerges from national convictions data is one of prosecutors following police departments' lead. Between 1986 and 2006 (the heart of the growth of Mass Incarceration), the Bureau of Justice Statistics published data from state courts about convictions for various felony offenses.[9] The convictions data matches up well with the arrest data described in the previous chapter. That is

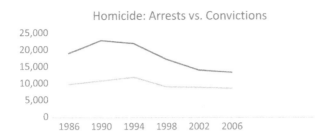

Figure 11.1 Homicide: Arrests versus convictions

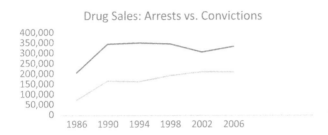

Figure 11.2 Drug sales: Arrests versus convictions

to be expected. Prosecutors and judges rarely initiate cases. They rely on the police. So, as Figure 11.1 reflects, the number of homicide cases that prosecutors charged leading to convictions (bottom line) tracks the number of arrests (top line). The gap between the two lines reflects cases where prosecutors (or other actors, such as judges or juries) determine that the evidence was insufficient.

Similar correspondence appears in Figure 11.2 between drug sale convictions (bottom line) and drug sale arrests (top line). This agreement between the drug sale lines is especially informative. As a practical matter, prosecutors should be expected to charge homicide cases so long as the evidence is sufficient. But they do not have to charge all the drug cases that police bring them. Yet the correspondence between the two lines suggests that prosecutors accepted the policy decision made by police and legislatures that drug crimes were worth the increased resources being devoted to them – so long as the evidence was sufficient to support a conviction (the consistent gap between the two lines). As police arrested more people for selling drugs, prosecutors prosecuted more folks, resulting in more convictions.

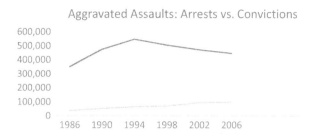

Figure 11.3 Aggravated assault: Arrests versus convictions

A similar although less distinct trend can be seen in aggravated assaults in Figure 11.3. As police arrested more people for aggravated assault (top line), prosecutors charged more aggravated assaults and courts reported more aggravated assault convictions (bottom line).

The large gap between the two lines reflects greater disagreement between police arrests and prosecutor charging and judicial convictions. Yet the general correspondence remains. Comparing 1986 to 2006, aggravated assault arrests went up by almost 100,000 and convictions increased by about 60,000.

These connections between arrests and convictions are critical to understanding the role that prosecutors played in Mass Incarceration. Prosecutors do not have to accept police charging recommendations. They can decline to prosecute the cases police bring them, or reduce (or increase) the charges recommended by police. For example, a common prosecutorial charging decision in my office was to reduce a felony assault arrest to a misdemeanor simple assault charge. And that's some of the space between the two lines in Figure 11.3: prosecutors reducing or rejecting aggravated assault arrests (the space also reflects court dismissals and acquittals). Yet there is little evidence that prosecutors altered their case screening philosophy over the period of Mass Incarceration. California, one of the biggest contributors to Mass Incarceration, is unusual among States in that it has kept data on the percentage of felony arrests declined by prosecutors since 1975. The percentage fluctuates, but not in a way that suggests any consistent shift in prosecutor behavior. The percentage of declinations averages around 14 percent in the 1970s, around 17 percent in the 1980s, back to 14 percent in the 1990s, 13 percent in the 2000s, and 15 percent in the 2010s.[10] A rigorous study of the federal system, which also provides solid data on declinations, found "little evidence of systematic change in the rate at which U.S. attorneys prosecuted criminal suspects."[11] Thus, the evidence we have, from two of the three largest contributors to Mass Incarceration, shows no sign of prosecutors altering their basic approach to case screening.

That does not mean that prosecutors did not change. It suggests that prosecutors moved in tandem with legislatures and police (and judges) – as all of these actors were becoming more severe. Sometimes prosecutors made the evidence for this consensus explicit. For example, after Congress passed the Sentencing Reform Act of 1984, abolishing parole, creating strict sentencing guidelines, and increasing penalties for federal crimes, Attorney General Richard Thornburgh issued a memo to federal prosecutors. The memo announced that the 1984 "Act was strongly supported by the Department of Justice" and warned against efforts by individual prosecutors to "seek to circumvent" its commands: It is "vitally important that federal prosecutors understand these guidelines and make them work." To ensure the consistency sought by the new sentencing scheme, Thornburgh directed federal prosecutors to "charge the most serious, readily provable offense or offenses consistent with the defendant's conduct" – a directive that would reappear in subsequent presidential administrations and become emblematic of prosecutorial severity. [12]

The apparent correspondence of police, prosecutor, and legislative desires is no surprise. The same factors that were operating on legislators and police during this period were also operating on prosecutors. In fact, a high degree of turnover in prosecutor jobs means that the decision makers themselves were frequently changing. One study in Wisconsin found that, out of "Wisconsin's 330 assistant district attorneys, 246 left their jobs between 2001 and 2007."[13] In a national survey of prosecutor offices in 2005, a third reported difficulties in retaining or recruiting attorneys.[14]

Evidence of changing attitudes appears in specific contexts as well, such as domestic violence. In her ground-breaking 1976 book, *Battered Wives*, Del Martin notes that domestic violence victims could bypass reluctant police by filing criminal complaints directly with District Attorney's Offices. But those offices took great lengths to avoid prosecution. In one example, Martin relates that San Francisco's District Attorney's Office referred such complaints to its Bureau of Family Relations, a team of nonlawyers who took pride in their "reconciliation record": "only eight of the several thousand cases processed by the Bureau during the fiscal year 1973–74 led to a formal complaint and prosecution."[15] After summarizing similar practices in a variety of offices, Martin concludes: "The lesson demonstrated in this section is depressingly familiar. Clearly, prosecutors resist trying cases of marital violence unless they cannot avoid doing so."

Just as legislatures were enacting mandatory arrest laws and police were taking domestic violence more seriously, legal professionals urged prosecution of the cases. Martin noted that the new San Francisco district attorney had pledged to assign felony complaints to the "assault team" staffed by prosecutors rather than social workers. The attorney general of the United States formed a Task Force on Family Violence, which issued a report in 1984:

> Progress against the problem of family violence must begin with the criminal justice system. Social service agencies, schools, churches, hospitals, businesses, and individual private citizens must do their part as well, but it is law enforcement that must respond to the calls for help, **prosecutors who must bring the perpetrators before the courts,** and judges who must impose penalties that balance the interest of the victims and the requirements of justice.

The report's first recommendation was that: "Family violence should be recognized and responded to as a criminal activity." Prosecutors were listening. The Orange County (California) District Attorney's Office, for example, prosecuted 4 felony domestic violence cases in 1989, a number that skyrocketed to 2,316 in 1999.[16]

Prosecutors' embrace of the increased number and changing mix of cases also comes through in Figure 11.4 in a broad comparison of serious arrests (top line) to convictions (bottom line).

Figure 11.4 and Table 11.1 show felony convictions generally increasing alongside the number of arrests and serious arrests. To better track "felony conviction" outcomes, the "serious arrests" category includes only arrest categories that most typically generate felony convictions.[17]

Table 11.1 *Conviction percentage*

Year	Arrests	Serious Arrests	Felony Convictions	FC/SA(%)
1980	10,458,260	3,821,860	N/A	N/A
1986	12,487,600	4,597,800	582,764	12.7
1990	14,217,170	5,085,070	829,344	16.3
2000	13,985,979	5,004,278	924,700	18.4
2006	14,382,852	5,250,024	1,132,290	21.5

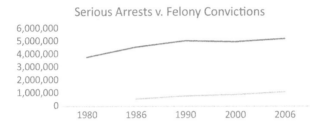

Figure 11.4 Serious arrests versus felony convictions

Serious arrests increased over the period and the percentage of those arrests that were becoming felony convictions (FC/SA) also increased – a change that becomes even more pronounced if drug possession arrests are excluded.[18] Several factors combine to explain this change:

- **Increased referrals of arrests to prosecutors.** Chapter 10 identified some evidence that police increased the percentage of arrests they were bringing to prosecutors over the period. (It is also possible that the quality of the arrests improved over time with increasing police funding and professionalism.)
- **More prosecutor staffing.** Just as legislators funded the hiring of more police, they funded the hiring of more prosecutors. Again, long-term data is spotty, but one survey found that the total employees in State prosecutor offices rose from 57,000 in 1992 to 78,000 in 2005, with prosecutors making up about a third of that staff.[19] California reported an even larger increase with the number of prosecutors growing by 84 percent between 1989 and 1999.[20] Better prosecution staffing likely reduced the number of cases that

were dismissed or declined due to resource constraints and bureaucratic oversights.

- **Increasing prevalence of criminal records.** As explained in more detail in Chapter 14, criminal justice actors seek and obtain longer punishments for repeat offenders and Mass Incarceration generated a steadily-expanding pool of offenders with criminal records.
- **New laws.** Prosecutors applied the new tools that legislators enacted to get "tougher" on crime described in Chapters 7 and 14, leading to more convictions and longer sentences.
- **Changing mix of arrests.** As noted in the previous chapter and explained below, a change in the type of cases police delivered to prosecutors increased the likelihood of felony convictions.

As Chapter 10 showed, the mix of arrests prosecutors received changed in important ways. As crime fell after 1990, police were not only still arresting lots of people, but they had altered the offenses they were arresting people for. The mix changed in two ways: (1) there were fewer "criminal justice system" arrests, that is, arrests for crimes like murder and robbery because there were fewer of those crimes and (2) the police shifted the mix of more discretionary arrests for crimes like gambling and drunkenness to arrests for weapons and drug offenses, and aggravated assault.

The change in the mix of arrests led to a change in the mix of convictions. Table 11.2 presents felony convictions in State court for major offense categories for selected years between 1986 and 2006.[21]

The table depicts two important trends: first, a sharp rise in total felony convictions. The biggest jump occurs in the earliest years in the

Table 11.2 *Convictions by crime*

Convictions	Total	Homicide	Robbery	Aggravated Assault	Drug Sales	Drug Possession
1986	582,764	9,854	42,305	38,245	76,437	(no data)
1990	829,344	10,896	47,446	53,861	168,360	106,253
1994	872,217	12,007	46,028	65,174	165,430	108,815
1998	927,717	9,158	38,784	71,060	195,183	119,443
2002	1,051,000	8,990	38,430	95,600	212,810	127,530
2006	1,132,290	8,670	41,740	100,560	212,490	165,360

chart, when arrests rose dramatically. But increases in convictions outpace the increases in arrests, particularly after 1990. Second, the mix of convictions is changing. From 1990 to 2006, crimes like homicide, rape, robbery, burglary, and car thefts all decreased in terms of their share of convictions. Convictions for crimes like aggravated assault, drug possession, drug sales, and weapons offenses took their place – as each of these crimes increased in terms of their share of convictions over the period.

While the shift might seem to be a wash because both sets of crimes include serious offenses, there is a difference. The new mix of arrests that police were delivering to prosecutor offices consisted of a high percentage of crimes that, when proven, generated long sentences *and* were relatively easy to prove.

Many of the new arrests pouring into the system were for offenses that legislators (and other officials) sought to punish with harsher sentences. Increasing punishments for these offenses increased the likelihood that the arrests would result in convictions and specifically felony (as opposed to misdemeanor) convictions. Most basically, increased penalties pushed offenses into felony territory, since the "felony" label depends on a crime's potential punishment. As the Bureau of Justice Statistics, the largest source of American crime statistics, explains: "Felonies are widely defined as crimes with the potential of being punished by more than 1 year in prison."[22] Just as important, longer sentences increased the downside risk of a conviction after trial for all offenses (the so-called trial penalty), increasing conviction percentages by making pleading guilty – to obtain prosecutorial concessions – more attractive.

The shift in the mix of arrests flowing into prosecutors' offices wasn't just in the direction of crimes that were being punished more severely. It was also a shift toward cases that were easy to prove. Many of the most serious cases, like robberies and rapes, are also the most difficult to prove in court. No matter how zealous the prosecutor, the likelihood of a conviction depends on the strength of the evidence. And once it becomes clear that a case (or a set of cases) will be difficult to prove, prosecutors become less likely to prosecute those cases, and more willing to decline, dismiss, or bargain them away. This explains one of the findings legal scholar Carissa Hessick presents in her recent book about plea bargaining. Based on files forwarded to her by an Ohio judge, Hessick reports that Ohio "prosecutors were repeatedly letting defendants accused of serious sex crimes plead guilty to charges that had nothing to do with sexual assault even though the prosecutors appeared to think that the defendants actually had committed sex crimes." It is unlikely that prosecutors agreed to these deals because they felt sympathy for sex offenders. Instead, the prosecutors feared that they would lose these cases (due to proof problems, victim non-cooperation, jury prejudice, etc.) and sought to ensure some consequences for the offenders through plea deals to lesser offenses.[23]

In cases centered on a civilian victim ("civilian cases") like robbery or rape, the government has less control over the evidence. Civilians often do not want to testify, sometimes don't show up to court, change their stories on the witness stand, and inject twists and turns that leave juries (and prosecutors) wondering what is really going on. That leads to reasonable doubt, which leads to dismissals and acquittals. The Bureau of Justice Statistics' study of felony cases prosecuted in large urban jurisdictions found that, in 1990, 52 percent of rape and 49 percent of robbery prosecutions ended in a felony conviction, with total conviction (misdemeanor or felony) percentages of 56 percent and 60 percent for those offenses respectively. That contrasted strongly with drug sale prosecutions, where 66 percent of prosecutions ended with a felony conviction, and the overall conviction percentage was 76 percent. Nonsale drug cases did not lead as frequently to felony convictions (49 percent), but that was primarily because more drug possession cases resulted in misdemeanor convictions (13 percent). The total conviction percentage for all drug cases of 69 percent, was the second highest of any of the studied offenses. Contrast that with the total conviction percentage for murder cases of 61 percent.[24] These percentages remained essentially the same in the 2000 survey and are particularly notable since they come from jurisdictions (large cities) where judge and jury resistance to drug prosecutions would be expected to be relatively strong.

The contrast in conviction percentages arises not just because civilian cases are difficult to prove, but because most noncivilian cases are easy to prove. Consider a typical drug or gun prosecution. The police stop someone, search their car, backpack, pockets, and the like, and find a bag of drugs or a gun. That's the whole case in under twenty words.

A typical drug *sale* case is a little more complicated but not much. The most common cases are completely police generated: an under-cover officer purchases drugs from a suspected drug dealer and a team of uniformed officers swoops in and makes an arrest. These cases are easy to prove both practically and legally. The typical drug or gun possession laws make it unlawful to possess heroin or cocaine or marijuana, or a handgun without a license. A traditional drug sale law is similarly broad: "It is unlawful for any person knowingly or intentionally to manufacture, distribute, or possess, with intent to manufacture or distribute, a controlled substance."[25] There are few legal defenses to having illegal drugs or an unlicensed gun in your coat, or selling drugs to an undercover officer. And police think about the evidence they need to "win" during the investigation itself. When the police bring a drug or gun arrest to the prosecutor, it is likely that the evidence is all in place. The witnesses are police officers. They get paid to show up at court, and since they testify all the time, they sound believable on the witness stand. These cases are tailor-made for trial and, especially, plea bargains. And just as more of these cases flowed into the courts, legislatures and judges increased the ease of prosecut-ing the cases and the severity of the punishments that followed. With little chance of an acquittal and a harsh penalty looming, defendants became increasingly attracted to guilty pleas.

Difficulty proving some, but not other cases, makes the mix of cases coming into prosecutors' offices especially important. Comparing 1990 to 2006, annual robbery arrests fell by 42,000 and forcible rape arrests fell by 15,000, while drug arrests increased by 800,000![26] With so many more easy-to-prove cases, like drug crimes, prosecutors were able to turn more of the arrests that police brought them into convic-tions, usually through resource-saving guilty pleas. And, as we will see in the next chapter, the easy-to-prove cases were also cases that could turn into significant jail or prison sentences.

The historical conviction rate data supports the points sketched out above. California, which offers the best data, reports that in 1975, 48.4 percent of the State's felony arrests led to a conviction. That percent-age increased, even as arrests skyrocketed, steadily climbing to over

Table 11.3 *California outcomes*

California	Felony Arrests	Police Release(%)	Declination(%)	Conviction(%)
1975	174,069	8.5	13.5	48.4
1985	240,978	9.5	16.5	58.3
1995	345,125	4.4	13.3	69.1
2005	319,587	3.2	12.2	71

Source: Crime in California Series(Table 37)
Note: Police Release = Police release arrested person without a referral to prosecutor;
Declination = Police referral declined by prosecutor

60 percent in 1989, and continuing to rise until plateauing at around 70 percent in the 1990s and beyond. As Table 11.3 shows, the primary driver of this change was the likelihood of a conviction in filed cases.[27]

Signs of this same trend appear in other sources as well. Federal authorities reported a 76 percent conviction rate in filed cases in 1975, rising to 81 percent in 1984,[28] 89 percent in 2000, and 91 percent in 2009.[29] Cities generally have relatively low conviction rates, but even those rates appear to have risen as Mass Incarceration peaked. A national study of large urban counties reported a 50 percent felony conviction percentage in filed cases in 1990, rising to 61 percent in 1994 and 59 percent in 2004 before slipping to 56 percent in 2006 and 54 percent in 2009 (the last year of the study).[30]

In sum, prosecutors contributed to Mass Incarceration by falling into step with the country's changing mood. When police introduced a new mix of arrests into the system, prosecutors did not balk at the changing nature of their caseloads. From a typical prosecutor's perspective, they kept doing what they had always done, deciding whether to charge the cases police brought them based primarily on the strength of the evidence. Many of these new cases were easy to prove *and* triggered harsh punishments. Prosecutors embraced this new leverage across the spectrum of crimes, asking for the longer sentences authorized by new laws and sentencing enhancements, leading to more convictions (often through guilty pleas) and more incarceration.

12 JUDGES TURNING CONVICTIONS INTO INCARCERATION

Sentencing is the next critical step after arrest and conviction. This chapter turns to the types of sentences that judges hand down and, with the next chapter, sketches the important role that judges play in Mass Incarceration. It shows that during the era of Mass Incarceration, judges sent more people to prison than they had in previous eras and for longer periods.

The first thing a judge must decide at sentencing is whether the defendant will be incarcerated. Unless a statute specifically provides otherwise, judges can, and often do, impose noncustodial sentences, that is, sentences that do not include any jail or prison time. For example, in 2000, State courts sentenced 32 percent of people convicted of a felony to something other than incarceration.[1] These sentences can be as simple as a fine or a period of probation. If a judge decides to incarcerate someone – the other 68 percent – determinate sentencing systems typically require the judge to assign a precise number indicating the length of that incarceration.

The data reflects that after the 1970s, across crime types, judges sentenced more and more people to prison. Sociologists Steven Raphael and Michael Stoll find that between 1984 and 2006, the probability tripled that someone arrested for rape/sexual assault, aggravated assault, larceny/fraud, and drug crimes would be sent to prison; for murder or burglary arrests, the rates of prison admission doubled; and the prison admission rates for robbery increased as well, although less dramatically.[2] Increased rates translate into higher numbers. Comparing the volume of admissions from 1970 to 2006, legal scholar Franklin Zimring offers startling estimates of annual incarceration increases across a variety of crime categories: drugs (+260,000 admissions), assault (+60,000), burglary (+60,000), theft (+60,000), robbery (+35,000), sex crimes (+35,000), and fraud (+30,000).[3]

The jump in admissions for drug offenses is especially revealing. The explosion in drug admissions reflects the powerful combination of two different phenomena: a jump in the number of arrests for drugs *plus* an increase in the likelihood of being incarcerated based on a drug arrest.

These changes in admissions translated into changes in the incarcerated population. In 1980, 6 percent of the State prison population and 25 percent of the federal prison population was serving time for a drug offense. By 2000, these numbers shot up to 20 percent (State) and 57 percent (federal), respectively.[4] Jail populations reflect the same trend, with 9 percent of jail inmates incarcerated for drug offenses in the early 1980s, increasing to over 20 percent in the 1990s and then plateauing at that level.[5] A similar trend appears with "public order" offenses, like unlawful gun possession, which accounted for only 4 percent of prisoners in 1979 but jumped to over 12 percent in 2018.[6]

Including federal and state prison and jail populations in their calculations, social scientists Mona Lynch and Anjuli Verma offer this jaw-dropping account of the numbers and the change over time:

> [S]ince 1980, the United States saw an increase of over 1,000 percent in the number of people in state and federal prisons and jails for drug law violations – from an estimated 41,000 people incarcerated for drug convictions in 1980 to an estimated 464,300 by year-end 2012. Simply put, the number of people incarcerated for drug law violations ... almost reaches the number of people incarcerated for all crimes in 1980.[7]

Many experts downplay the drug war's significance by pointing out that fewer than 25 percent of the people incarcerated at any given time in America are incarcerated for drugs. This is an important point. But it obscures both the dramatic increase in drug convictions over time and the oversized role drug crime plays in *admissions*.

People convicted of State drug crimes are typically sentenced to relatively short terms, rotating in and out of prison against a backdrop of other prisoners who are incarcerated for longer terms for less frequent but more serious crimes like rape and murder. As a result, drug offenses make up a larger percentage of the people *ever* incarcerated than they do of the people incarcerated at any particular time. And that percentage increased dramatically over the period of Mass Incarceration.

Overall, the increase in prison admissions over time reflects two different trends occurring simultaneously: a general increase in penal severity and a shift in the type of offenses coming before judges. Across the range of crimes, more people were being sent to prison for incidents that would not previously have led to incarceration. In addition, the mix of crimes for which people were going to prison changed, with a sharp swing toward drug and weapons offenses.

That is the story of admissions. But admissions are just the beginning. At the same time that more people are being incarcerated, sentences are getting longer. This story is harder to show with raw data because what we really care about is not the sentence length (or range) *announced* by the judge, but the actual time served. And with the number and mix of cases changing over time, comparing average sentence lengths in 2000 to those in 1980 would be misleading.

The good news is that researchers have long been interested in sentence lengths. There is an abundance of high-quality research on the question and a general consensus on the answer. Perhaps the most influential account comes from sociologists Allen Beck and Alfred Blumstein. They conclude that while increases in admissions drove the prison boom in the 1980s, that changed in the 1990s when longer sentences took over. Between 1990 and 2000, as "the state incarceration rate grew by 55 percent," Beck and Blumstein find that increasing "time served replaces commitments" as the leading contributor to Mass Incarceration.[8] Raphael and Stoll, writing in 2013, similarly documented "substantial increases in the amount of time that those sentenced to prison can expect to serve today relative to years past in both the state and federal prison systems." They illustrate the point with specifics: "[I]n 1984 an inmate convicted of murder or manslaughter could expect to serve 9.2 years. By 2004 this figure had increased to 14.27 years." Average time served for rape increased from 5 to 8 years; for robbery, from 3.5 to 5 years. Those convicted of aggravated assault served almost a full year longer in 2004 than they did in 1984.[9] The PEW Research Center similarly found an increase in time served during this period and that "[t]he growth in time served was remarkably similar across crime types":

"Offenders released in 2009 served:

For drug crimes: 2.2 years, up from 1.6 years in 1990 (a 36 percent increase)
For property crimes: 2.3 years up from 1.8 years in 1990 (a 24 percent increase)
For violent crimes: 5.0 years up from 3.7 years in 1990 (a 37 percent increase)"[10]

The trend toward longer sentences is most dramatically illustrated in the federal system, where comparison is easiest because of the availability of federal data and the relative homogeneity of federal crimes. PEW Researchers report that "[t]he average length of time served by federal inmates more than doubled from 1988 to 2012, rising from 17.9 to 37.5 months," with steep rises occurring across crime types, especially for drug convictions.[11]

The consensus among researchers that prison sentences increased over the period of Mass Incarceration fits the narrative presented in Chapter 7. Legislators sought to close the "revolving door" and enacted laws designed to ensure that result. They achieved their purpose. In at least one instance, the match between the forecasted effect of the new laws and reality was prescient. In 1987, the US Sentencing Commission reported to Congress on the likely impact of new federal criminal sentencing laws. The Commission projected that the number of federal prisoners would jump from 42,000 in 1987 to 156,000 by 2002.[12] The actual number of federal prisoners in 2002 was 151,618.[13]

Multiple actors contributed to the longer sentences, including prosecutors who selected charges and negotiated plea deals, legislators who rewrote the sentencing laws, and parole boards who resisted early release. But judges' contributions cannot be overlooked. Some scholars downplay the role of judges in sentencing because so many convictions result from guilty pleas (not trials). For example, legal scholar Franklin Zimring writes, "In court systems where the vast majority of felony case dispositions are the product of negotiated guilty pleas, the defendant's criminal sentence is usually determined long before the judge who issues the formal sentence is involved in the case."[14]

But judges play a role in sentencing even in plea-bargained cases. This point is repeatedly demonstrated by empirical studies that find variation in sentence lengths depending on the assigned judge. For example, one 2016 study of sentences in Texas found that the sentences imposed, which were "to a very large extent plea bargained sentences," were "strongly influenced by the judges deciding the case." The authors added:

> [T]he effect attributed to any given judge tends to be relatively constant across the counties over which such a judge has jurisdiction. That our estimated judge-specific effects do not seem to vary with the counties where the cases are prosecuted provides further support for the interpretation that they indeed reflect the sentencing behavior of the judges, rather than the influence of prosecutors or other agents involved in the plea negotiations.[15]

Another recent North Carolina study summarized its findings as follows: "[T]he vast majority of criminal cases in North Carolina are resolved via plea bargain, 97% in our data. Even though sentences must be agreed to by prosecutors and defendants, judges still have enormous impact on the outcomes. ... Later in the paper we show that judge-specific effects vary substantially across judges."[16]

A 2012 analysis of the sentences in over 370,000 cases in the federal courts, where approximately 95 percent of convictions result from guilty pleas, similarly found significant disparities based on the sentencing judge, concluding that "the typical sentence handed down by a federal district court judge can be very different than the typical sentences handed down for similar cases by other judges within the same courthouse."[17]

Judicial influence on plea-bargained sentences is no surprise to anyone who has worked in the criminal courts. Prosecutors and defense attorneys do not negotiate plea deals in a vacuum. In American courtrooms, judges preside, and that includes oversight of plea bargains. In fact, judges involve themselves directly in plea negotiations in many American jurisdictions. For example, recent investigative reporting in Baltimore revealed that despite the fact that plea agreements were formally entered into between the prosecution and defendant, judges had the final say. For example, in one case, a defendant was charged with "possessing a firearm [an assault rifle] in a drug offense," a crime punishable by a five-year mandatory minimum sentence. The prosecutor offered a guilty plea to a lesser offense and an eight-year suspended sentence with the defendant serving four years in prison. The defense attorney objected that the proposal was "kind of high," and the judge responded: "Today only, I'll give him eight and [all but] two [suspended]" – meaning the defendant would receive two years in prison not the four requested by the prosecutor.[18]

Someone looking at the outcome in the Baltimore case, without seeing the informal colloquy set out above, would characterize this as a classic instance where the defendant, faced with a harsh mandatory minimum sentence, had no choice but to plead guilty on the prosecutor's terms. In fact, the defendant ended up with a different sentence than what the prosecutor sought because of the judge's intervention. Direct judicial involvement in plea negotiations, although barred in many jurisdictions, is common in a substantial minority as documented by legal scholars Nancy King and Ron Wright in their 2016 study of ten such States, including two of the largest contributors to Mass Incarceration: California and Florida.[19]

Judges influence plea deals even when they are not directly involved in negotiations. For example, the Federal Rules of Criminal Procedure forbid judicial involvement, stating: "The court must not participate in these discussions." The typical process in these jurisdictions is that the defendant agrees to plead guilty to one or more charges in exchange for the prosecutor's agreement to dismiss other charges. Often plea bargains include a recommended sentence, or an agreement by the prosecutor not to oppose or seek a certain sentence. But judges are not bound by the parties' sentencing recommendations. This is such an important aspect of plea bargaining that judges must warn defendants about it, or risk any resulting conviction being thrown out on appeal. The federal rules of criminal procedure – and analogous State rules – command that for typical plea deals, "the court must advise the defendant that the defendant has no right to withdraw the plea if the court does not follow the [parties'] recommendation or request."[20]

Sometimes plea agreements do include a specific "stipulated" sentence agreed to by the parties. But judges can still reject sentences even for these stipulated deals by rejecting the plea deal itself. Again, the representative federal rule makes this clear, stating: "[T]he court may accept the [stipulated] agreement, reject it, or defer a decision until the court has reviewed the presentence report." And while formal rejections of plea bargains may be unusual, they don't need to be common (or formal) for prosecutors and defense attorneys to get the message. Cases fall into familiar patterns, and both prosecutors and defense attorneys regularly appear before the same judge. That means that whenever a judge reacts (formally or informally) to a plea agreement by pushing for more or less severity that reaction sets a new bar for the cases that follow. Consequently, judges can have a significant impact on plea bargained sentences even in jurisdictions where they are excluded from the bargaining process.

Of course, neither the increasingly harsh sentences imposed over the era of Mass Incarceration nor the increase in time served was solely a function of judicial action. Prosecutors contributed to longer sentences through charging. And legislators contributed in a variety of ways. The most dramatic was that legislators replaced indeterminate sentencing with determinate sentences, and eliminated parole. This required judges to pronounce a precise term of imprisonment at sentencing. In an era when politicians and the public were calling for longer sentences, this precision created a kind of report card. Voters and government officials tasked with appointing, promoting, or reviewing judges could use this report card to penalize those perceived to be "soft" on crime. Judges could not help but be influenced by these dynamics.

Legislators also took some sentences out of judges' hands entirely. They paid special attention to crimes that judges weren't already treating harshly, like drugs, gun possession, child pornography, and repeat offenders. As the legislators recognized, mandatory sentencing laws matter most when they mandate sentences that judges would not otherwise impose.

The legislative reduction of judicial discretion through mandatory sentencing laws angered some judges. In 2004, federal judge Paul Cassell sentenced a drug defendant to fifty-five years in prison, while issuing a fiery opinion denouncing the statutorily-mandated sentence as "cruel, unjust, and even irrational."[21] The judge in the *Tigano* case discussed in Chapter 7 similarly expressed reservations about the sentence he was required to impose, saying: "I do not believe he should be punished by imprisonment of 20 years. I feel that that is much greater than is necessary." By overriding judicial objections like these, mandatory sentencing laws enforced judicial uniformity, and minimized the ability of judges to sentence leniently. Harsh mandatory sentencing laws had subtler effects as well. Among other things, they made becoming a judge less attractive for those who were not inclined toward harsh sentencing. Cassell resigned from the bench not long after the opinion quoted above.[22] Federal judge J. Lawrence Irving cited the severity of sentencing laws in his resignation in 1990, telling the *New York Times*, "I just can't, in good conscience, continue to do this."[23] Many judges no doubt silently recoiled at having to sign their name to orders that sent people to prison for years for things like selling a small bag of crack cocaine. With these judges leaving the bench and similarly minded attorneys less likely to seek judge (or prosecutor) positions, the criminal courts skewed further toward severity.

Judges willing to persevere found the increased severity to be contagious. Increasing sentences for some crimes – especially for crimes that might not seem gravely serious like transporting drugs or possessing weapons – creates pressure to increase the sentences for others. With precise sentences, judges, reporters, and the public naturally came to view sentences as signals of how seriously society viewed a crime (or offender) relative to other crimes (or offenders). Here is how I explained the phenomenon to the 2020 annual meeting of elected Louisiana prosecutors in a (subsequently transcribed) presentation:

> Severity is contextual. There's a guy in Norway who killed 77 people in 2011, an atrocious crime. Norway sentenced him to 21 years. Why 21 years? That's the max in Norway. You can imagine at the sentencing hearing, the judge saying, "This is an atrocious crime. I'm giving you the max." Obviously, that's not the max in the United States – not even close.
>
> Compare that to the notorious case from Louisiana in 1996 where someone stole a jacket and gets life without the possibility of parole. It's a totally different world. In the United States,

the max is through the roof for things that nobody would describe as atrocious crimes. Ratcheting up severity for some crimes pushes severity up for all crimes. If you're giving out huge sentences for drug crimes or habitual offenders, that pushes the ceiling higher for murderers or rapists. For an American judge to express outrage, the judge has to compete with life sentences for stealing a jacket. A judge that just sentenced a guy to life for theft is going to have a hard time imposing a lower sentence for an armed robbery, murder, or rape. That pressure affects legislators, judges, police, and prosecutors.

> The above excerpt references the 1996 case of Timothy Jackson, who shoplifted a $159 jacket from a department store and was sentenced to life in prison under Louisiana's repeat-offender law. Repeat offender laws are the focus of Chapter 14.[24]

As suggested in the Norway example, the wholesale upward shift of the scale of American punishment can be seen in comparisons to other countries. Writing in 2003, James Whitman noted that "American convicts . . . serve sentences roughly five to ten times as long as similarly situated French ones; and almost certainly even longer by comparison to German convicts."[25] A Vera Institute study similarly notes that:

In 2006 in Germany, 75 percent of prison sentences were for 12 months or less and 92 percent of sentences were for two years or less [and] only a very small percentage of those sentenced ever went to prison. Similarly, in the Netherlands in 2012, the vast majority of sentences (91 percent) were for one year or less, going up to 95 percent if sentences of two years or less are included. In contrast, the average length of stay in American prisons is approximately 3 years.[26]

13 JUDICIAL INTERPRETATION

Judges play a role in enabling Mass Incarceration beyond imposing longer sentences. Judges also set the boundaries of American criminal law. They do this in two ways: (1) judges interpret the criminal laws that legislators enact and (2) judges ensure that the processes the government uses to lock people up comport with state and federal constitutions.

13.1 INTERPRETING THE LAWS

It is a foundational principle of American law that a person can only be imprisoned for behavior that was specifically prohibited by a then-existing criminal law. That is why prosecutors must specify which criminal law(s) they believe the defendant violated at the outset of any criminal prosecution. And while a jury is the ultimate barrier to a conviction, judges too can dismiss a prosecution if the government's proof does not sufficiently establish a violation of the law. For example, a jury convicted former Virginia Governor Bob McDonnell of public corruption in 2014, but the Supreme Court later rejected the federal prosecutors' view of the applicable law and threw out McDonnell's conviction.

Many of the legal fights in criminal court are disputes about precisely what a law prohibits. Does federal law prohibit, for example:

1. paying money to college basketball coaches to steer players to a particular sports agent or
2. throwing a stock of recently caught fish back into the water just before Fish and Wildlife agents can measure them?[1]

These are questions that must ultimately be resolved by judges when –
as is often the case – the applicable criminal law is unclear.

As noted in Part II, legislators generally try to help law enforcement
by writing broad laws. That's why it is illegal not just to steal a car but
to drive one without the owner's permission; or to "distribute" (not just
sell) illegal drugs or child pornography. Still there are many circumstances where the law's application is not clear, leaving space for
judicial interpretation. As Mass Incarceration spread across the nation,
judges frequently interpreted criminal laws broadly, making it easier,
not harder, to convict.

The best way to illustrate the point is with specific examples.
California, like all United States jurisdictions, prohibits burglary: the
ancient crime of entering a house to take what is inside. But as with
most modern statutes, California's burglary statute (section 459 of the
State's penal code) reflects herculean efforts to ensure that it applies to
every possible burglary scenario:

> Every person who **enters** any house, room, apartment, tenement,
> shop, warehouse, store, mill, barn, stable, outhouse or other build-
> ing, tent, vessel, floating home, railroad car, locked or sealed cargo
> container, trailer coach, inhabited camper, vehicle, when the doors
> are locked, aircraft, or mine or any underground portion thereof,
> with intent to commit grand or petit larceny or any felony is guilty
> of burglary.

California's modern burglary statute protects almost any enclosure
where items might be found. By including locked cars, the statute
makes the common occurrence of stealing from parked cars a burglary.

But California's burglary statute is even broader than it looks
because of how judges, in cases like *People* v. *Valencia*, interpret the
word "enters." In 1998, Cuahutemoc Valencia "removed a window
screen from a bathroom window of [a] house and tried unsuccessfully
to open the window itself." Unable to open the window, Valencia drove
away, but having been observed by neighbors, was soon arrested. After
a jury convicted Valencia of burglary, the California courts had to
decide whether this really was a burglary – a felony punishable by five
years in prison. Legally speaking, the question was, did Valencia *enter*
the house when he removed a window screen? The California Court of

Appeal said yes: "The issue before us is whether penetration into the area behind a window screen amounts to an entry of a building within the meaning of the burglary statute when the window itself is closed and is not penetrated. As we shall explain, we conclude that it does."[2] This ruling may seem technical, but California courts regularly rely on it to uphold felony burglary convictions for people who try, but fail, to get into enclosures.

The point here is not whether removing a screen should be a crime or even whether it should count as the felony offense of "burglary." The point is that the California burglary statute requires the prosecution to prove that a person "enters a house," and the California courts interpreted that statute to allow convictions of people who did not, in fact, *enter* a house. This is all the more surprising because it seems to violate "the rule of lenity." The rule of lenity is a long-standing legal principle that requires that ambiguity in criminal laws must be interpreted against the government. In the present context, the rule should dictate that if it is not clear that a person who removes a window screen "enters a house," the defendant wins. But, as critics such as legal scholar Shon Hopwood have noted, the "current rule of lenity diverges significantly from historical practice," with modern judges rarely applying the rule to benefit criminal defendants.[3]

Examples can be found in many areas of the criminal law. Chapter 10 noted the outsized role of aggravated assault charges in Mass Incarceration. The distinction between an aggravated and simple assault is important because the former is a felony (not misdemeanor) offense with longer penalties. One way an assault becomes aggravated is through the use of a deadly or dangerous weapon. Obvious examples are knives and guns and even baseball bats. But what about shoes? It may seem like a silly question, but it is an important one because assaults with shoes (i.e., kicking) are common. Are shoes dangerous weapons? Courts frequently say yes. For example, in the District of Columbia in 2003, a defendant was convicted of aggravated assault based on proof "that he kicked the complainant in the buttocks with one of his Timberland walking or hiking boots." The D.C. courts affirmed a felony conviction based on this conduct for "assault with a dangerous weapon" because a "Timberland boot, used to kick someone, has intrinsically greater potential to cause serious injury than do, say, ... tennis shoes."[4] Why tennis shoes? Because the opinion relied on an earlier decision from 1992, where the same court held that a defendant who kicked someone in the head while "wearing white sneakers" was guilty of the offense of assault "while armed with a dangerous weapon, namely, a shod foot."[5] That case, in turn, relied on a Massachusetts case that held that a defendant who kicked a person with boots was similarly guilty of aggravated assault "by means of a dangerous weapon."[6] In accepting the government's argument that sneakers constituted a deadly weapon, an Indiana court in 2011 summarized a variety of other States' case law on the question, reporting a general consensus that "kicking with a 'shod foot' constitutes an assault with a 'deadly weapon.'"[7]

Here is another example that illustrates how subtle yet consequential these rulings can be. Simple assault and shoplifting are both misdemeanors, typically punished by short jail stays or no incarceration at all. But if a person commits a simple assault during a theft, the offense becomes a robbery, a felony typically punished with a prison term. Robbery is generally defined as theft by use of force or fear. But what if a person is detected shoplifting a coat, drops the coat and then, in the process of fleeing the store, hits a store employee who tries to detain him. Is the shoplifter guilty of two misdemeanors (shoplifting and assault) or a felony (robbery)? The way courts answer these questions is they look at the applicable statutory language. In the case that presented this question, the judges were applying a Texas law that defines robbery as the use of force "in the course of committing theft." The shoplifter argued that he was no longer committing ("in the course of") a theft when he hit the store employee. You can guess what the court said. When asked questions like these, American courts regularly gave the answer most favorable to the prosecution, concluding, in this case, that the offense was a felony (robbery), not two misdemeanors (shoplifting and assault) – and upholding the sentence of seven years in prison.[8]

It is easiest to look at the data and connect the increase in prison admissions to the most direct actors involved: police officers making arrests, prosecutors filing charges, trial judges imposing sentences. But behind those actors are other actors, legislators who write broad laws and appellate judges who stretch those laws to enable the maximum punishments.

13.2 INTERPRETING THE CONSTITUTION

Judges do more than determine what the laws mean. They also decide whether the application of those laws violates the limits of State and federal constitutions. And here, criminal defendants should find an ally. The nation's founders grew up on stories of English treason prosecutions of famous figures like Sir Walter Raleigh, who was beheaded in 1618. And when folks like George Mason (who lodged in the celebrated Raleigh Tavern in Williamsburg, Virginia) and Thomas Jefferson (who had a portrait of Raleigh in his Monticello home)[9] heard these stories, they identified with Raleigh, not the Crown. Worried that they could fall prey to similar injustices, the country's founders placed a number of rights designed to undermine the government's ability to throw them in jail in the federal and State constitutions. Among these rights were a right to a jury trial, a right to an attorney, a right to confront witnesses, the right not to incriminate themselves, a right to due process, and a prohibition of cruel and unusual punishments. It is a great irony that Mass Incarceration arose in a country whose founding documents included such seemingly powerful obstacles to criminal prosecution. But rights must be interpreted. And almost every step of the way, modern judges interpreted these rights in a manner that expanded the reach of the criminal law.

The 1999 California case *People* v. *Taylor* illustrates this point. There, police saw an impoverished man, Gregory Taylor, "attempt to pry open the metal security screen over [a] church's kitchen door." Taylor, who claimed he only wanted food, was convicted of burglary. More importantly, this was Taylor's third "strike" and, applying California's three strikes law, the judge sentenced him to life in prison.[10] As an appellate judge pointed out in reviewing the case: "Taylor received a longer sentence than the fictional Jean Valjean – twenty-five years to life – over the same proverbial 'loaf of bread.'" California's three strikes law (discussed in the next chapter) shoulders the most blame. But it takes a village to send someone to prison, and the entire village came out for the *Taylor* case. The police had to arrest Taylor and bring this trivial case to prosecutors. The prosecutors decided to charge the case as a felony burglary and to introduce proof of Taylor's prior "strikes." The courts had to recognize a failed effort to enter – in this case using a board to try to pry open a metal security door – as an "entry" and thus a burglary.

Still more was required. Despite all of its severity, California's three strikes law permits trial courts to "strike a strike" in the interest of justice, an action that would have dramatically reduced the sentence. The judge in Taylor's case declined to do so. Standing between Taylor and a life sentence was yet one last legal obstacle. The Eighth Amendment to the federal Constitution prohibits "cruel and unusual" punishment, and California's State constitution prohibits punishments that are "cruel or unusual." Isn't a life sentence for kind-of-trying to steal something from a church cruel or unusual, or both? Not according to American judges.

Perhaps the most profound fact about Taylor's sentence is that his lawyer did not even raise the legal argument that its imposition was "cruel or unusual." That's probably because the argument was doomed. Even with the many tools at their disposal, courts have shown little interest in pushing back against the rising tide of Mass Incarceration. In fact, they generally seem fully supportive. For example, in an early case rejecting a challenge to the voter-passed three strikes law, a California appeals court suggested that these penalties could not be "cruel or unusual" because they were so popular:

> It may be inferred from the results of the election that well over two-thirds of California voters do not consider it cruel or unusual punishment for a recidivist offender convicted of a nonviolent, nonserious felony with prior convictions for violent or serious felonies ... to receive a sentence of 25 years to life. While it is conceivable that a sentence violative of the cruel or unusual punishment prohibition might be approved by the electorate, such is highly unlikely .... Rather, the enactment of the statute and its appropriate application to [the defendant] results from a need to deter offenders who repeatedly commit crimes serious enough to be classified as felonies and to segregate those offenders from the rest of society for an extended period of time.[11]

The California courts' rulings were ultimately validated by the highest court in the land in the 2003 case *Ewing* v. *California*. In that case,

> Gary Ewing walked into the pro shop of the El Segundo Golf Course in Los Angeles County on March 12, 2000. He walked

out with three golf clubs, priced at $399 apiece, concealed in his pants leg. A shop employee, whose suspicions were aroused when he observed Ewing limp out of the pro shop, telephoned the police. The police apprehended Ewing in the parking lot.[12]

The conviction represented Ewing's third strike, and that meant a life sentence. Ewing did challenge the sentence as cruel and unusual, and the case made it all the way to the US Supreme Court. In an opinion by Justice Sandra Day O'Connor, the Court delivered its verdict: "We hold that Ewing's sentence of 25 years to life in prison, imposed for the offense of felony grand theft under the three strikes law, is not grossly disproportionate and therefore does not violate the Eighth Amendment's prohibition on cruel and unusual punishments." Rulings like these eliminated an important potential roadblock to Mass Incarceration by making it almost impossible for defendants to claim that punishments were too severe or, more precisely, unconstitutionally disproportionate to their offense.

Interestingly, American courts are more likely to declare sentences to be "cruel and unusual" if they deviate from the incarceration norm. American legislatures and trial judges avoid (once common) shaming and corporal punishments, in part, because they have become "unusual," making their legal status uncertain. That was on the mind of Judge Vaughn Walker who, in 2003, required a person convicted of stealing mail to stand outside a post office wearing a signboard stating, "I stole mail. This is my punishment."[13] Still, Judge Walker emphasized that such a punishment was preferable to the usual one, a prison sentence. An appeals court upheld the sentence, but a dissenting judge signaled its tenuous status, writing: "There is precious little federal authority on sentences that include shaming components, perhaps indicative of a recognition that whatever legal justification may be marshaled in support of sentences involving public humiliation, they simply have no place in the majesty of an Article III courtroom."[14] The dissenting judge was right about one thing. Judge Walker's sentence is a rarity. There is only one kind of serious punishment that American judges can impose without worrying about a constitutional challenge: imprisonment. And not coincidentally, that is the type of sentence that has become the most abundant.

American courts also work to keep juries unaware of the lengthy sentences that guilty verdicts enable. The operating principal was most recently articulated in a 1994 opinion, where the Supreme Court rejected a defendant's argument that the jury should be informed about the consequences of its potential verdict. The Court explained "when a jury has no sentencing function, it should be admonished to reach its verdict without regard to what sentence might be imposed." (In most American jurisdictions, juries do not impose sentences and so have no "sentencing function.")

The Court explained its ruling as a matter of logic:

> The principle that juries are not to consider the consequences of their verdicts is a reflection of the basic division of labor in our legal system between judge and jury. The jury's function is to find the facts and to decide whether, on those facts, the defendant is guilty of the crime charged. The judge, by contrast, imposes sentence on the defendant after the jury has arrived at a guilty verdict. Information regarding the consequences of a verdict is therefore irrelevant to the jury's task.[15]

This ruling matters because juries might convict less if they knew, in cases like those involving California's three strikes law, that a guilty verdict would lead to a draconian sentence. That might even cause prosecutors to avoid triggering severe punishments in borderline cases, and push legislatures to moderate statutory severity. Indeed, in the colonial era, jurors knew that a guilty verdict for many offenses meant death. As a result, they frequently tailored their verdicts to avoid a death sentence. Courts seek to prevent today's jurors from similarly evading disproportionate punishments by preventing them from learning about sentencing consequences. In fact, in the *Taylor* case discussed above, after convicting Taylor and learning his fate, several jurors offered to testify at his sentencing hearing in (futile) opposition to imposition of the life sentence mandated by California's three strikes law.

American courts' reluctance to deem lengthy prison sentences "cruel and unusual," and their efforts to keep juries unaware of those sentences, are straightforward contributors to Mass Incarceration. Other rulings contribute in predictable ways. Chapter 17 highlights court rulings that diluted the constitutional rights to a "speedy trial" and the prohibition of "excessive bail," enabling pretrial jail populations to spike. Another, less obvious contributor is the courts' refusal to set boundaries on the substantive reach of criminal law. The best illustration of this point is a 1962 case where the Supreme Court did set a boundary, *Robinson* v. *California*. In that case, Lawrence Robinson was convicted under a criminal law that made it unlawful "either to use narcotics, or to be addicted to the use of narcotics."[16] The Supreme Court rejected the conviction and ninety-day jail sentence Robinson received on the ground that a statute prohibiting the status of being addicted to narcotics "inflicts a cruel and unusual punishment." Criminalizing addiction, the Court explained, was analogous to making it unlawful to have an illness. The most important aspect of the *Robinson* ruling, however, is how unusual it is. Aside from situations like *Robinson*, where a person is punished for a status, not an act, American courts refuse to set limits on the substance of criminal law. A logical extension of the principle that a person cannot be criminally punished for being addicted to drugs is that an addict cannot be criminally prosecuted for possessing drugs. But the courts never made that connection. In fact, there is no rule that conduct must be harmful, dangerous, or immoral to be punished by imprisonment. The courts' reluctance to recognize any such limits permits legislatures to criminalize even relatively benign conduct and punish that conduct severely. In 2006 alone, State courts convicted over 165,000 people of a felony for drug possession, and incarcerated over 60 percent in jail (31 percent) or prison (33 percent).[17]

American courts also shied away from regulating the most important procedural development in American criminal law: plea bargaining. About 95 percent of convictions in America come from guilty pleas, not trials. Part of the explanation for that high percentage is the courts' reluctance to set limits. In fact, some experts trace the dawn of Mass Incarceration to a 1978 check forgery case in Kentucky, *Bordenkircher* v. *Hayes*. There, Paul Hayes passed a forged $88 check. The prosecutor offered Hayes, who had a criminal record, a deal: plead guilty and the prosecutor would recommend a five-year sentence. The prosecutor warned Hayes that, if he turned down the offer, the prosecutor would seek an indictment under the State's Habitual Criminal Act – a statute that mandated a life prison term for repeat offenders. The prosecutor later explained that he wanted Hayes to plead guilty to "save the court the inconvenience and necessity of a trial, and taking up this time." Hayes turned down the offer. The prosecutor followed through on his promise. A jury convicted and Hayes was sentenced to life in prison.[18]

Hayes appealed, arguing that the prosecutor's action in seeking the additional indictment was an unconstitutional punishment for Hayes's exercising his constitutional right to a jury trial. The Supreme Court rejected this claim, explaining: "[T]he course of conduct engaged in by the prosecutor in this case, which no more than openly presented the defendant with the unpleasant alternatives of forgoing trial or facing charges on which he was plainly subject to prosecution, did not violate the [Constitution]." In reaching this ruling, the Court quoted this telling observation from an earlier case: "Whatever might be the situation in an ideal world, the fact is that the guilty plea and the often concomitant plea bargain are important components of this country's criminal justice system. Properly administered, they can benefit all concerned."

The Supreme Court recognized that the facts of *Bordenkircher*, while extreme, differed in degree not in kind from the routine plea bargaining that prosecutors, defense attorneys, and trial judges had come to rely on to manage their caseloads and (sometimes) work around draconian sentencing laws. A different ruling would have jeopardized that system.

Thirty years after *Bordenkircher*, a Supreme Court majority issued an opinion that wryly stated that plea bargaining "is not some adjunct to the criminal justice system; it *is* the criminal justice system."[19] Left out of the opinion is the fact that the Court was no innocent bystander to this development. Its refusal to set boundaries on plea bargaining makes the practice attractive, especially to attorneys and trial judges dealing with heavy caseloads. And the more plea bargaining that goes on, the more cases the system can process, and the more people it can incarcerate.

American judges generally downplay their role in Mass Incarceration. Judges claim that they merely enforce the laws enacted by legislators and that legislators have forced their hands with mandatory minimum sentences and sentencing guidelines. Any blame about the outcomes of particular cases, judges say, falls to police and prosecutors who overload their dockets and legislators who tie their hands. Chief Justice John Roberts famously told the senators at his confirmation hearing that all judges do is "call balls and strikes." But the courts' role has not been as passive as this suggests. This is apparent in the way that courts interpret criminal laws, the abandonment of the rule of lenity, and the long sentences handed down by trial judges and upheld on appeal. But it can also be seen in the courts' reluctance to create boundaries despite the constitutional authority to do so. The Fourth Amendment's prohibition of "unreasonable" searches and seizures could be a powerful obstacle to the Drug War. The Fifth Amendment's prohibition of compelled self-incrimination and the Sixth Amendment's guarantee of a trial "by an impartial jury" could limit plea bargaining. The Eighth Amendment's prohibition of "cruel and unusual punishments" could rein in long sentences and ensure humane prison and jail conditions. The prohibition of "excessive bail" and "speedy trial" guarantee could reduce pretrial detention. The Fifth and Fourteenth Amendments' command that defendants receive "due process" could block extortionate law enforcement practices like those in Ferguson, Missouri. The relative rarity of these kinds of decisions suggests that courts were not neutral observers to the rise of Mass Incarceration. They chose a side. And more often than not, that side was incarceration.

14 PUNISHING REPEAT OFFENSES

Abstract arguments about crime and punishment typically focus on single, isolated offenses. But a key question for any criminal justice system is how to treat people who come before courts for their second, third, fourth, fifth time and beyond? The prevalence of these cases is one of the reasons that police, prosecutors, and judges often do not consider the system as harsh as it appears to outsiders. In their experience, many of the folks who get locked up received multiple chances to avoid incarceration.

While some people serving time in prison or jail have no prior record of criminal offenses, repeat offenders (or, more precisely, repeat arrestees) are the norm. A Bureau of Justice Statistics (BJS) 2009 study of arrestees in large cities found that 75 percent of those arrested for a felony offense had been arrested previously, and 60 percent had a prior conviction. Of those with an arrest record, over half had five or more prior arrests and more than a third had ten or more arrests.[1] Of those with a prior conviction, almost a third (29 percent) had five or more previous convictions.

A record of prior incarceration is the norm, not the exception, in American prisons. A recent BJS publication offered the following insight: "Thirty percent of state and federal prisoners reported that they had 5 or more incarcerations prior to the offense for which they were being held in 2016, including 12% who had 10 or more prior incarcerations. Less than a quarter of prisoners reported no history of prior incarcerations in 2016 (22%)."[2]

These same patterns show up in prison releases. The BJS examined a random sample of folks released in 2008 from prisons in twenty-four states and found that of the 73,600 people studied, "82% were arrested at least once during the 10 years following release."[3] The percentage was even higher (90%) for those under the age of twenty-five.

These numbers are not static. In fact, one of the most important feedback loops fueling Mass Incarceration is the increasing number of people with prior convictions. In 2017, researchers studying the growing numbers of Americans with prior convictions found that what had once been an unusual occurrence was becoming commonplace, especially in certain communities: "The total number of non–African Americans with felony convictions grew from 2.5% of the adult population in 1980 to more than 6% in 2010. For African Americans, people with felony convictions tripled, from 7.6% of adults in 1980 to approximately 23% in 2010."[4]

This increase in the number of people with prior convictions predictably translated into an increase in the number of defendants coming before prosecutors and courts with criminal records. The BJS survey of large cities reported that in 1990, 54 percent of defendants arrested for a felony had a prior conviction, rising to 58 percent in 2000, and 60 percent in 2009 (the last year of the series). The number of defendants with ten or more prior convictions rose from 7 percent in 1990 to 14 percent in 2009.[5]

Prior records fuel Mass Incarceration in a variety of ways, specifically: (1) police and prosecutors are less likely to give breaks to people with criminal records; (2) judges impose longer sentences on repeat offenders; and (3) people who commit a crime while on probation or parole are often sent directly to prison or jail.

In addition to each of the mechanisms just mentioned, legislators seeking to close the revolving door enacted special laws to crack down on repeat offenders. "Three strikes" laws are the most dramatic example. By 1996, at least half the States had adopted three strikes laws that ratcheted up penalties for each "strike," that is, conviction.[6] The laws typically maxed out with a particularly dramatic sentence, like life imprisonment, for the third offense. Some repeat offender laws apply across conviction types, while others target specific types of convictions. For example, Congress enacted the Armed Career Criminal Act in 1984. That law imposes a minimum fifteen-year sentence for anyone who violates the federal law prohibiting possession of a firearm by a felon if the person was previously convicted of three violent or serious drug offenses.[7] In the *Tigano* case referenced in Chapter 8, a federal statute doubled Tigano's mandatory sentence for growing over 1,000 marijuana plants (from ten to twenty years) because he had a prior felony drug conviction.[8] The enhancement could have been even steeper. In 1986, Congress enacted a provision that punished drug offenses like Tigano's with a mandatory life sentence if the defendant had more than one prior felony drug conviction.[9]

The relative contribution of the various repeat offender laws to Mass Incarceration depends on their scope and the degree to which they push sentences higher than what judges are already imposing. By these criteria, the most impactful repeat offender law is California's three strikes law, enacted in 1994.

The California law defines a broad set of "serious" or "violent" crimes as "strikes." Anyone with a prior "strike" who is convicted of a new felony has their sentence doubled. If the defendant has two prior strikes, the law dictates a twenty-five-year-to-life sentence for the new felony – meaning the defendant must serve twenty-five years before becoming eligible for (but not entitled to) parole.[10] What made California's three-strikes law unusual was that third strikes were not limited to violent or serious felonies. The third strike could be any of the broad variety of California felonies, including drug possession or theft. As then–Los Angeles District Attorney Gil Garcetti, an opponent of the law, complained, "the way the initiative is worded, a three-time felon could be sent to prison for life without committing any violent crimes."[11] This made California's law more impactful than most three-strikes laws, both because it applied so broadly and because it mandated much higher sentences than a judge would normally impose.

As Figure 14.1, a 2005 chart prepared by California's Legislative Analyst's Office (CLAO), shows, tens of thousands of defendants were sentenced to lengthy prison terms under the three strikes law.[12] Garcetti's critique proved prescient as the CLAO also determined that 56 percent of Three Strike sentences followed a third offense that was considered both "nonserious" and "nonviolent" even under the law's narrow definitions of those terms.

In 1995, Jerry Dewayne Williams famously received a life sentence for stealing a slice of pepperoni pizza, a petty theft that, due to another

**Growth in the Three Strikes Inmate
Population in State Prison**

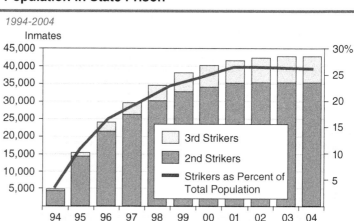

Figure 14.1 Growth in the Three Strikes prison population

recidivism law, became a felony because Williams had prior convictions. In an effort to blunt criticism, the California prosecutor handling the case, Deputy District Attorney Bill Gravlin, emphasized that the sentence was based on the totality of Williams's offenses (including earlier convictions for robbery, attempted robbery, car theft and drug possession). Gravlin argued: "The people of California are sick of revolving-door justice, they're sick of judges who are soft on crime. It is wrong to focus on the last offense."[13]

Gravlin would later write a letter to the editor of the *Los Angeles Times*, criticizing Los Angeles District Attorney George Gascon, who, upon his 2020 election as a "progressive prosecutor," announced a policy of declining to invoke sentencing enhancements like the one that sent Williams to prison. Gravlin wrote, "Refusing to prosecute a particular enhancement in all cases is inconsistent with Gascon's oath of office, which requires him to enforce the laws of the state."[14]

While the pizza-theft case received a lot of attention as something of an outlier, even a typical California three-strikes case reflects the law's oversized impact. For example, in 2003, Antwoine Bealer threatened the employees of a Wendy's with a knife in an effort to rob the restaurant. Bealer obtained some money from a register but was arrested before he could leave. Bealer pled guilty to two felonies: aggravated assault and robbery. That gave Bealer two "strikes." (The California Supreme court ruled in 1997 that a single incident could give rise to multiple "strikes.")[15] Since this was Bealer's first offense, the three strikes law had no immediate impact. In fact, the trial court gave him a second chance, sentencing him to probation with no jail time. Less than a year later, Bealer robbed a gas station with a real-looking but plastic gun, leaving with $200 before being captured by police as he drove away. After a jury convicted Bealer of robbery, the judge sentenced him to twenty-five years to life as required by the three-strikes law, plus an additional five years for violating the terms of his 2003 probation.[16]

The stark contrast between Bealer's first and second sentencing illustrates the power of a three-strikes law. Bealer received no jail time in his first case, even though the first case was more serious than his second. When Bealer committed another crime while on probation, he would expect to receive a harsher sentence. But in California, the three strikes law took that decision out of the judge's hands and dictated that the second chance Bealer had already received would be his last.

> In 2012, a California voter initiative modified the three strikes law so that nonserious, nonviolent crimes would no longer trigger a life sentence. That change helps defendants like Williams but not Bealer.

Repeat offender laws are particularly impactful in an era of Mass Incarceration because, with more and more cases moving through the system, more and more of the people coming to the attention of police, prosecutors, and judges have prior convictions. Even without the laws referenced above, the proliferation of criminal records in the wake of Mass Incarceration increased severity at every step of the process. A criminal record is a factor in whether someone is arrested, referred for prosecution, booked into jail, held pending trial; changes the evidence introduced at trial; and influences sentencing, probation/parole revocations, early release, and clemency. At every one of these decision points, the increased prevalence of prior records pushed decision-makers toward severity.

In sum, the treatment of repeat offenders is a critical and often overlooked element of Mass Incarceration. Laws like those described above, combined with less-forgiving attitudes on the part of police, prosecutors, and judges, resulted in harsher treatment and longer sentences for people arrested and convicted of second, third, and fourth offenses. And this severity extended to more and more people as the churning wheels of Mass Incarceration ensured that more and more people caught up in the system had criminal records.

15 THE PAROLE-AND-PROBATION-TO-PRISON PIPELINE

Recidivism laws, like the three strikes laws discussed in the previous chapter, are one way to eliminate second and third chances, dictating lengthy sentences for repeat offenses. Another way that the criminal law punishes people who have offended one too many times is through probation and parole revocations. While severely understudied, parole and probation revocations generate about a third of prison admissions and possibly more. And perhaps no change better illustrates the change from a criminal justice to a criminal legal system than the increasing volume of incarceration generated through the parole and probation revocation process.

Judges often sentence people to probation rather than incarceration. For example, in 2006, 27 percent of defendants sentenced for a felony offense in State court received a sentence of probation only, a percentage that increases dramatically for misdemeanor offenses. Judges also routinely use probation as a supplemental punishment, imposing a period of probation to follow a custodial sentence: for example, thirty days in jail plus two years' probation. Altogether, judges place millions of Americans on probation: just over 1 million (total) in 1980 rising to over 4 million by 2002.[1] The formula was illustrated in Antwoine Bealer's case discussed in Chapter 14. After his first conviction, Bealer, like thousands of defendants across America, was not locked up even though his offense was serious. Instead, Bealer received a five-year suspended sentence – meaning that he didn't have to serve any actual ("active") incarceration. But a custodial sentence still loomed over his head. If Bealer violated the terms of his probation, the judge could impose the five previously suspended years.

One of the most common ways that people violate the terms of probation is to commit a new offense, as Bealer did. But it is not the only way. When defendants are placed on probation, they agree to comply with a series of conditions. One common condition is drug testing. Others involve curfews and obtaining employment. Defendants who violate the terms of probation, even if those violations aren't themselves crimes, can be sent to jail or prison for so-called technical violations.

Once caught in the net of government supervision, it can be difficult to get out. Consider the case of Robert Williams. Williams was convicted of drug and gun charges in 2008 as a teenager and served about a year in prison in Pennsylvania. His 2009 release came with seven years of probation. Although Williams seemed to have turned his life around, the authorities continued to bring him back before the judge who had originally sentenced him, for technical violations of his probation.

Probation expands the reasons that someone can be incarcerated, and makes the process easier for the government. When a probation officer, police officer, or prosecutor notifies the court of an alleged violation, there is no requirement of a formal trial. The normal evidence rules don't apply. The standard of proof is lower. The judge, not a jury, decides. Often a judge simply looks at the evidence the government presents of the alleged violation – such as a probation officer's report – and decides to send the defendant to jail or prison. In Williams's case, the judge decided to send him to prison over and over again. A few more months in prison in 2014. Again in 2016. And a few years in 2018. Each time, the judge resentenced Williams, adding new probation periods that ensured that Williams remained under court supervision even after serving additional time – all based on a crime that occurred in 2007.

Williams's violations ranged from positive drug tests to unauthorized travel to fighting to traffic infractions. Williams's story came to light because he is famous. He is better known as the rap artist Meek Mill. Mill wrote a column for the *New York Times* highlighting his experience and calling for reform.[2] In describing the 2018 violation that sent him to prison, Mill explained:

My crime? Popping a wheelie on a motorcycle in Manhattan. Even though the charge was dismissed in a New York City court, a

Philadelphia-based judge still deemed my interaction with the police to be a technical violation of my probation – stemming from a 2007 arrest – and sentenced me to two to four years in prison despite the fact that I didn't commit a crime.

Probation isn't the only system that works this way. States also release people on parole before the end of their prison term or, as in California, impose parole supervision as an add-on to a completed sentence. Even as parole systems were dismantled across the country, the number of Americans on parole increased from 220,438 in 1980 to 878,900 in 2019.[3]

The term *parole* comes from the French. Traditionally, prisoners of war could be released on their *parole d'honneur* – a solemn promise not to take up arms again for the duration of the conflict. In the prison context, parole means release with a promise to abide by a series of conditions. Again, the most important condition is a promise not to break the law. But there are many more conditions: no drugs, no alcohol, stay away from certain people or areas, get counseling, get a job, check in regularly, obey curfew, and so on. Violations of these terms can mean a return to prison. In 1999, California reported that its prison population included 65,000 parole violators: 39,000 (60 percent) who had their parole revoked for committing a new crime and 26,000 (40 percent) for technical violations. Perhaps most remarkably, parole violators constituted 40 percent of the State's total prison population.[4]

As Mill's account suggests, parole and probation violations are not necessary to punish people who commit crimes. People on probation or parole who commit new crimes can be punished just like everyone else – after a trial or guilty plea, with a new sentence tailored to the new offense. They can even be sentenced to longer terms for committing the new crime while on probation or parole. But as explained in Chapter 8, catching and punishing folks for crime can be hard for the government. Probation and parole revocations are shortcuts to incarceration. Probation and parole violations are the most meaningful, when, as in Mill's case, the government cannot successfully prosecute the new offense. If the new offense is not a stand-alone crime, or a jury wouldn't convict, or the witnesses don't cooperate, probation and parole violations offer a streamlined alternative. Technically, people

2017

New Cases   Violations

Figure 15.1 Old versus new cases

who go to prison for parole or probation violations aren't being punished for the new violation. They are being punished for their original crime.

One of the striking things about the number of people in American prisons is how many of them are there for violating conditions of release. In 2017, for example, there were 418,579 people admitted to prison on new court commitments (i.e., convictions of new crimes) and 174,210 admitted (30 percent) to prison for violations of the conditions of release (see Figure 15.1). The percentage was essentially unchanged (29 percent) in 2019.[5] This tracks an analysis of a large data set of State prisoners released in 2008, which found that almost a third (32 percent) were serving time for violating terms of release – that is, violations of probation or parole. In some States, violations of conditions of release are the primary source of new prisoners. As the BJS reported, in 2019, "Violations of post-custody supervision accounted for . . . the majority of admissions by six states: Washington (75%), Vermont (64 %), Idaho (62%), Utah (57%), New Hampshire (56%), and Arkansas (52%)."[6] These estimates are for postcustody supervision and so leave out folks sent to prison or jail for violating noncustodial probation terms. At a minimum, parole and probation revocations generate about a third of the inflow of people into America's prisons and jails.

As already indicated, parole revocations became a notable contributor to California's high incarceration numbers. A 2008 study by sociologists Ryken Grattet, Joan Petersilia, and Jeffrey Lin unearthed the many layers to the problem. First, the State had been incarcerating thousands of people for years, almost all of whom were eventually released. Second, California used parole to punish, not reward, inmates, placing almost everyone who served prison time on parole upon release, usually for three years. This created a large pool of folks under parole supervision, about 120,000 at any given time.[7] Third, parole violation decisions were not made by a judge, but by a corrections official – a deputy commissioner at the Board of Parole Hearings using a low "preponderance of the evidence" standard. Fourth, strict regulations required parole officers to trigger revocations for every violation for parolees who had originally committed a "serious" or "violent" offense.

In the early 1990s, California authorities recognized that sky-high parole violations were a problem. In 1992, Republican Governor Pete Wilson's administration adopted new policies designed to reduce the number of people sent to prison for parole violations. The *Los Angeles Times* reported that the policy seemed to be working: "the percentage of parolees returned to prison dropped, from a high of 67% in 1989 to 39.2% in 1993."[8] But some parolees who benefited from this policy committed serious crimes. For example, in 1993, Glen Cornwell killed William Reagan during a robbery. William Reagan's daughter, Robin, subsequently lobbied for tougher parole revocation rules, noting that parole officials gave Cornwell a break when he violated his parole a few months before the killing. With bipartisan support, California enacted the tougher rules, including those referenced in the preceding paragraph – commonly called the "Robin Reagan rules." California's parole revocation numbers returned to their previous highs.

California illustrates how parole can go from a mechanism for reducing incarceration to a means of increasing it. Parole was originally intended to allow government officials to reduce prison populations by letting people out prior to the expiration of their sentence. When California abolished early parole release for almost all offenses in 1977, this pressure release valve disappeared. And then things got worse. California imposed an additional period of parole supervision on the back end of completed prison sentences. And the State created policies that encouraged sending parolees back to prison. That meant California prisoners were not being released early *and* yet were still being sent back to prison for parole revocations. In terms of increasing incarceration, it was the worst of both worlds. And it was exactly what was intended when California designed this new system in the late 1970s. As legal scholar Sarah Mayeux explains, amid alarm about the "revolving door" of the then-existing system, "California parole officers offered themselves as a workaround, a way of sending dangerous people to prison without having to go through the plea bargaining and trial process."[9] A similar pattern played out in the federal system, which abolished parole while adding a system of "supervised release" onto the ends of completed prison sentences. Other jurisdictions retained a traditional parole system that allowed early releases, but released people less often and revoked the parole of those who were released more frequently.

Criminologist Jeremy Travis is one of the few modern scholars highlighting the importance of parole releases and revocations – what Travis calls "back-end sentencing." He reports that in 1980, 17 percent of prison admissions resulted from parole violations. By 2000, the percentage had grown to 35 percent, setting a new normal. Travis offers a powerful summary of the extent of that change: "about as many people were returned to prison for parole violations in 2000 as were admitted in 1980 for all reasons."[10]

16 DISAPPEARING PARDONS

One of the bedrock powers of any government is the power to pardon people for criminal offenses. This power is made explicit in State and federal constitutions. For example,

- The US Constitution states, "The President ... shall have Power to grant Reprieves and Pardons for Offenses against the United States, except in Cases of impeachment."
- The Virginia Constitution says that the governor shall have the power "to grant reprieves and pardons after conviction."
- The Florida Constitution has an entire section dedicated to "Clemency" that authorizes the governor to "grant full or conditional pardons, restore civil rights, commute punishment, and remit fines and forfeiture for offenses."

Historian James Whitman notes that, historically, governors used pardons to maintain low prison populations. He relates the report of an English observer in 1835 that prisoners in New York "felt unduly wronged" if they did not receive a pardon after serving half of their sentences, a belief reinforced by the existence of "semiannual clemency sessions which resulted in the release of forty to fifty convicts simultaneously."[1] One explanation for the demise of executive clemency was its replacement with more formal types of executive lenience, such as parole.[2] As noted in Chapters 7 and 15, however, American jurisdictions would later severely restrict parole. And when that happened, a traditional safeguard against bloated prison populations – the pardon power – did not reemerge.

In 2003, Supreme Court Justice Anthony Kennedy addressed the American Bar Association (ABA), urging a variety of criminal justice reforms. Among the changes he sought was a resurrection of the pardon power: "Pardons have become infrequent. A people confident in its laws and institutions should not be ashamed of mercy.... I hope more lawyers involved in the pardon process will say to Chief Executives, 'Mr. President,' or 'Your Excellency, the Governor, this young man has not served his full sentence, but he has served long enough. Give him what only you can give him.... Give him liberty.'" In response to Kennedy's address, the ABA formed a commission, the Justice Kennedy Commission, to report on the issues raised. Canvassing the State pardon process, the commission's report explained:

> In the states, the practice of pardoning varies [but] two things appear to be true: 1) in almost every jurisdiction the instance of pardoning decreased markedly after 1990; and 2) the vitality of the pardon power in a particular state jurisdiction varies depending upon the extent to which its decision-maker is insulated from politics.... Ironically, [the] pardon has continued to perform a useful role in mitigating sentences only in jurisdictions that also have a healthy parole system, with the two forms of early release often administered by the same personnel.[3]

Figure 16.1, produced by the Pew Research Center from Department of Justice data, highlights the pardons and commutations (sentence reductions) granted by US presidents.[4] The chart shows that, as federal prisons filled, pardons dwindled. This can be most easily observed in the percentage of clemency requests granted. For example, Calvin Coolidge (1,691), Herbert Hoover (1,077), and Barack Obama (1,927) granted a similar number of requests, but the percentages differed dramatically. Because Coolidge and Hoover presided over a system with many fewer people in federal custody, their grant rates (21 percent and 25 percent) – which were low for their eras – eclipsed Obama's (5 percent), which was high for his. A comparison to the overall federal prison population makes the trend even more striking. During the Coolidge and Hoover administrations there were about 11,000 federal prisoners. Granting mercy to over 1,000 people convicted of federal crimes impacted a large share of the federal system. By the time Obama took office, the federal prison population exceeded 200,000, meaning that Obama's commutations made only a ripple in a large pond. Updating the chart to the end of President Trump's term

Trump used clemency power less often than nearly every other modern president

Clemency statistics, by president

President	Term	Pardons	Commutations	Other	Total clemency	Total requests	Requests granted
Trump	2017-21	143	94	0	237	11,611	2%
Obama	2009-17	212	1,715	0	1,927	36,544	5
G.W. Bush	2001-09	189	11	0	200	11,074	2
Clinton	1993-01	396	61	2	459	7,489	6
Bush	1989-93	74	3	0	77	1,466	5
Reagan	1981-89	393	13	0	406	3,404	12
Carter	1977-81	534	29	3	566	2,627	22
Ford	1974-77	382	22	5	409	1,527	27
Nixon	1969-74	863	60	3	926	2,591	36
Johnson	1963-69	960	226	1	1,187	4,537	26
Kennedy	1961-63	472	100	3	575	1,749	33
Eisenhower	1953-61	1,110	47	0	1,157	4,100	28
Truman	1945-53	1,913	118	13	2,044	5,030	41
FDR	1933-45	2,819	488	489	3,796	13,541	28
Hoover	1929-33	672	405	121	1,198	4,774	25
Coolidge	1923-29	773	773	145	1,691	8,046	21
Harding	1921-23	300	386	87	773	2,461	31
Wilson	1913-21	1,087	1,366	374	2,827	7,454	38
Taft	1909-13	383	361	87	831	2,111	39
Roosevelt	1901-09	668	363	68	1,099	4,513	24
McKinley	1897-01	291	123	32	446	1,473	30

Note: "Other" refers to remissions, which reduce financial penalties, and respites, which are temporary reprieves often granted for medical reasons. Pardons and commutations under Trump are through the end of his term, but requests are only through the end of 2020. Totals for McKinley include fiscal 1900 and 1901 only.
Source: U.S. Department of Justice data, accessed Jan. 22, 2021.

PEW RESEARCH CENTER

Figure 16.1 Federal pardons

reflects an even more dramatic decrease, with Trump granting 144 requests, or about 1.4 percent of petitions received.

Before Trump, the lowest grant rate was George W. Bush, who had also been reluctant to issue pardons as governor of Texas. As reported in the *Fort Worth Telegram*, then–Governor Bush was "deeply embarrassed" when one of his first pardons, of a police officer with a marijuana conviction, backfired. Just months later, the officer "was back in jail, accused of stealing cocaine from a drug bust."

As data from Texas shows, Bush's pardon record was particularly stingy, and yet roughly in line with modern Texas governors. Table 16.1 shows the full or partial pardons issued by each of the last six Texas governors.[5]

There is no comprehensive data on State pardons, but the window into the declining number of Texas pardons appears to be representative. In a press release declaring that he had pardoned three prisoners

Table 16.1 *Texas pardons*

Pardons	Years in Office	Total Pardons	Pardons/Year
Greg Abbott	2016–present	38	6
Rick Perry	2000–2015	225	15
George W. Bush	1995–2000	21	4
Ann Richards	1991–1995	70	14
Mark White	1983–1987	500	100
Bill Clements	1979–1983, 1987–1991	822	82

in 2005, California Governor Arnold Schwarzenegger listed the pardons granted by former governors:

Arnold Schwarzenegger	2003–2005	3
Grey Davis	1999–2003	0
Pete Wilson	1991–1999	13
George Deukmejian	1983–1991	328
Gerry Brown	1975–1983	403
Ronald Reagan	1967–1975	575

The press release reveals two things, (1) the decreasing number of pardons over time and (2) Governor Schwarzenegger's apparent belief that granting even a handful of pardons required political cover in the form of contrasting his action with the lenience of previous administrations, and particularly that of conservative icon Ronald Reagan.

Since the numbers are low, it is tempting to view the decline of pardons as a minor component of the Mass Incarceration story. But one reason that the numbers are low is that, in the heyday of pardons, far fewer people were locked up. Executive clemency was once a powerful obstacle to excessive imprisonment. It is a last resort, with few strings attached, that can reduce the warehousing of people in prisons and jails. And it once functioned that way. But in the era of Mass Incarceration, executive clemency was one more structural safe-guard that failed. As America's prisons filled, pardons became less, not more, frequent.

17 THE MINDLESSNESS OF JAIL

American incarceration takes two distinct forms. People locked up for a short time are typically placed in a local jail, not a State prison. The primary benefits of jails are logistical. Jails are close to the police stations that generate arrests and the courts that process them. For prisoners, jails are nearer to home, family, and friends. There is, however, little to do in jails, since jails are intended for short-term stays. People locked up for longer periods, generally more than a year, are sent to a prison. Prisons are usually larger and more centralized and thus likely to be farther from the scene of the arrest, the sentencing court, and the prisoner's home and loved ones. Since prisons are intended for longer stays, they have, or at least should have, more programs, like jobs and education.

Most of the popular focus of Mass Incarceration is on prison populations. These populations are easier to measure since they are more stable. And people in prison are more dramatically affected by incarceration since they serve longer sentences, typically for more serious offenses. But jails are important too. The breathtaking growth of jail populations is an especially troubling aspect of Mass Incarceration. This is because the system is at its most mindless when it is filling jails. In fact, most of the people in jail haven't been convicted of any crime. They are waiting for their cases to proceed through the system.

In 1978, there were 158,000 people locked up in America's jails. By 2019 that number was 734,500, down from a high of 785,000 in 2008.[1] And since people cycle in and out of jail relatively quickly, those numbers represent only a portion of the total number of individuals who serve time in jail each year. In 2019, the average length of a jail stay was twenty-six days.[2]

Jails have two distinct functions. One function is to detain people during the delay between an arrest and a (potential) trial. In 2019, 65 percent of the people held in jail – 480,700 inmates – fell into this status. These pretrial detainees are responsible for the majority of the growth of jail populations over time. In 1978, States held about 67,000 people in pretrial detention (42 percent of the overall jail population).[3] The other purpose of jail is to provide a local detention center for people who have been convicted and ordered to serve short sentences. This accounted for the remaining 35 percent of prisoners in 2019, or 253,700 people.

Pretrial detention is largely a function of bureaucratic delay. And this is another area where changing police arrest policies appear to have made a substantial difference. The Vera Institute of Justice estimates that in 1975, only 51 percent of arrests involved a jail admission, with police frequently releasing arrestees rather than booking them into jail. By 2012, police were booking 95 percent of arrestees into jail.[4] That jarring statistic is even more important than it appears. Arrestees who are released pending a future court date can (and typically do) come to court voluntarily, demonstrating that they can be trusted to return for future hearings without court-imposed conditions or confinement. Folks who are detained until their initial hearings do not get that opportunity. Further, people who are detained have understandable trouble preparing their defense and are more likely to plead guilty.

Pretrial detention is most problematic in jurisdictions with over-crowded courts. Crowded dockets extend the time between arrest and hearings and the ultimate resolution of the case. Resolution does not necessarily mean trial or even a guilty plea. Many cases are simply dismissed outright by prosecutors, but in some jurisdictions, this does not happen for weeks or months. A below-the-radar reform that can reduce jail populations is forcing prosecutors to screen cases either before people are arrested or immediately after.[5] Even when necessary, pretrial detention should be brief. For example, Nebraska reported in 1995 that 80 percent of its jail population consisted of pretrial detain-ees, but almost half of that group (48 percent) ended up being held for fewer than twenty-four hours.[6]

In theory, defendants detained in jail must be tried or released in a timely manner. It says so right in the Constitution: "In all criminal prosecutions, the accused shall enjoy the right to a *speedy* and public trial." In practice, what counts as a "speedy" trial is determined by a multifactor legal test that indulges lengthy delays so long as the prosecution can point to reasons other than its own negligence. In 2009, the Supreme Court overturned a Vermont court's ruling that a three-year delay between arrest and trial violated the speedy trial right. In its ruling, the Supreme Court candidly summarized the right's watered-down status:

> The speedy-trial right is amorphous, slippery, and necessarily relative. It is consistent with delays and dependent upon circumstances. In [an earlier case], this Court refused to quantify the right into a specified number of days or months or to hinge the right on a defendant's explicit request for a speedy trial. Rejecting such inflexible approaches, we established a balancing test, in which the conduct of both the prosecution and the defendant are weighed.[7]

In the earlier case referenced in the quote, the Supreme Court held that a five-year delay between arrest and trial, during which the prosecution sought sixteen separate postponements, was consistent with the constitutional requirement of a "speedy trial."[8]

Delays between arrest and trial are problematic for a variety of reasons, but the most obvious injustices arise when defendants are held in jail throughout the delay. There are two ways that this comes about. The first is that a judge determines that pretrial detention is necessary because the person is either a flight risk or dangerous or both. The second is that a judge sets a bail amount – a cash bond that the person must deposit with the court to obtain release.

The thinking behind cash bail is simple. Money is a way to incentivize defendants to come to court. A judge can require the defendant to put up say $5,000, with the understanding that if the defendant does not show up for a later hearing, the money will be forfeited. In one of its rare discussions of bail, the Supreme Court in 1951 endorsed the practice, explaining: "Like the ancient practice of securing the oaths of responsible persons to stand as sureties for the accused, the modern practice of requiring a bail bond or the deposit of a sum of money subject to forfeiture serves as additional assurance of the presence of an accused."

The problem with cash bail is that it ties pretrial release to wealth. It is more likely that poor people will end up stuck in jail, either because they cannot afford to post bail or they are unwilling to sacrifice the money necessary to do so. Again, as a theoretical matter, defendants forced by financial reasons to wait in jail for their cases to be resolved should be rare, since a cash bond is supposed to guarantee an appearance, not coerce detention. And again, the topic is addressed in the Constitution, which states: "Excessive bail shall not be required." But the courts have concluded that a bail amount is not "excessive" simply because it exceeds the defendant's ability to pay.[9] This leads to a system where judges can use bail not to guarantee a released defendant's appearance at a later hearing but to decrease the likelihood that the defendant is released at all.

There has long been an exception. Washington, D.C., abolished cash bail in the 1990s. In its place, the District created a pretrial services agency that screens defendants and identifies the least restrictive conditions of release. This last point is critical. Simply abolishing cash bail does not mean that fewer people will be detained pending trial. Instead of setting high bail amounts, judges can order that defendants be detained until trial, that is, "held without bail." To reduce unnecessary pretrial detention, it is important to create a mechanism (or at least a mindset) that pushes judges to release defendants. Hints of that mindset can be seen in the Pretrial Services Agency for the District of Columbia's description of itself:

> The Pretrial Services Agency for the District of Columbia is the Federal agency responsible for gathering information about newly arrested defendants and preparing the recommendations considered by the Court in deciding release options. We recommend the least restrictive conditions that promote public safety and return to court.[10]

By depriving judges of the option of imposing cash bail, and offering them the assistance of an agency designed to help defendants return to court, the District dramatically reduced pretrial detention. Here is a summary of the District's success in a 2017 report by the Pretrial Justice Institute:

> In Washington, DC, 92% of people who are arrested are released pretrial and no one is detained because of an inability to pay. These

results are largely due to the District of Columbia Pretrial Services Agency (PSA), [which] operates 24 hours a day, promoting court appearance and public safety through the use of public safety assessments and graduated supervision levels.

The Institute reports that 89 percent of those released before trial were not rearrested and 98 percent were not rearrested on a crime of violence while they were out in the community pending trial.[11]

The District's experience suggests that most pretrial detention – the bulk of modern jail populations – is unnecessary. As discussed in Chapter 9, New Jersey abolished cash bail in 2017, adopting a model similar to that of the District, with similar success.

The other piece of reducing jail populations is eliminating jail stays imposed for violating probation or committing minor crimes, or both, a goal that parallels the overarching goal of reducing prison populations. The good news about jail populations is that because jail stays are relatively short, jail populations can change rapidly. In fact, the Bureau of Justice Statistics recorded a sharp decline in jail populations from 734,500 in 2019 to 549,100 in 2020, a reduction of 185,400 people. The Bureau explained that this was due to "both a reduction in admissions to jails and expedited releases in response to the COVID-19 pandemic."[12] This reduction may be temporary. Still, the ability to swiftly reduce jail populations points to a weakness in the edifice of Mass Incarceration.

PART IV

The Road to Recovery

The next chapters turn to reform. Most criminal justice experts agree that substantial change is needed to reduce the incarcerated population. There are, however, differing articulations of the ultimate goal and little precision about how to get there. Disentangling the two threads of criminal law enforcement in the United States can help. As explained throughout the book, there are, in essence, two parallel systems. One is the core system for addressing serious, often violent crimes like homicides, identifying those who commit such crimes and allotting appropriate punishments. This system is fairly characterized as the criminal **justice** system. The other is primarily a policy tool designed to address societal problems like drug abuse. This criminal **legal** system seeks to achieve each era's distinctive policy goals by imposing punishment for violations of essentially regulatory laws. We can dramatically cut back on this second system, while preserving, and moderating the severity of, the first. That would return the country to a criminal justice system not unlike the model that existed up until the 1970s. All that is needed is to undo the changes described in Parts II and III, recasting those Parts as a blueprint for reform.

18 WHAT SUCCESS LOOKS LIKE

While there is broad agreement that this country incarcerates too many people, there is a distressing lack of clarity about how to address the problem. At one end of the spectrum are "abolitionists," who view American criminal law enforcement, like slavery, as an illegitimate institution that can only be abolished, not reformed. Broadly speaking, abolitionists want to get rid of prisons, defund the police, and adopt noncoercive strategies to deal with crime. Or, as Woods Ervin, an organizer with Critical Resistance, a prominent abolitionist organization, explains, "abolition is a political vision with a goal of eliminating imprisonment, policing, and surveillance and creating lasting alternatives to punishment and imprisonment."[1] Abolitionists contrast their approach with that of "reformers." Reformers view the criminal justice system with more optimism or, at least, as a necessary evil. They seek changes to, not the elimination of, existing law enforcement architecture. Abolitionists think reformers are too timid. Reformers think abolitionists are impractical.

One problem with this debate is that the true disagreement is unclear. Both the reform and the abolition sides want change, but neither offers a clear picture of what success looks like. Reformers want to improve the criminal justice system, and abolitionists want to replace the existing system with something different. Depending on the depth of the reforms, the nature of the replacement, and the context in which all of this takes place, these goals may be overlapping. Working toward a future where prisons aren't needed sounds similar to reforms that seek to dramatically shrink incarcerated populations through reductions in crime and punishment. Or, consider the case of Camden, New Jersey, which disbanded its police force in 2012, and

immediately reconstituted a new, reformed police force. Is that abolition, reform, or both?

Policy makers seeking to implement change require precise bench-
marks to describe and measure progress. This is especially true with
respect to reducing incarceration, a context where some progress is
already being made. The number of people in prisons and jails has
decreased in recent years. The pattern varies by jurisdiction, but the
trend is clear. For example, in June 2020, California had 113,403 people
in its prisons, a substantial drop from 162,369 inmates in June 2011. As
recently as 2018, Oklahoma held 27,121 people in prison, a number that
dropped to 22,580 in July 2020.[2] With crime decreasing and widespread criticism of Mass Incarceration, we should expect further reductions. As this happens, people will start asking, "Are we there yet?" It is
important for policy makers to have something to say.

One clear benchmark is a return to the incarceration levels that
preceded Mass Incarceration. A return to the 1970s (for this purpose
only) offers several benefits. First, it is transformative. Returning to the
1970s would mean going from 2 million to 300,000 people locked up.
That's an 85 percent drop. This is not incremental or "reformist
reform." Second, it is logical. For most of its history, the United
States incarcerated about the same percentage of people. After the
1970s, the country made a series of changes that led to Mass
Incarceration. We can unwind those changes, taking us back to where
we deviated from both historical and comparative norms. Third, it is
not scary. Abolishing long-standing institutions requires a leap of faith
that many people are unwilling to take because, as bad as the current
system is, the replacement might be worse – particularly as compared
to a "reformed" system. By contrast, we know what we had in the
1970s. It was a flawed system, but it was one the country had long
accepted. Fourth, it is concrete. With a clear goal in mind, we can
measure how close we are to success and identify the steps that are
most likely to get us the rest of the way. This is especially important
because as prison populations drop, there will be increasing pressure to
declare victory and pivot to other priorities.

The precise goal spelled out above meshes with the framework of
this book to generate a blueprint for transformation. We can think of
the laws and enforcement mechanisms circa 1970 as a rough core of a

functioning criminal justice system. As long as serious crimes are prevalent in our society, we need a place where people can go for justice – an alternative to vigilantism and civil disorder. We need a criminal justice system. Beyond that, most of the things we added since the 1970s – like most of the federal law enforcement apparatus, an aggressive drug war, harsh determinate sentencing, mandatory minimum sentences, frequent parole/probation revocations – can be reassessed with a skeptical eye. There will be pushback, of course. But a question that can blunt the criticism is: If this or that law or enforcement policy is so important, why didn't we need it in the country's first 200 years?

The precise mechanisms of change range from a steady rollback of policies and laws to a nationwide reconciliation process touching every State, modeled on the closing of federal military bases after the Cold War. Even though every base (like every criminal punishment) has its supporters, the Base Realignment and Closure process shuttered over 350 bases, saving the country an estimated $12 billion a year.[3] The keys to this success were broad recommendations that addressed the whole problem at once. Similarly, an expert commission in each State, like those suggested by legal scholar Rachel Barkow in her book *Prisoners of Politics*, could review the criminal laws and enforcement procedures and, as this book suggests, skeptically reassess the need for anything that became more punitive after January 1, 1970. The commission could then propose a comprehensive slate of reforms.

The specific tactics will necessarily vary by jurisdiction, but the goal remains the same: to dial back each local system to its pre–Mass Incarceration analog. Mass Incarceration arose from expanding the road to prison's on-ramps and shrinking its off-ramps. Reversing course means undoing those changes. There are countless levers of reform, laws that need to change, and choices that can be viewed in a different light. No one change will undo a phenomenon that unfolded over half a century, but every change will contribute.

Connecticut offers an early model of success. Some of the most optimistic reformers are urging States to "cut-50" by which they mean to reduce the number of people incarcerated by half. Connecticut has already achieved this goal. In 2008, the State held almost 20,000 prisoners. By early 2020 (pre-Covid), that number was down to 12,000 people, and in January 2022, it was under 10,000.[4]

Connecticut offers a model for how to durably reduce incarceration and raises some notes of caution. Connecticut, like most States, experienced a reduction in violent crime in the past decades. That helped the State reduce prison admissions. In addition, Connecticut has a functional parole system that never stopped releasing people. In 2008, for example, Connecticut held 3,096 parole hearings and granted 81 percent of requests for parole.[5] This meant that when the State later shifted its correctional policies to decrease severity, it did not have a backlog of prisoners sentenced under earlier policies. By 2018, the Connecticut parole grant rate shrank to 50 percent, but that's still high enough to make a real difference. Importantly, Connecticut's parole board is not generating lots of new prison admissions either. Revocations have gone down. And Connecticut continues to issue pardons: 767 pardons in 2018. In essence, Connecticut kept more of its 1970s criminal justice infrastructure than other places, adopting the opposite approach of States like California. When crime started dropping and attitudes softened, Connecticut was able to nimbly shift gears and shrink its prison population. The flexibility that Connecticut's criminal justice system permits – the same flexibility that existed across the country until the 1970s – allowed the State to substantially reduce incarceration when crime went down.

But there are some caveats to this success story. The first is that Connecticut's success is tied to a reduction in crime. In 1994, Connecticut recorded a high of 216 murders and 149,085 so-called Index crimes (serious offenses). By 2010, there were 132 murders and only about 88,000 Index crimes.[6] Less serious crime means fewer serious cases, and that helps to reduce prison admissions and long sentences. The problem isn't that Connecticut is unique in terms of the crime drop. Crime has been decreasing across the country for decades. The problem is that we don't know what will happen to the kind of progress we see in Connecticut when crime inevitably ticks back up.

There's another caveat. Connecticut deserves credit for decreasing its prison population. But the State is nowhere near 1970s levels of incarceration. In 1977, Connecticut locked up 3,063 people.[7] Against a backdrop of modest population growth, Connecticut's incarcerated population increased by 534 percent between 1977 and 2008. It is progress that the State has since cut this population in half to about 10,000. But that is still over three times what it was in the 1970s. To get back to 1970s levels, Connecticut – like the rest of the country – still has a long way to go.

The biggest challenge is changing the attitudes described in Part II. While there is some consensus that we have gone overboard with punishment, even many critics of Mass Incarceration seem to view the problem as narrower than it really is. They point to some crimes that are punished too harshly, while zealously supporting the punishment of other existing crimes and even advocating for new punishments.[8] A key insight into a future without Mass Incarceration is to see that this kind of thinking – *this* crime or *that* person needs to be punished severely – is how we got here. Everybody wants the government to punish someone. The arguments are rarely frivolous. In isolation, each argument for severity can sound compelling. Add up all these arguments and you get Mass Incarceration.

The path back to the 1970s depends on re-creating the once-prevalent consensus that incarceration is rarely (if ever) the solution, especially to achieve policy goals, as opposed to justice. Most obviously, the expanding criminal legal system is a mistake. Criminal law is a disastrous way to express our collective condemnation of the many things we dislike or seek to discourage. And even with respect to actual - justice-focused crimes, the answer is usually less punishment, not more.

The next chapters discuss ways to get more States to embrace the model offered by Connecticut and beyond. Of course, each State will take a different course. And, as in 1970, each State will end up with a different incarceration rate. But we know that every State can return to its 1970s levels of incarceration, because they have been there before. The blueprint is clear. Parts II and III identified the changes that generated Mass Incarceration. Getting back to the 1970s requires reversing those changes.

19 (MOSTLY) ABOLISH THE FEDS

A return to the 1970s would mean a dramatic reduction in federal law enforcement and federal prisoners. While the vast majority of criminal prosecutions happen at the State and local level, the federal government is just as important a contributor to Mass Incarceration as the largest State. And it is the easiest place to see that Mass Incarceration is about policies, not crime.

Federal prison growth is almost entirely a policy choice made after the 1970s. In 1979, federal correctional facilities incarcerated 26,371 people.[1] In 2019, that number was 175,116 (dropping to 152,156 in 2020).[2] The growth in federal prison populations is particularly notable since States can and do prosecute almost all the same offenses that the federal government prosecutes. If we trust the States, there is little need for a parallel federal system. Why do we have one? Part of it is that we don't totally trust the States. In fact, the Department of Justice (DOJ) was created in 1870 to bring order to areas of the post–Civil War South that were characterized by the lawless and brutal treatment of formerly enslaved persons. But that's not the role the DOJ plays today. Now, the best explanation for most of federal criminal law enforcement is that "fighting crime" is popular, and federal politicians don't want to be left out.

Federal law enforcement is needed when the States are unable or unwilling to address a particular crime. As a consequence of this narrow purpose, the federal government was a bit player with respect to criminal law for most of the country's history. And those humble origins almost resurfaced just as Mass Incarceration was gaining steam. As State prisons started to fill, DOJ statisticians noted an interesting trend. Federal prison populations were dropping. They explained:

The 1980 gain in prison population was limited to State facilities. The number of prisoners under the jurisdiction of Federal authorities fell by almost 8 percent to 24,363, continuing a decline begun in 1978 that has reduced the Federal prison population by one-fourth in 3 years. It results in large part from a decision by Federal law enforcement authorities to concentrate their resources on white collar crime, leaving the apprehension, prosecution, and confinement of bank robbers, interstate auto thieves, and certain drug offenders to State and local authorities.[3]

The drop did not last. In 1980 the federal prison population (24,363) roughly matched that of the highest incarcerating States: Texas (29,886), California (24,579), New York (21,819), and Florida (20,742). And while each jurisdiction's prison populations ballooned in the years that followed, the federal population experienced the most growth of all. By 2018, the federal prison population was higher than any other State, twice that of Florida, and almost five times that of New York.

Diagnosis of the federal system is relatively easy. The reason we have so many federal prisoners has little connection to criminal justice. After 1980, Congress and various presidents directed federal law enforcement agents to target drugs, guns, and border offenses. The more federal agents looked for those offenses, the more they found. And in recent years, that's most of what federal law enforcement does – feed a vast criminal legal system that has only small pockets of justice-focused enforcement.

Table 19.1 gives a breakdown of the overall arrests by federal law enforcement in 2019 by offense ("Supervision" is violations of conditions of release).

Drug, weapons, immigration, and supervision **arrests** account for over 85 percent of total federal arrests. Table 19.2 shows federal prosecutions concluded in 2019.

Drug, weapons, immigration, and misdemeanor **prosecutions** accounted for almost 80 percent of federal prosecutions.[4]

Table 19.1 *Federal arrests*

Federal 2019	Total	Drug	Weapons	Immigration	Supervision
Arrests	206,630	24,432	11,629	117,425	23,266

Table 19.2 *Federal prosecutions*

Federal 2019	Total	Drug	Weapons	Immigration	Misdemeanor
Prosecutions	84,782	22,158	9,511	29,348	6,239

Drug convictions are an even bigger contributor to the federal Mass Incarceration story than these numbers reflect because they often lead to lengthy prison time. The number of federal drug convictions steadily increased over the past decades, rising 134 percent from 1980 to 1986 (5,000 to 12,000), while all other federal convictions rose only 27 percent.[5] By 1999, the federal system was churning out over 25,000 drug convictions per year, with judges sending almost 90 percent of those defendants to prison.[6] That's because while federal law enforcement officials were ramping up arrests and prosecutions, Congress increased the penalties for federal crimes, especially for drug and weapons offenses. A 1992 government report noted that "nearly all mandatory sentences imposed (94% during 1984–90) were for drug-law and weapons violations specified in 4 statutes."[7] Mandatory minimum sentences are most impactful when they push judges to sentence higher than they ordinarily would. Drug and weapons offenses are a prime example. Thus, even as law enforcement officials widened the net to bring more and more drug cases into the system, prosecutors and judges increased the percentage of those convicted of federal drug crimes who were sentenced to incarceration.[8] By 1990, there were over 25,000 people in federal prison for drug offenses,[9] a number that shot up to 69,000 in 1999,[10] and 97,000 by 2009.[11] The percentage of federal prisoners who were incarcerated for drug offenses steadily increased from 16 percent in 1970 to 61 percent in 1994.[12]

Apart from drug offenses, the most commonly prosecuted federal crimes involve guns and immigration, primarily involving two narrow circumstances. For guns, most federal prosecutions involve 18 U.S.C. § 922(g), which prohibits the possession of a firearm by a person with a prior felony conviction. In 2018, there were 6,719 federal convictions for this offense – nearing 10 percent of all the federal convictions that year. Almost every offender (97.6 percent) was sentenced to prison, with an average sentence of over five years; 54 percent of those convicted of the offense were Black.[13]

Most criminal immigration cases are so-called reentry cases. Under 8 U.S.C. § 1326, anyone who has been denied admission to or deported from the United States and "thereafter enters, attempts to enter, or is at any time found in, the United States" can be imprisoned for up to two years. The punishment jumps to ten or even twenty years if the prior deportation was triggered by certain criminal convictions. The Federal Sentencing Commission issued a report on this offense in 2015. It found that there were over 22,000 federal criminal immigration cases in 2013, and over 18,000 (83 percent) were illegal reentry cases. The commission reported that almost all (98 percent) of the defendants were Hispanic, and the average sentence imposed for illegal entry was eighteen months in federal prison.[14] The thousands of defendants sentenced to prison terms for weapons possession and immigration offenses in recent decades is a sharp departure from past practice. In 1980, for example, federal prisons held a total of 907 people convicted of immigration offenses and 737 people convicted for weapons possession.[15] In 2010, those numbers had climbed to 13,676 (immigration) and 10,822 (weapons) respectively.

As these numbers show, the federal system is almost exclusively a criminal legal, not justice, system. The vast majority of federal prisoners are incarcerated for committing a handful of drug, gun, and immigration offenses that federal agents frequently encounter and easily solve, and that federal prosecutors can prove with little effort, leading to resource-saving guilty pleas. And these are offenses that Congress and judges punish harshly. As a result, there is a surprisingly small amount of justice happening at the Department of Justice and a lot of enforcing the law.

A return to the 1970s would mean that the federal government would abandon its decades-long focus on drug, weapons, and criminal immigration enforcement, reversing the explosion of these convictions and emptying federal prisons. The Department of Justice would return to its core mission, focusing on cases that are beyond the ability (or will) of States to prosecute. The immigration system would still function, but – as it did in the 1970s – through civil and administrative hearings, not criminal courts. And the States could choose to step in wherever the federal government's presence was missed, prosecuting any of the drug or gun cases abandoned by federal authorities under State laws that criminalize that same conduct.

20 LESS CRIME, PART 1
Changing the Rules

One of the easiest ways to reduce crime is to shrink the footprint of the criminal law. The most obvious candidates are the parts of the criminal infrastructure that I have been calling the criminal legal system: pretrial detention, the war on drugs, parole and probation revocations, repeat offending laws, and so on. The best way to shrink the criminal legal system is to change the law so that violations of essentially regulatory rules do not lead to incarceration.

This is a natural process. There will always be laws that were enacted with the hope of deterring socially undesirable activity that ultimately prove ineffective or unnecessary. For example, in the 1920s, federal courts were crowded with two kinds of cases: alcohol cases that poured into the courts during Prohibition and draft resistance cases.[1] Federal dockets no longer contain any of these cases. The government no longer prosecutes people for refusing to register for Selective Service,[2] and in 1933, the nation ended its experiment with Prohibition.

Eliminating laws that criminalize common conduct reduce crime in two ways, both illustrated by the end of Prohibition. First, the repeal of laws that prohibited the purchase, sale, and manufacture of alcohol removed the criminal label from a commonly engaged in activity. Second, by eliminating a vast underground market, the repeal of Prohibition put an end to a broad swath of crimes indirectly fostered by that market, from bribery and tax evasion to weapons possession and murder.[3]

The closest modern analog to the repeal of Prohibition is an end to the drug war. Whatever the motives behind the aggressive use of incarceration to reduce drug abuse, it is clear that this strategy has failed. Over the course of the drug war, drug use has not declined and prices for illicit drugs have actually fallen. For example, the DEA reports that the retail price of heroin in the United States plummeted from over $3,000 per gram in 1981 to under $500 per gram in 2012.[4] In light of findings like these, there is no reason to think that incarcerating people decreases the availability or use of illicit drugs in this country. In fact, the evidence is to the contrary. In 2014, Pew researchers studied the effectiveness of the drug war by looking at variations in enforcement aggressiveness in various States. Their "analysis found no statistically significant relationship between state drug imprisonment rates and three indicators of state drug problems: self-reported drug use, drug overdose deaths, and drug arrests."[5]

Bowing to this logic, some States have decriminalized some drug offenses. As this movement gathers momentum, it could put a large dent in Mass Incarceration. Much like the end of alcohol prohibition, the end of the drug war could reduce Mass Incarceration in two ways. It would eliminate the laws that lead to thousands of drug convictions, as well as numerous parole and probation revocations. Second, it would generate indirect effects, reducing the ancillary crimes – and policing excesses – that accompany the underground drug market. As just one example, the Department of Justice estimates that about 5 percent of homicides involve drug trafficking.[6]

There is no single policy change that has as much potential to scale back Mass Incarceration as drug decriminalization. We would, in essence, return to the 1970s, where drug use was common (as it is today), enforcement infrequent, and few drug offenders wound up in prison. Decriminalizing drugs does not mean that the government must take a hands-off approach to the problem of drug abuse. There is a broad spectrum of approaches to address disfavored conduct. For example, cigarettes are harmful. But in light of the widespread desire to smoke, the government regulates cigarettes with age limits and heavy taxes in an effort to discourage smoking. The approach is similar to that taken before and after Prohibition with respect to alcohol.

The government often seeks to discourage activities without relying on criminal prosecution and incarceration. This is effectively the approach to traffic violations. There are tens of thousands of traffic fatalities in the United States every year.[7] Yet broad efforts to enforce traffic safety laws rarely lead to jail or prison time. Consequently, general traffic enforcement does not contribute significantly to Mass Incarceration. The same is true for parking laws, local zoning regulations, and defaults on financial obligations. Refusing to register with the Selective Service is still a federal crime punishable by up to five years in prison.[8] Draft compliance cases used to make up a substantial portion of the federal criminal docket. But those cases are gone now. Even with the Selective Service law still on the books, the government relies on noncriminal sanctions, like college financial aid eligibility, to incentivize compliance.[9]

The logic of drug decriminalization applies more broadly to a host of criminal legal system offenses that are best understood as efforts to reduce harmful behaviors like gun possession, drunk driving, and parole and probation violations. Decriminalization does not mean the government gives up on the underlying social problem. It means that the government abandons incarceration as the answer. This might be objectionable if there was evidence that incarceration helped to solve these problems. But there is typically no such evidence. The logic arguably extends even to unequivocally abhorrent and harmful behavior like domestic violence. A 1984 Minnesota study that suggested that arrests reduced domestic violence helped spark the efforts to use criminal law to put an end to domestic abuse. But later studies failed to replicate the Minnesota finding, and some found that domestic violence arrests actually increased violence. A 2020 meta-analysis of the many studies on the effectiveness of arrests in reducing domestic violence found little evidence to support the status quo. The authors summarized their findings as follows:

> The purpose of the current meta-analysis was to synthesize the results of the Minneapolis DV experiment, the replications, and other studies using experimental and quasi-experimental research designs to examine whether arrest for DV is effective in reducing repeat offending. The results of the meta-analysis suggest that the mandatory arrest policies adopted by police departments in the 1980s and 1990s did not produce the desired deterrent effect sought by law enforcement agencies and advocates alike.[10]

Again, an argument that incarceration is rarely the answer does not mean that the government should give up on the problem. The argument suggests only that the government change tactics, shifting resources to other more effective tools.[11]

There are other offenses that contribute to clogged courts and jail stays without any evidence of effectiveness. A prime example is the "crime" of driving on a suspended license. Jurisdictions originally used driver's license suspensions to prevent dangerous drivers from getting behind the wheel. But today, almost every State uses driver's license suspensions to collect revenue, such as unpaid court fines or child support. And, as we saw in Chapter 9's discussion of policing in Ferguson, Missouri, these fees and fines can spiral out of control. The problem with the effort to use driver's license suspensions to force people to pay unpaid debts is obvious. Many people cannot afford to pay and yet have little choice but to continue driving to meet work and family obligations. Plus, the likelihood of getting stopped on any trip is low, so people risk driving even after their license is suspended.

The number of people with suspended licenses is shockingly high. One study in North Carolina, for example, found "1,225,000 individuals with active driver's license suspensions" in the State – about 15 percent of North Carolina drivers. In 2021, the Kansas Department of Revenue reported that 227,794 Kansans had a suspended license, 8 percent of the State's population. The overwhelming majority of these suspensions result from either failing to appear at a court proceeding or failing to comply with court payment orders. Large pools of drivers with suspended licenses lead to large numbers of arrests and cases. The North Carolina study found that the State filed about 160,000 driving-on-a-suspended-license charges per year, over a five-year period (2013–2017).[12]

Driving on a suspended license is another commonly committed criminal offense that is frequently detected and easily proven. But it is a crime generated by the government. Consequently, this crime can be dramatically reduced by reducing the frequency of driver's license suspensions, and eliminating suspensions that are unrelated to driving competency. Again, some States are already taking the lead on this reform. But the reforms vary, sometimes in ways that undercut their promise. Virginia, for example, recently eliminated driver's license suspensions for failure to pay court fines and costs, but retained them for failure to pay tolls and child support. There will always be people who owe money, and creditors who want them to pay. As the abolition of debtor's prisons recognized, however, that is a problem better left to civil, not criminal, law.

21 LESS CRIME, PART 2
Decreased Offending

One important piece of the return to the 1970s is to return to 1970s levels of crime. The good news is we are already well on our way. As Figure 21.1, from the PEW Research Center, shows, the United States has been enjoying steady declines in the crime rate since the 1990s.[1]

Decreasing crime undermines Mass Incarceration on a variety of levels. Most obviously, less crime means fewer people to arrest and convict and imprison. It also reduces populist pressures for increased severity. But the reverse is true as well. Increased crime can prove fatal to reform. For example, in 2016, Alaska passed comprehensive criminal justice reform. Then, Republican Mike Dunleavy exploited a perception of rising crime in the wake of that legislation to win election as governor on a "Make Alaska Safe Again" platform. In 2019, under Dunleavy's leadership, Alaska undid the 2016 reforms.

In recent years, there has been an uptick in certain serious crimes.[2] Time will tell if this is a statistical blip influenced by Covid lockdowns and a summer of police shootings and protests or a long-lasting phenomenon. It is important to emphasize that the uptick is not yet on the order of the dramatic crime surge the nation faced decades ago, but it is also important not to underestimate the risk rising crime poses to reform efforts.

Careful attention to the government's response to serious crime is an important ingredient for lasting progress. Failures to reduce and respond to true criminal justice events like homicides jeopardize the prospects for reform. Homicide clearance rates would benefit from a return to the 1970s. As noted in Chapter 10, police solved about 80 percent of homicides in 1976, but only about 60 percent in 2019, with many of the jurisdictions with the most homicides reporting much lower clearance rates.[3] Homicides are high-profile tragedies that tear

U.S. violent and property crime rates have plunged since 1990s, regardless of data source

Trends in U.S. violent and property crime, 1993-2019

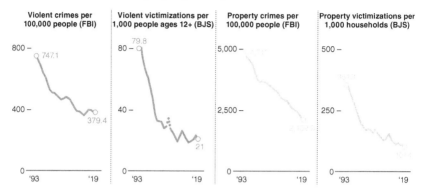

Note: FBI figures include reported crimes only. Bureau of Justice Statistics (BJS) figures include unreported and reported crimes. 2006 BJS estimates are not comparable to those in other years due to methodological changes. Source: U.S. Bureau of Justice Statistics (BJS), Federal Bureau of Investigation (FBI).

PEW RESEARCH CENTER

Figure 21.1 Falling crime

the fabric of society. When the government fails to respond adequately, the consequences can be far-reaching.[4] Most starkly, people lose faith in formal institutions and turn to vigilantism, generating new cycles of violence. These cycles increase pressure for residents to carry weapons as a form of self-defense. At the same time, citizens urge the government to respond to perceived disorder with new laws, aggressive policing, and vigorous prosecution of the few offenders who are caught. Every homicide and every shooting creates a risk of restarting new cycles of crime and punitive responses like those that generated Mass Incarceration.

The most effective tactics in the battle against Mass Incarceration include efforts to reduce violent crime, and especially homicide. These efforts should include elements from inside and outside the criminal law. Importantly, one intervention that many researchers believe can reduce crime is better policing. In a recent study of 242 large US cities over the period of 1981–2018, researchers at the National Bureau of Economic Research found that "each additional police officer hired abates between 0.06 and 0.1 homicides."[5] Of course, simply adding police officers to the payroll is not a targeted strategy. And there is no reason to think that police officers or *armed* police officers are the only way to operationalize this effect. It may simply be a question of resources, enlisting people, whether police or other individuals with the means and expertise to address the problem of violence, and deploying them to act in whatever ways prove most effective.

Reducing violent crime is not as difficult as it may seem. Gun violence is often concentrated in small areas, with a few individuals, what crime researcher Thomas Abt calls "the violent few," responsible for a vastly disproportionate percentage of shootings. This explains why one of the most promising strategies for reducing violence is "focused deterrence." This strategy identifies the few folks suspected of driving the violence and offers them options designed to avoid violent inter-actions going forward. Importantly, these strategies also place the potentially violent person on notice of the law enforcement apparatus that is ready to step in if they continue on a violent path. These methods are intrusive and potentially overbearing. But if reducing violence is a critical step to dramatically reduced incarceration, the primary question may be: What works? As Abt – who has studied this question exten-sively – explains, "nothing works as well to reduce urban violence as focused deterrence"; "it does not work perfectly, it does not work every time, but it works better, on average, than anything else out there."[6]

There are many crime-reduction strategies that have nothing to do with criminal law. One way to reduce crime is to make it more difficult. One of the biggest recent success stories in crime reduction is a drop in car theft. In 2000, while I was trying to figure out how to successfully prosecute car thefts in D.C. Superior Court, America had over 1 mil-lion reported car thefts. By 2018, the number dropped below 750,000. That's 250,000 annual felonies that disappeared. The rate of car thefts dropped almost in half. Researchers believe that technology deserves the credit. The main evidence for this is that car thefts began to skew toward older cars. That's counterintuitive. Car thieves should prefer new cars since they are more valuable.[7] Lots of people are trying to reform the criminal justice system, but one of the most effective reforms came from car companies. They reduced incarceration by making it harder to steal cars.

After a lengthy decline, car thefts trended up in 2020, not because car thieves figured out how to defeat security measures but reportedly because bored "lockdown" teenagers and others looking to avoid using public transportation noticed that car owners often leave their key fobs in their cars.[8]

Other technologies help by increasing the likelihood of detection. Recall that research shows that deterrence is effective when people think they will be caught. That suggests that technology that increases the likelihood of detection can deter crime better than punishment after the fact. Technologies along these lines include increased surveillance and lighting in public areas as well as DNA databases.[9] A recent systematic analysis of public surveillance cameras concluded that "CCTV is associated with a modest and significant reduction in crime," particularly in combination with other strategies such as active monitoring.[10] A randomized experiment of lighting in New York City housing projects found a substantial reduction in crime without a corresponding increase in arrests.[11] Other technologies, such as automated traffic enforcement, offer a window into a possible future of widespread deterrence without criminal penalties. Since the punishment for traffic offenses is typically noncustodial, automating traffic enforcement would increase detection and deterrence, without increasing incarceration. And it could dramatically reduce the number of interactions between civilians and police, leading to fewer police shootings and fewer overall arrests.

A lot of the people who worry about Mass Incarceration also worry about new law enforcement technology. But it can be a mistake to view these as similar problems. New technologies that deter crime *and* reduce incarceration can be a powerful ally in the fight against Mass Incarceration.[12]

There are also technologies that reduce crime in completely unobjectionable ways. For example, in many jurisdictions, it is a criminal offense to fail to appear for a court hearing. Even when a new charge isn't filed, a warrant will typically issue. Warrants are remarkably prevalent and often lead to additional offenses. Police stop people, find out they have a warrant, and then arrest them on the warrant. The arrest gives the police authority to search, and these searches often lead to drugs. In a 2016 case that followed that pattern, Supreme Court Justice Sonia Sotomayor highlighted the abundance of warrants. Justice Sotomayor wrote that Utah, where the case occurred, had 180,000 misdemeanor warrants in its database; and a 2014 survey of forty states revealed 7.8 million outstanding warrants.[13] One way to reduce the number of warrants is for judges to stop casually issuing them. But another is to remind people about their court dates or other obligations. A study in New York City found that sending reminder texts to defendants decreased court "no-shows" by 26 percent. That's fewer warrants, fewer arrests, and less "crime."[14]

The urgent need to reduce incarceration makes it hard to overlook any effective strategies, including those that reduce crime. Less crime means fewer arrests and fewer convictions, and perhaps most importantly, fewer stories about crime to fuel "tough on crime" politics. A focus on what works leads, of course, to social programs that give people who currently have few options alternative paths to success, like jobs and education. In fact, something like a universal basic income could offer those pathways, while also making financial alternatives to incarceration, like the income-based "day fines" prevalent in some European countries, more attractive. A focus on what works also points to crime detection and prevention measures that many critics of Mass Incarceration may disfavor. As the past two decades have shown, crime reduction won't eliminate Mass Incarceration. But it makes change easier and may even be a necessary component of lasting reform.

22 REDUCING ADMISSIONS AND SHORTENING STAYS

In 1970, there were approximately 200,000 people in state and federal prisons and an incarceration rate of about 96 persons per 100,000 population.[1] A variety of steps will be required to get back to these numbers. The previous chapters discuss ways to shrink the pool of people caught up in the criminal justice system by reducing the scope of American criminal law and decreasing offending. This chapter discusses ways to limit the number of people incarcerated from the remaining pool of law breakers. The two basic steps are (1) decreasing the number of admissions to prison/jail and (2) reducing the time served for those who are incarcerated.

22.1 REDUCING ADMISSIONS

The most immediate step toward reducing prison populations is to reduce new admissions to prisons and jails. The good news is that because it takes a village to incarcerate someone, there are many different mechanisms for reducing admissions.

Jail and prison admissions begin with police. That means that police can shrink the incarcerated population by bringing fewer cases to the courts. The easiest reform is doing nothing more often. Many prison and jail admissions are generated through police initiatives, like "buy-bust" operations that use undercover officers to purchase drugs or solicit prostitution. There is no evidence that these policing measures solve the underlying problems they purport to address, but they reliably generate arrests, prosecutions, and incarceration. Reform is easiest in this criminal-legal-system context because it just means decreasing police activity. The other major category of cases arises from civilian-initiated complaints. Police cannot as easily do nothing in this context, but they can move toward more informal problem solving. The instinct to cabin police discretion through formal policies, like mandatory arrest requirements, may stem from noble intentions. But pushing police to treat legal infractions as formal criminal matters has a terrible side effect. It funnels more and more people into the system, including many who do not need to be there. A notable risk of this dynamic arises with the practice of placing police officers in schools, inevitably increasing the application of formal criminal processes to school disciplinary issues.

Some cases, like homicides, must go through the courts, even if punishments for those offenses are drastically reduced. But many cases that currently clog court dockets never should have been brought into the system in the first place. Jurisdictions wary of leaving too much discretion in the hands of the police can create formal prearrest diversion programs like Project Lead in Seattle. As described on the Seattle government web site: "LEAD diverts individuals who are engaged in low-level drug crime, prostitution, and crimes of poverty away from the criminal legal system – bypassing prosecution and jail time – and connects them with intensive case managers who can provide crisis response, immediate psychosocial assessment, and long term wrap-around services including substance use disorder treatment and housing."[2] The primary value of these programs is that they address social problems outside of a criminal law framework, rather than attempting to address problems within that framework.

Next, prosecutors can say no (to police) more often. While the celebrated image of the American prosecutor is that of a public servant seeking justice for serious offenses, one of the most important things American prosecutors do is dismiss cases. Most obviously, prosecutors should assertively dismiss cases with weak evidence. Justice is never served by the prosecution of the innocent, and to ensure that the innocent are not prosecuted, prosecutors must err on the side of dismissing cases even in circumstances where the defendant may be guilty. That is not all. In the current context of crowded courts and Mass Incarceration, prosecutors could also jealously guard the criminal courts' limited capacity by routinely dismissing criminal legal system cases where little is achieved through prosecution.

Outright dismissals are preferable in this context to diversion programs that, unlike Project LEAD, are embedded within the criminal justice architecture. Although often better than formal prosecution, diversion programs, like drug courts and other treatment-based alternatives to incarceration, are ultimately powered by incarceration. I saw this firsthand in Washington, D.C.'s drug court. It was unlike any of my other assignments. The prosecutor in drug court hardly does anything. Drug court locks people up all by itself.

For anyone who is addicted, hard drugs are exceedingly difficult to quit. Drug court may help some folks get "clean," but for many, it is just another lane on the road to incarceration. Studies show that defendants can get locked up longer in drug court than regular court. For example, a study of New York drug courts revealed that, in five of the six jurisdictions studied, participants who were unable to succeed in the drug court program ended up with substantially longer sentences than those in a control group who did not participate.[3] In one jurisdiction (the Bronx), felony drug court participants generally (not just those who were unable to succeed in the program) were incarcerated longer than a comparison group who did not participate, and the disparity was even worse for those who failed the drug court program. Thus, while it is important to help people who are addicted to drugs, that assistance doesn't need to go through the criminal courts. Drug courts are powered by incarceration and may, in fact, be counterproductive to the extent they sap energy from decriminalization efforts.

Drug decriminalization is the most obvious way to reverse the rise in jail and prison admissions. As already noted in Chapter 12, incarceration for drug offenses skyrocketed after the 1970s. Letting the criminal justice system bow out of the Drug War isn't the silver bullet that ends Mass Incarceration. But it's a bullet. About 20 percent of the people locked up at any one time in this country – around 450,000 people – are locked up for drugs.[4] And as noted in Chapter 12, that number masks a far larger number of folks rotating in and out of prison, as well as an unknown number of prisoners locked up for non-drug crimes that would not have occurred but for the illicit market for drugs (e.g., drug-trafficking-related homicides).

While some States are decriminalizing marijuana, there seems to be little momentum for broader drug decriminalization. To the extent that drugs remain illegal in this country, however, there can still be increased resistance to incarcerating people for drug crimes. Legislators can ensure that drug possession or even sale is a misdemeanor (or just an "infraction") not a felony offense, and remove mandatory minimum sentences for drug crimes. Police can arrest fewer people for drug sales and possession. There is, in fact, an informal punishment readily at hand: seizing and destroying illicit drugs the police come across. Prosecutors can decline to prosecute drug cases, instead prioritizing justice-focused prosecutions. Judges can decline to sentence drug offenders to jail and prison. Probation and parole officers can decline to trigger parole and probation revocations based on drug offenses or tests.

This multitiered effort to ratchet back the involvement of the criminal justice system in the war on drugs can be applied in a number of analogous areas. Due to an absence of alternatives, policy makers turned to the criminal courts to solve everything from shoplifting to drunk driving to domestic violence. The point is not to single out any of these causes as unworthy. They are all important. The question policy makers need to revisit is whether the criminal courts and especially incarceration are the right tools for addressing them.

While there is an increasing focus on prosecutorial dismissals, judges too can dismiss cases. In a recent study, legal scholar Anna Roberts identified nineteen States with statutes that allow judges to dismiss prosecutions in the interest of justice.[5] Minnesota's statute is representative, stating: "The court may order a criminal action, whether prosecuted upon indictment or complaint, to be dismissed. The court may order dismissal of an action either on its own motion or upon motion of the prosecuting attorney and in furtherance of justice."

Beyond dismissals, judges can, like their predecessors in the 1970s, focus on the in-out of custody decision as the most important aspect of sentencing. Judges attuned to the solemnity of this landmark would sentence someone to incarceration – any incarceration – only when there is a strong justification for doing so. In a world of plea bargains, judges can impose nonincarceration preferences by rejecting plea deals, and imposing nonincarceration sentences whenever pleas preserve judicial discretion, and after trial, setting a new benchmark for future plea deals. And judges can resist the urge to incarcerate defendants pending trial and for violations of conditions of release.

As noted in Chapter 14, one of the drivers of Mass Incarceration is the explosion in the number of admissions to prison and jail through probation and parole violations. In the late 1970s, 80 percent of prisoners were newly sentenced as opposed to people sent back to prison for violations of probation or parole.[6] In the era of Mass Incarceration, the percentage of prison and jail admissions for new crimes dropped as parole and probation revocations surged. Judges have a role to play, but so do parole boards and probation officers, who manage these important checkpoints on the road to prison.

Jail populations may be the lowest-hanging fruit. As mentioned in Chapter 9, New Jersey recently revised its pretrial detention laws after determining that people who were unable to afford bail made up 40 percent of the State's jail population. The State abandoned the cash-bail model and created a pretrial services agency that works with judges to set conditions designed to encourage release, not detention. The reforms worked. By the end of 2018, New Jersey's jail population dropped by 6,000. Now, only about 5 percent of people who are arrested in New Jersey are detained pending trial, and there has been essentially no change in the rate at which defendants appear for trial, and no evidence that the reforms have led to more crime.[7] As noted in Chapter 17, the District of Columbia has a similar pretrial release system. Other jurisdictions can copy these models. Police can also return to defaulting to citation releases rather than custodial arrests, as noted in Chapter 10.

While details will vary by jurisdiction, the key theme for reducing prison and jail admissions is robust resistance to the idea that criminal courts and incarceration can solve society's problems. In important ways, the criminal legal system is the enemy of the criminal justice system. A true justice system can be preserved, and flourish, as the criminal legal system recedes. Criminal courts can once again be viewed narrowly, as an extreme form of governmental intrusion reserved for the most heinous offenses from which society cannot move forward without an official reckoning and some form of formal justice. Policy makers can approach everything else as a policy problem, requiring thoughtful and even intrusive regulation but rarely incarceration.

Some police and prosecutors and judges and legislators are beginning to get the message. This is most obvious in the "progressive prosecutor" movement, a group of prosecutors elected in a variety of jurisdictions across the country on a platform of dismantling Mass Incarceration from the inside. Journalist Emily Bazelon estimates that 12 percent of the population lives in a jurisdiction with a reform prosecutor.[8] Widespread change will require broader buy-in, however.

Experts have proposed a variety of ideas to get government officials, and the voters who support them, to reduce their reliance on incarceration. One of the simplest is for judges, prosecutors, and other government officials to visit prisons. The thinking is that if people had a better idea of what it means to send someone to prison, they would be reluctant to impose incarceration. There is no obvious reason prison visits should be limited to government officials. Other potential audiences include jurors, civic and church groups, and high school and college classes.

Some experts think that financial incentives could make a difference. In a lot of places, the local county whose employees (police, prosecutors, judges, probation officers) decide whether someone should go to prison and for how long are able to offload the financial costs of that decision to the State. One study found that when California shifted the costs of incarcerating juvenile offenders to local counties, county probation officers recommended incarceration less often, resulting in fewer locked-up kids. Similar reforms seek to get financial information to the judges who are deciding sentences. In Missouri, judges have a tool that informs them of the financial costs of any prison sentence they consider imposing. And Philadelphia's progressive prosecutor instructs his attorneys to include the financial costs of prison in their sentencing recommendations. More information about financial costs, and a better alignment of those costs with the actors who generate them, could reduce unnecessary incarceration.[9]

A bolder approach is to actually increase the costs of incarceration. Trying to reduce the prevalence of something by making it more expensive is a common regulatory tactic. For example, governments tax cigarettes and alcohol at a high rate to decrease their use. Taxing local governments for sending people to prison or jail uses the same logic. In economic terms, we can think of incarceration like pollution, as a negative side effect of some other goal (justice). One way to regulate pollution is to tax it. Another is to set a jurisdiction-wide cap on prisoners. This would disincentivize incarceration but leave it to local authorities to map their own paths toward the goal. Something like a prison cap already exists in Minnesota, where the State's Sentencing Commission adjusts its sentencing guidelines to ensure that prisons do not exceed 95 percent of capacity.[10]

22.2 REDUCING TIME SERVED

Decreasing new admissions to jail and prison is a key step toward escaping the era of Mass Incarceration. The other step is reducing time served. One of the reasons the sustained crime drop hasn't emptied the nation's prisons is that there is a huge backlog. We have been warehousing people in prison for decades. Even if America stopped sending people to prison and jails tomorrow, we would continue to owe a national prison debt, a backlog of ongoing prison sentences imposed by past generations. No matter how sharply we reduce admissions, we need to reckon with the past. As noted in Chapter 12, prison sentences increased substantially over the past decades. In fact, there are more people serving life sentences today than there were prisoners in 1970.[11] To get back to the model of the 1970s requires reducing sentence lengths for new offenses, and retroactively reducing the sentences imposed in the past.

There are two levers for reducing sentence lengths: (1) reducing the actual sentences announced by judges and (2) increasing the frequency of early release. There are some easy cases – people in jail or prison for offenses that are not serious or harmful. There are also hundreds of thousands of folks locked up not as a form of justice, but because they broke the law, that is, violating the rules of the criminal legal system. And, of course, the most difficult cases involve people serving long sentences for the most serious crimes, and those who continue to commit crimes after receiving second, third, and fourth chances.

One answer lies in the past. A critical lesson of the study of American Mass Incarceration is the subtle genius of indeterminate sentencing. Indeterminate sentencing is an antidote to an apparent hallmark of American society: populist penal severity. Even if we accept that a kind of punitive populism is inevitable, we can still work to reduce its effects. One way to do that is to change the timing of the critical sentence-length decision.

It is hardest to resist severe and punitive reactions in the shadow of an offense. The harm is fresh and interest from the media and the community is at its peak. Politicians who benefit politically from severity and suffer from lenience are least likely to resist the punitive pressures in this moment. And in the States, (almost all chief) prosecutors, (most) judges, and (all) legislators stand for election.[12] As the American experience demonstrates, it is dangerous to rely on these political actors to stem the country's punitive instincts, especially when those instincts are at their height. That's the genius of indeterminate sentencing. It places the real sentence-length decision in the hands of nonelected actors and allows them to make those decisions well after the offense. Indeterminate sentencing allows elected prosecutors and judges to vent community outrage by sending serious offenders "to the penitentiary." But it then offers a kind of safety valve that can be used, if needed, to reduce incarceration at a later date. Whether viewed in terms of the passions relating to a particular case or a particular era, this delay allows the initial wave of punitive populism to subside, and permits later adjustments toward lenience.

Indeterminate sentencing also ties into two of the most powerful theoretical justifications for punishment: deterrence and incapacitation. Even when prison is the answer, these justifications for punishment rarely support long, predetermined sentences. With respect to deterring offenders, there is little evidence that severe punishments are effective. People don't commit crime because they only expect to get a short prison sentence. In the moment when they break a law, people often aren't thinking rationally. And even if they are, they don't expect to get caught. Thus, an indeterminate prison sentence, or a one-year sentence can be just as effective a deterrent as a five-, ten- or twenty-year sentence.

With respect to incapacitation – keeping people in prison so they cannot commit additional crimes – an indeterminate parole-based system makes the most sense, not a determinative "truth-in-senten-cing" system that incarcerates people long after they are likely to reoffend. Imposing long predetermined prison terms has predictably led to a dramatic leap in elderly prisoners. PEW Researchers found, for example, that between 1999 and 2016, the number of prisoners aged fifty and over increased by 280 percent.[13]

Our aging prison population cannot be justified as a means of incapacitating dangerous folks. Most people age out of crime, and especially violent crime. As a comprehensive review of the academic literature explains, the existing research "suggests that individuals over the age of 55 are among the least likely to commit crime."[14] And a revealing entry in a federal government report on prison growth notes: "During World War II, the prison population declined by nearly 50,000 in 5 years as most of the pool of potential offenders was drafted."[15] This is where parole boards can be most active, releasing older prisoners who present the smallest likelihood of reoffending. In addition, programs like the Federal Residential Drug Abuse Treatment Program (RDAP), which pairs treatment with the promise of sentence reduction, have shown promising results in helping prisoners avoid substance abuse and rearrest upon release.[16] Programs like these can be used to reduce time served and reduce reoffending, attacking Mass Incarceration from two directions simultaneously.

There is little to say about retribution, the third and most amorph-ous theoretical justification for incarceration. To the extent someone "deserves" a period of incarceration, there is no way to objectively assess how long that sentence must be. The best we can do is to argue about relative sentence lengths.

If long prison sentences aren't necessary for deterrence or incapaci-tation, they are only doing one thing: sending a message. The problem is that we are not clear about what that message is, and we have no idea if anyone, besides the prisoner, hears it. Recall from Chapter 12 that sentence lengths grew, in part, due to a punishment auction where sentences increased for some crimes and others followed. To get back to the 1970s model, the entire spectrum of sentences should be ratcheted down. The longest sentences will continue to be imposed for the most heinous crimes, like murder. Yet all sentences can be shorter. One straightforward proposal is to make twenty-one years the longest possible sentence, as in the Norway example cited in Chapter 12. Long sentences serve a purpose. They assure people that society takes serious crimes seriously. But relative, not absolute, sentence length is the key to this symbolic exercise.

CONCLUSION

In 1992, McDonald's introduced a popular menu option that allowed customers to "Supersize" their orders. Around that same time, the United States supersized its criminal justice system. But it wasn't like McDonald's. At McDonald's, the supersized order comes all at once. Voters would have balked had they gotten Mass Incarceration all at once. People could digest Mass Incarceration because it happened slowly, over time. It would be like ordering McDonald's every week for forty years and getting a slightly larger burger each time. You could go from eating a tiny burger to a massive one without noticing the change.

Looking back now, it is easy to see that something is wrong. But it is harder to identify exactly when and where things went off track. That's because there are so many pieces to Mass Incarceration, each playing out differently in different jurisdictions and eras. Another reason commentators struggle to identify what went wrong is that *we* are the villains of this story (never a popular message). Over the past few decades, government officials and cheering voters latched on to the criminal justice system as a Swiss army knife policy tool that could solve society's problems. People sometimes disagreed about *which* crimes mattered the most, but everyone pushed the government to crack down on someone and something. "Lock them up" is not just an applause line at political campaign rallies. It has become our country's unofficial motto.

We try to eliminate drug addiction by jailing people who use drugs or sell them. We protect stores from theft by prosecuting shoplifters. We try to stop sex trafficking by arresting sex workers and their customers. We crack down on shootings by criminalizing gun possession and imposing mandatory minimum sentences for anyone who illegally possesses a weapon. Drunk driving, assault, political corruption, police brutality, illegal immigration – the list goes on. The politicians preach that harsh criminal laws can save us. Voters say, "amen."

After decades of stagnation, change is finally in the air. People are waking up to the human costs of so much policing and so much incarceration. And there are reasons for optimism. Unlike many other problems like climate change or pandemics, this is a problem we can fix unilaterally. We control all the levers that control incarceration. In fact, mostly we need to just stop doing things that make the problem worse. The clearest path to recovery from Mass Incarceration is to stop doing the things we started doing after the 1970s that increased incarceration. And the best part about this prescription is that there is little evidence that we will lose anything if we do . . . except our overcrowded prisons and jails.

NOTES

Introduction

1 The US data comes from the Bureau of Justice Statistics' (BJS) publication Prisoners in 2019. The BJS publishes an annual report summarizing the number of prisoners held in the U.S. The reports are available at: bjs.ojp.gov/library/publications/list?series_filter=Prisoners
European data comes from *The World Prison Brief*, available at www.prisonstudies.org/world-prison-brief-data

2 The decline is reported in Prisoners in 2020, along with a caveat that it is a result of Covid-19, see BJS, Prisoners in 2020 1 (2021), bjs.ojp.gov/content/pub/pdf/p20st.pdf For signs of reversal, see Vera Institute of Justice, People in Jail and Prison in 2020, Figure 1, www.vera.org/downloads/publications/people-in-jail-and-prison-in-2020.pdf.

3 The clearance rate for homicides comes from data gathered by the D.C. Policy Center, Murder Accountability Project, www.dcpolicycenter.org/publications/dc-above-average-murder-clearance-rate/

4 Peter Slevin, Police Informant's Killer Gets Maximum Sentence, *Wash. Post*, 1999.

5 The testimony comes from *Arizona* v. *Gant*, 556 U.S. 332, 337 (2009) and is recounted in the opinion: "When asked at the suppression hearing why the search was conducted, Officer Griffith responded: 'Because the law says we can do it.'"

6 Clearance rates and sources are covered in more depth in Chapter 7. The rate for rape comes from the Bureau of Justice Statistics (BJS), Rape and Sexual Assault, 1992–2000.

7 The Tables I.1 and I.2 and data come from the U.S. Attorneys' Annual Statistical Report 2000 at 22, 27–28, www.justice.gov/sites/default/files/usao/legacy/2009/06/08/00statrpt.pdf.

8 The 2020 data and conclusion regarding the impact of Covid-19 come from the BJS publication, Prisoners 2020, bjs.ojp.gov/content/pub/pdf/p20st.pdf at 1.

Chapter 1

1 The State data comes from Bureau of Justice Statistics, State Corrections Expenditures, FY 1982–2010 by Tracey Kyckelhahn, bjs.ojp.gov/content/pub/pdf/scefy8210.pdf (State); the federal data from the PEW Research Center, Federal Prison System Shows Dramatic Long-Term Growth, at 1, www.pewtrusts.org/~/media/assets/2015/02/pew_federal_prison_growth.pdf. Both totals are inflation adjusted.

2 Alfred Blumstein & Jacqueline Cohen, A Theory of the Stability of Punishment, 64 *Journal of Criminal Law & Criminology* 198 (1973). The article uses the term "imprisonment rate," but the authors do not specify whether their calculations exclude jail populations.

3 The 2020 rate is based on a midyear assessment by the Vera Institute of Justice, People in Jail and Prison in 2020, by Jacob Kang-Brown, Chase Montagnet, and Jasmine Heiss, www.vera.org/downloads/publications/people-in-jail-and-prison-in-2020.pdf, Table 2 (midyear 2020 total incarceration rate).

4 "The World Prison Brief (WPB) is a unique database that provides free access to information about prison systems throughout the world. Country information is updated on a monthly basis, using data largely derived from governmental or other official sources." www.prisonstudies.org/highest-to-lowest/prison-population-total?field_region_taxonomy_tid=All; see also www.pewresearch.org/fact-tank/2021/08/16/americas-incarceration-rate-lowest-since-1995/; www.prisonstudies.org/sites/default/files/resources/downloads/wppl_12.pdf; Paul Mazerolle et al., Exploring Imprisonment across Cross-National Contexts, in *The Oxford Handbook of Prisons and Imprisonment* 80 (2018) ("[T]here are around 10.2 million people incarcerated world-wide, with around half of those in the United States, China, and Russia. When population is taken into account, the highest incarceration rate is found in the United States at 716 persons per 100,000."). For the caveats regarding China in Table 1.1, see www.prisonstudies.org/country/china, and for the execution data, see https://deathpenaltyinfo.org/policy-issues/international/executions-around-the-world.

5 A review of these studies can be found in Don Stemen, "Reconsidering Incarceration: New Directions for Reducing Crime," 19 *Federal Sentencing Reporter* 221–24 (April 2007).

6 National Research Council, *The Growth of Incarceration in the United* States 4 (2014).

7 Further discussion of this data is included in Chapter 9.

8 James Comey, *A Higher Loyalty* (2018). For further disagreement with Comey's objection, see Alice Ristroph, An Intellectual History of Mass Incarceration, 60 *Boston College Law Review* 1949, 1998 (2019)

("millions of separate proceedings can nonetheless add up to a mass phenomenon").

9 Michelle Alexander, *The New Jim Crow* 15 (2020 ed.).

10 The estimate regarding immigration detainees comes from TRAC Immigration, trac.syr.edu/immigration/quickfacts/, while the data on civil commitments comes from Megan Testa and Sara West, Civil Commitment in the United States, *Psychiatry* (2010); see www.ncbi.nlm.nih.gov/pmc/art icles/PMC3392176/.

Chapter 2

1 Evelyn J. Patterson, The Dose-Response of Time Served in Prison on Mortality: New York State, 1989–2003, *American Journal of Public Health*, (Nov. 2012), ajph.aphapublications.org/doi/abs/10.2105/AJPH.2012 .301148

2 *Florence* v. *Bd. of Chosen Freeholders of Cty. of Burlington*, 566 U.S. 318, 324 (2012).

3 *Ruiz* v. *Estelle*, 503 F. Supp. 1265, 1280 (S.D. Tex. 1980).

4 *Brown* v. *Plata*, 563 U.S. 493, 502 (2011).

Chapter 3

1 Data is from Bureau of Justice Statistics, Prisoners 2019 and Historical Statistics on Prisoners in State and Federal Institutions, Yearend 1925–1986 (1973), https://bjs.ojp.gov/content/pub/pdf/hspsfiy25–86.pdf.

2 Franklin Zimring, *The Insidious Momentum of American Mass Incarceration* 18 (2020).

Chapter 4

1 For a summary of this literature, see Sergio Herzog, The Relationship between Public Perceptions of Crime Seriousness and Support for Plea-Bargaining Practices in Israel: A Factorial-Survey Approach, 94 *Journal of Criminal Law & Criminology* 103, 106–7 (2003); Andrew von Hirsch, *Past or Future Crimes: Deservedness and Dangerousness in the Sentencing of Criminals* 76 (1985); Michael O'Connell and Anthony Whelan, Taking Wrongs Seriously: Public Perceptions of Crime Seriousness, 36 *British Journal of Criminology* 299, 301 (1996).

2 The National Crime Severity Survey is available at bjs.ojp.gov/content/pub/ pdf/nscs.pdf. The quoted text comes from p. vi. For an illuminating discussion of the long history of efforts to draw lines like the one proposed in this section, from John Stuart Mill to H. L. A. Hart to Herbert Packer and

beyond, see Bernard E. Harcourt, The Collapse of the Harm Principle, 90 *Journal of Criminal Law & Criminology* 109, 136 (1999).

3 All of the offenses listed in this chart are for State prisoners and the data comes from BJS, *Prisoners 2011* (Table 9) (2010 data) and BJS, *Prisoners in 1994* (Table 14) (reporting 1980–93 data). Federal totals include all federal prison inmates and are from *Prisoners 1994* (Table 13) (reporting number of federal prisoners for selected years from 1980 to 1993) and *Prisoners 2011* (Table 1). The Prisoners series is available at: bjs.ojp.gov/library/publications/list?series_filter=Prisoners. Pretrial detention numbers compare 1978 and 2010 and come from BJS, *Jail Inmates at Midyear 2010*, and BJS, *Jail Inmates 1984* (Table 1) (providing data for 1978), bjs.ojp.gov/content/pub/pdf/jim10st.pdf; bjs.ojp.gov/library/publications/jail-inmates-1984-0.

Chapter 5

1 Michelle Alexander, *The New Jim Crow* 52 (2020 ed.) ("Beginning in the 1960s, crime rates rose in the United States for a period of about ten years. Reported street crime quadrupled, and homicide rates nearly doubled."); National Research Council, *The Growth of Incarceration in the United States* 46 (2014).

2 John J. Donohue, Understanding the Time Path of Crime, 88 *Journal of Criminal Law & Criminology* 1423, 1425 (1998).

3 The quote and data come from BJS, Homicide Trends in the United States, 1980-2008, www.bjs.gov/content/pub/pdf/htus8008.pdf. The chart, intended to show rough trends, reflects data from every ten-year period and so does not reflect trends within each decade.

4 The CDC reported about 5 homicide deaths per 100,000 people in the 1950s and 1960s, rising to 9 per 100,000 in 1970, peaking at 10 per 100,000 in 1980 through 1990 and finally falling back to 5 or 6 per 100,000 after 2000. www.cdc.gov/nchs/data/hus/2019/005-508.pdf.

5 The graph reflects the prison incarceration rate per 100,000 persons versus the total crime index rate per 100,000 residents. Data is from the *Sourcebook of Criminal Statistics*, Tables 3.106.2012 and 6.28.2102. For a similar comparison, see www.pewtrusts.org/-/media/legacy/uploadedfiles/wwwpewtrustsorg/reports/state-based_policy/pspprisonprojections0207pdf.pdf at 23.

6 Clay F. Richards, Fears about Crime Jump Poll: Almost Half Have Been Victims, *Newsday*, Dec. 16, 1993, at 5.

7 NYPD, *Police Strategy No. 1: Getting Guns off the Streets of New York* 6 (1994).

8 Erin Grinshteyn and David Hemenway, Violent Death Rates: The US Compared with Other High Income OECD Countries, 2010, p. 271 (2016), www.amjmed.com/article/S0002-9343(15)01030-X/pdf.

9   Zelia Gallo, Nicola Lacey, David Soskice, Comparing Serious Violent Crime in the United States and England and Wales: Why It Matters, and How It Can Be Done, in *American Exceptionalism in Crime and Punishment* (Kevin R. Reitz ed., 2018).

Chapter 6

1   PEW Research Center, Interdiction and Incarceration Still Top Remedies, March 21, 2001, www.people-press.org/2001/03/21/interdiction-and-incarceration-still-top-remedies/.
2   Historical Gallup polling data on crime can be accessed online, news.gallup.com/poll/1603/crime.aspx.
3   John J. Donohue, Comey, Trump, and the Puzzling Pattern of Crime in 2015 and Beyond, 117 *Columbia Law Review* 1297 (2017).
4   Texas crime poll summary reports from Michael C. Campbell, Politics, Prisons, and Law Enforcement: An Examination of the Emergence of "Law and Order" Politics in Texas, 2011 *Law & Society Review* 643.
5   Rich Simon & Claudia Luther, Edward Kennedy Dies at 77; 'Liberal Lion of the Senate,' *L.A. Times*, Aug. 26, 2009, www.latimes.com/local/obituaries/la-me-ted-kennedy26-2009aug26-story.html.
6   Edward M. Kennedy, Punishing the Offenders, *N.Y. Times*, Dec. 6, 1975, www.nytimes.com/1975/12/06/archives/punishing-the-offenders.htm.l
7   Carissa Hessick, *Punishment without Trial* (2021).
8   See Joint Committee on New York Drug Law Evaluation, *The Nation's Toughest Drug Law: Evaluating the New York Experience* 4 (1977), www.ojp.gov/pdffiles1/Digitization/43315NCJRS.pdf.
9   Michael L. Rubinstein, Stevens H. Clarke & Teresa J. White, *Alaska Bans Plea Bargaining* 12 (1980).
10 Cal. Penal Code § 1192.7(a)(2) (West 2015).
11 George Skelton, A Father's Crusade Born from Pain, *L.A. Times*, Dec. 9, 1993, www.latimes.com/archives/la-xpm-1993-12-09-mn-65402-story.html.
12 Dan Morain, Lawmakers Jump on '3 Strikes' Bandwagon, *L.A. Times*, Jan. 31, 1994.
13 Dan Morain, Legislators Maneuver on Prison Bond Issue, *L.A. Times*, June 3, 1996, at A3.
14 Corin Hoggard, Man Who Inspired Three Strikes Law Sentenced to Life in Prison for Most Recent Act of Violence, *ABC30*, March 5, 2018, abc30.com/man-who-inspired-three-strikes-law-sentenced-to-life-in-prison-for-most-recent-act-of-violence/3177651/.
15 Peter Applebome, Arkansas Execution Raises Questions on Governor's Politics, *N.Y. Times*, Jan. 25, 1992, www.nytimes.com/1992/01/25/us/1992-campaign-death-penalty-arkansas-execution-raises-questions-governor-s.html.

16 David B. Holian, He's Stealing My Issues! Clinton's Crime Rhetoric and the Dynamics of Issue Ownership, 26(2) *Political Behavior* (June 2004), pp. 95–124, 108.

17 Michael Kramer, Frying Them Isn't the Answer, *Time*, March 14, 1994, content.time.com/time/subscriber/article/0,33009,980318,00.html.

18 James Forman Jr., *Locking Up Our Own* 10 (2017); Michelle Alexander, *The New Jim Crow* 53 (2020 ed.) ("some black activists began to join calls for 'law and order' and expressed support for harsh responses to lawbreakers").

19 Paul Glastris & Jeannye Thornton, A New Civil Rights Frontier, *U.S. News & World Report*, Jan 17, 1994 (Jesse Jackson quote).

20 The Clinton quote is reported in Elizabeth Hinton, Julilly Kohler-Hausmann and Vesla M. Weaver, Did Blacks Really Endorse the 1994 Crime Bill? *N.Y. Times*, April 13, 2016, www.nytimes.com/2016/04/13/opinion/did-blacks-really-endorse-the-1994-crime-bill.html. The authors point out that many members of Congressional Black Caucus criticized the Crime Bill and sought changes but acknowledge that "26 of the 38 voting members [ultimately] supported the legislation." For further analysis, see Yolanda Young, Analysis: Black Leaders Supported Clinton's Crime Bill, NBC News, April 8, 2016, www.nbcnews.com/news/nbcblk/analysis-black-leaders-supported-clinton-s-crime-bill-n552961; and Karen Hosler, Black Caucus Yields on Crime Bill, *Baltimore Sun*, Aug. 18, 1994, www.baltimoresun.com/news/bs-xpm-1994-08-18-1994230118-story.html.

21 Sheryl Gay Stolberg and Astead W. Herndon, 'Lock the S.O.B.s Up': Joe Biden and the Era of Mass Incarceration, *N.Y. Times*, June 25, 2019 www.nytimes.com/2019/06/25/us/joe-biden-crime-laws.html. For further analysis of the rise of the "law and order" political agenda in national politics, see Elizabeth Hinton, *From the War on Poverty to the War on Crime: The Making of Mass Incarceration in America* (2016); and Naomi Murakawa, *The First Civil Right: How Liberals Built Prison America* (2014).

22 The Final Report of the President's Task Force on Victims of Crime was published in December 1982 and is available at ovc.ojp.gov/library/publications/final-report-presidents-task-force-victims-crime. The Report states (p. 24) "[a] substantial proportion of the crimes committed in this country are committed by defendants who have been released on bail or their own recognizance" (p. 30); it recommends "truth in sentencing" and "sentencing guidelines" and that "Legislation should be proposed and enacted to abolish parole and limit judicial discretion in sentencing" (p. 29). Commentary and the "milestone" quote can be found in A Retrospective of the 1982 President's Task Force on Victims of Crime, available at www.ncjrs.gov/ovc_archives/ncvrw/2005/pg4d.html

23 For discussion of the ad, see Doug Criss, This Is the 30-Year-Old Willie Horton Ad Everybody Is Talking about Today, *CNN*, November 1, 2018, www.cnn.com/2018/11/01/politics/willie-horton-ad-1988-explainer-trnd/

index.html; Robin Toner, Prison Furloughs in Massachusetts Threaten Dukakis Record on Crime, *N.Y. Times*, July 5, 1988, www.nytimes.com/ 1988/07/05/us/prison-furloughs-in-massachusetts-threaten-dukakis-record-on-crime.html; Peter Baker, Bush Made Willie Horton an Issue in 1988, and the Racial Scars Are Still Fresh, *N.Y. Times*, Dec. 3, 2018, www.nytimes .com/2018/12/03/us/politics/bush-willie-horton.html, and to see the ad itself, see www.youtube.com/watch?v=PmwhdDv8VrM. For the Dukakis response, see Michael Oreskes, Dukakis, in TV Ads, Strikes Back in Kind, *N.Y. Times*, Oct. 22, 1988, www.nytimes.com/1988/10/22/us/dukakis-in-tv-ads-strikes-back-in-kind.html.

24 These quotes come from Michael C. Campbell, Ornery Alligators and Soap on a Rope: Texas Prosecutors and Punishment Reform in the Lone Star State, *Theoretical Criminology* (2011) and Campbell, Politics, Prisons, and Law Enforcement, at 657.

25 For a comprehensive discussion of Arizona, see Mona Lynch, *Sunbelt Justice: Arizona and the Transformation of American Punishment* 96, 154–55 (2009). For information regarding the pardon, see Pat Flannery, Boyhood Pal Helped Symington Get Pardon, *Ariz. Republic*, Feb. 25, 2001, A1.

26 Daniel M. Weintraub, Woman Blames Parole Policy in Father's Slaying, *L.A. Times*, February 4, 1994, A3.

27 For the Singel story and its ongoing impact, see Mark Singel, I Pardoned A Convict Who Killed Again: Here's Why I Still Believe in Mercy, *American Magazine*, July 24, 2017, www.americamagazine.org/pardon; Joseph Berger, Accused Serial Killer and 92 Days of Freedom, *N.Y. Times*, April 4, 1995, www.nytimes.com/1995/04/04/nyregion/accused-serial-killer-and-92-days-of-freedom.html, Benjamin H. Smith, Who Is Reginald McFadden, and How Did His Killing Spree Affect The Pennsylvania Legal System? *Oxygen*, www .oxygen.com/kim-kardashian-west-the-justice-project/crime-news/reginald-mcfadden-murders-pennsylvania-law. An-Li Herring, As Political Tides Shift, Chances At Commutation Rise For Pennsylvania Lifers, *WESA*, September 9, 2019, www.wesa.fm/post/political-tides-shift-chances-commu tation-rise-pennsylvania-lifers#stream/0; NYU State Clemency Project, The Demise of Clemency for Lifers in Pennsylvania, at 6, www.law.nyu.edu/sites/ default/files/CACL%20Clemency%20PA_Accessible.pdf. For the changes to Massachusetts program, see Beth Schwartzapfel and Bill Keller, Willie Horton Revisited, *The Marshall Project*, May 13, 2015, www .themarshallproject.org/2015/05/13/willie-horton-revisited.

28 The report is available at web.archive.org/web/20051116023319/http://www .cjpc.state.tx.us/reports/bienrep/BiennialReport1999.pdf.

29 See Maggie Astor, California Voters Remove Judge Aaron Persky, Who Gave a 6-Month Sentence for Sexual Assault, *N.Y. Times*, June 6, 2018, www .nytimes.com/2018/06/06/us/politics/judge-persky-brock-turner-recall.html

Chapter 7

1 US Department of Justice, Violent Crime Control and Law Enforcement Act of 1994, Fact Sheet, www.ncjrs.gov/txtfiles/billfs.txt.

2 S. Rep. 98-225 (1983) at *37. This document is accessible online at www.fd.org/sites/default/files/criminal_defense_topics/essential_topics/sentencing_resources/deconstructing_the_guidelines/legislative-history-of-the-comprehensive-crime-control-act-of-1983.pdf

3 See Jeremy Travis, *But They All Come Back: Facing the Challenges of Prisoner Reentry* (2005).

4 *People* v. *Tower*, 308 N.Y. 123, 125 (1954).

5 S. Rep. 98-225 (1983) at *37.

6 James Q. Whitman, *Harsh Justice* 53 (2005).

7 Edward M. Kennedy, Justice in Sentencing, *N.Y. Times*, July 29, 1977, www.nytimes.com/1977/07/29/archives/justice-in-sentencing.html.

8 O. J. Keller, The Criminal Personality or Lombraso Revisited, *Federal Probation* 43 (March 1980).

9 Robert Martinson, What Works? – Questions and Answers about Prison Reform, 1974 *Public Interest* 22 (Spring 1984).

10 Lee Wohlfert, Criminologist Bob Martinson Offers a Crime-Stopper: Put a Cop on Each Ex-Con, *People*, February 23, 1976, people.com/archive/criminologist-bob-martinson-offers-a-crime-stopper-put-a-cop-on-each-ex-con-vol-5-no-7/.

11 S. Rep. 98-225 (1983) at *40 and fn. 138.

12 The clip is available here: www.youtube.com/watch?v=io__Rz61ZBM. See also National Research Council, *The Growth of Incarceration in the United States* 3 (2014): "These changes in sentencing reflected a consensus that viewed incarceration as a key instrument for crime control."

13 Robert Martinson, New Findings, New Views: A Note of Caution Regarding Sentencing Reform, 7 *Hofstra Law Review* 243 (1979) (recantation); see Francis T. Cullen, Rehabilitation: Beyond Nothing Works, 42 *Crime & Justice* 299, 327 (2013) (providing quote).

14 The description of the crime and punishment of Joseph Rozzo come from *In re Rozzo*, 72 Cal. Rptr. 3d 58, 63 (Ct. App. 2008).

15 *In re Rodriguez*, 14 Cal. 3d 639, 644 (1975).

16 Cal Penal Code § 213 (second degree robbery).

17 *People* v. *Jefferson*, 21 Cal. 4th 86, 95 (1999).

18 For an official history of the Washington law, see sgc.wa.gov/sites/default/files/public/sgc/documents/historical.pdf.

19 BJS, Offenders Returning to Federal Prison, 1986-97 1–2 (2000), bjs.ojp.gov/content/pub/pdf/orfp97.pdf; see also BJS, *Federal Sentencing in Transition, 1986–1990* 3 (1992).

20 For a discussion of the aggravated assault sentencing framework, see *People* v. *Wingo*, 14 Cal. 3d 169, 173 (1975).

21 For the Minnesota guidelines, see Minnesota Court Rules ("Sentencing Guidelines") and for departure criteria, see Part D, available at www .revisor.mn.gov/court_rules/sg/id/2/.

22 *United States* v. *Wellman*, 716 F. Supp. 2d 447, 452 n.8 (S.D.W. Va. 2010); www.ussc.gov/sites/default/files/pdf/research-and-publications/research-projects-and-surveys/sex-offenses/20091030_History_Child_Pornography_ Guidelines.pdf.

23 Washington State Sentencing Guidelines Commission, Sentencing Reform Act: Historical Background, sgc.wa.gov/sites/default/files/public/sgc/docu ments/historical.pdf.

24 BJS, Prison Admissions and Releases, 1981, bjs.ojp.gov/content/pub/pdf/ par81.pdf.

25 For a discussion of the complex "ex post facto" restrictions to changing early release laws, see *Weaver* v. *Graham*, 450 U.S. 24, 35 (1981).

26 BJS, Truth in Sentencing in State Prisons, in *Bureau of Justice Statistics Special Report* at 8, 11 (1999), bjs.ojp.gov/content/pub/pdf/tssp.pdf.

27 George Allen, Abolishing Parole Saves Lives and Property, 59(4) *Corrections Today* 22 (1997).

28 Anne Gearan, Sticking to a Promise, *Roanoke Times*, Sept. 15, 1994, scholar.lib .vt.edu/VA-news/ROA-Times/issues/1994/rt0994/940915/09150042.htm.

29 William J. Sabol et al., Influences of Truth-in-Sentencing Reforms on Changes in States' Sentencing Practices and Prison Populations, July 2002 at Table 1.5, www.ojp.gov/pdffiles1/nij/grants/195161.pdf; Joan Petersilia, *Parole and Prisoner Reentry in the United States*, 26 *Crime & Justice* 479, 495 (1999).

30 Carl Reynolds, Sentencing and Corrections: From Crowding to Equilibrium (and Back Again?), 69 *Texas Bar Journal* 232, 234 (2006).

31 For discussion of Michigan, Missouri, and Georgia parole changes, see Nazgol Ghandnoosh, Delaying a Second Chance, *The Sentencing Project*, 2017, www.sentencingproject.org/publications/delaying-second-chance-declining-prospects-parole-life-sentences/.

32 Jeremy Travis & Sarah Lawrence, *Beyond the Prison Gates: The State of Parole in America* at 25, webarchive.urban.org/UploadedPDF/310583_Beyond_ prison_gates.pdf.

33 In fact, Allen dramatically reduced the availability of good time credits but did not eliminate it completely. George Allen, Abolishing Parole Saves Lives and Property, *Corrections Today* 59(4):22 (1997).

34 United States General Accounting Office, Truth in Sentencing, Availability of Federal Grants Influenced Laws in Some States, Feb. 1998, www.govinfo .gov/content/pkg/GAOREPORTS-GGD-98-42/pdf/GAOREPORTS-GGD-98-42.pdf

35 California Department of Corrections and Rehabilitation, Suitability Hearing Summary, www.cdcr.ca.gov/bph/2020/01/09/suitability-hearing-summary-

cy-1978-through-cy-2018/ See also Kathryne M. Young et al., Predicting
Parole Grants: An Analysis of Suitability Hearings for California's Lifer
Inmates, 28(4) *Federal Sentencing Reporter* 268 (April 2016).

36 Statement on the Presidential Commission on Drunk Driving, April 5, 1983,
www.reaganlibrary.gov/archives/speech/statement-presidential-commission-
drunk-driving.

37 Rachel Barkow, *Prisoners of Politics*, 29–30 (2019).

38 For the Michigan study, see James Copland et al., Overcriminalizing the
Wolverine State, Mackinac Center, Oct. 2014, at 3–4, www.mackinac.org/
archives/2014/S2014-06.pdf; for North Carolina, see James Copland and
Rafael Mangual, North Carolina Overcriminalization, Manhattan Institute,
August 2017, at 3, media4.manhattan-institute.org/sites/default/files/IB-JC-
0717.pdf. For the North Carolina law, see General Assembly of North
Carolina, Session 2015, Session Law 2016-113, Senate Bill 770, www
.ncleg.net/enactedlegislation/sessionlaws/pdf/2015-2016/sl2016-113.pdf; the
Michigan example is at Michigan Compiled Laws § 324.80143, the federal
laws are 18 U.S.C. § 924(g) and Crime Control Act of 1990, Pub. L. No.
101–647, 104 Stat. 4789, Title III, § 323(a), (b) (1990).

39 Money Laundering Control Act of 1986.

40 For a discussion of the enhancement and an interview with a prosecutor who
related that "a gang enhancement would permit the admission of gang evidence against a defendant, and thus, it served primarily as an evidentiary
function when it was used," see Erin R. Yoshino, California's Criminal Gang
Enhancements: Lessons from Interviews with Practitioners, 18 *Southern
California Review of Law & Social Justice* 117, 133 (2008).

41 Totals are rounded to the nearest percentage. The 2019 data comes from
BJS, *Prisoners 2020*, Table 14 and combine theft (3 percent) and motor
vehicle theft (0.8 percent) into a single total. Table data is calculated from
raw numbers in *Prisoners 2000* and *Prisoners 1994* (which includes in
Table 14 raw numbers for 1980). The Prisoners series is available at: bjs
.ojp.gov/library/publications/list?series_filter=Prisoners.

42 *People* v. *Bronzino*, 25 A.D.2d 685, 685 (N.Y. App. Div. 1966).

43 Assembly Subcommittee on Drunk Driving, Drunk Driving Reform in New
York State 1980–1984, May 2, 1984, www.ojp.gov/pdffiles1/Digitization/
96572NCJRS.pdf

44 Edward Louis Fiandach, *New York Driving While Intoxicated* § 1:6 (3d ed.).

45 The arrest data can be accessed at the following website, data.ny.gov/d/rikd-
mt35/visualization; the increase in convictions is reflected in the previously
referenced Assembly report.

46 BJS, DWI Offenders under Correctional Supervision, 1999, bjs.ojp.gov/
content/pub/pdf/dwiocs.pdf.

47 Or. Laws 1977, ch. 845, § 1 (codified at ORS 133.055(2) (1977); Aya
Gruber, *The Feminist War on Crime* 82 (2021) ("by 1991, around half the
states had some form of proarrest DV statute").

48 Act of May 26, 1991, ch. 542, § 9, 1991 Tex. Sess. Law Serv. 1880 (Vernon) (emphasis added) (to be codified as an amendment to Tex. Code Crim. Proc. art. 14.03(b)).

49 Utah Code § 77-36-2.7.

50 Fla. Stat. 741.2901.

51 N.J. Rev Stat § 2C:25-24.

52 Violent Crime Control and Law Enforcement Act of 1994, U.S. Department of Justice, Fact Sheet, www.ncjrs.gov/txtfiles/billfs.txt.

53 Naomi Murakawa, *The First Civil Right: How Liberals Built Prison American* 116 (2014).

54 *United States* v. *Angelos*, 433 F.3d 738, 743 (10th Cir. 2006).

55 For an in-depth look at this history, see David A. Sklansky, Cocaine, Race, and Equal Protection, 47 *Stanford Law Review* 1283, 1288 (1995). Congress removed the five-year mandatory minimum sentence for distributing five grams of crack in the Fair Sentencing Act of 2010.

56 Jennifer Walwyn, Targeting Gang Crime: An Analysis of California Penal Code Section 12022.53 and Vicarious Liability for Gang Members, 50 *UCLA Law Review* 685, 693 (2002). California substantially enhanced the enhancement in 2000. Erin R. Yoshino, California's Criminal Gang Enhancements: Lessons from Interviews with Practitioners, 18 *Southern California Review of Law & Social Just*ice 117, 133 (2008).

57 Beth Bjerregaard, The Constitutionality of Anti-Gang Legislation, 21 *Campbell Law Review* 31, 32 (1998).

Chapter 8

1 Franklin Zimring, *The Insidious Momentum of American Mass Incarceration* 20 (2020).

2 Jessica Neptune, Harshest in the Nation: The Rockefeller Drug Laws and the Widening Embrace of Punitive Politics, *Political Science* (June 2012), pdfs.semanticscholar.org/bd84/c91152348b83911cb8aa7ae82b4a48 f2c6e7.pdf.

3 See *United States* v. *Angelos*, 345 F. Supp. 2d 1227, 1233 (D. Utah 2004) (quoting 114 Cong. Rec. 22, 231–48 , Statement of Rep. Poff).

4 Cal. Penal Code § 186.21.

5 National Institute of Justice, Five Things about Deterrence 1 (2016), www .ojp.gov/pdffiles1/nij/247350.pdf. The research is summarized in Daniel S. Nagin, Deterrence in the Twenty-First Century: Crime and Justice, 42(1) *Crime and Justice in America, 1975–2025* 199-263 (August 2013).

6 FBI, UCR National Clearance Data, ucr.fbi.gov/crime-in-the-u.s/2018/ crime-in-the-u.s.-2018/topic-pages/clearance-browse-by/national-data.

7 Detroit clearance rate was obtained from a NPR database of data reported to the FBI: www.npr.org/2015/03/30/395799413/how-many-crimes-do-your-police-clear-now-you-can-find-out.

8 Anne Dowling et al., Frequency of Alcohol-Impaired Driving in New York State, *Traffic Injury Prevention* 124 (2011).
9 Pew Research Center, What the Data Says (and Doesn't Say) about Crime in the United States, Nov. 20, 2020, www.pewresearch.org/fact-tank/2020/11/20/facts-about-crime-in-the-u-s/ft_20-11-12_crimeintheus_4/
10 Crime & Delinquency in California, 1996, (Table 15 and p. 24 reflect 1991-6 data), oag.ca.gov/sites/all/files/agweb/pdfs/cjsc/publications/candd/cd96-full-report.pdf; Crime in California, 2001, at 30, oag.ca.gov/sites/all/files/agweb/pdfs/cjsc/publications/misc/cinc-full-report.pdf; Crime in California, 2002, at 22 (decreasing through 2002), oag.ca.gov/sites/all/files/agweb/pdfs/cjsc/publications/candd/cd02-full-report.pdf
11 Percentages vary by jurisdiction and time. The chart is based on estimates that about 50 percent of robberies are reported (see BJS, Criminal Victimization, 2019, bjs.ojp.gov/content/pub/pdf/cv19.pdf, Table 6 which shows a 62 percent reporting rate in 2018 and 47 percent reporting rate in 2019), about 30 percent of reported robberies lead to arrest (FBI estimate earlier in this chapter), a generic estimate that prosecutors charge about 66 percent of felony arrests (see Chapter 11), and the finding from BJS, Felony Defendants in Large Urban Counties 2009, that 59 percent of charged robberies resulted in felony convictions, bjs.ojp.gov/content/pub/pdf/fdluc09.pdf.
12 BJS, Criminal Victimization, 2020, Table 4, bjs.ojp.gov/sites/g/files/xyckuh236/files/media/document/cv20.pdf.
13 D.C. Code § 22–3215.
14 See *Agnew* v. *United States*, 813 A.2d 192, 195 (D.C. 2002) (car was borrowed from aunt).
15 *Thomas* v. *United States*, 553 A.2d 1206, 1206 (D.C. 1989).
16 Jeffrey Bellin, Waiting for Justice, *Slate*, Feb. 7, 2018.
17 161 Cong Rec. S955–02, S963 (daily ed. Feb. 12, 2015) (Sen. Grassley).

Chapter 9

1 Nationwide statistics come from BJS, Prisoners series, or U.S. Census Bureau unless otherwise indicated. I use the term "Hispanic" to mirror the use of the same term by these sources from which the data comes. All State figures from Vera, trends.vera.org/, and located by searching for States. The site reports that the data was last updated in 2021. For official confirmation, see Mississippi Department of Corrections, FY 2019, Annual Report at 59 (reporting that 61.9 percent of inmates were Black), www.mdoc.ms.gov/Admin-Finance/Documents/201920Annual%20Report.pdf.
2 See John Gramlich, The Gap between the Number of Blacks and Whites in Prison Is Shrinking, Pew Research Center, April 30, 2019, www.pewresearch.org/fact-tank/2019/04/30/shrinking-gap-between-number-of-blacks-and-whites-in-prison/; and John Gramlich, Black Imprisonment

Rate in the U.S. Has Fallen by a Third since 2006, Pew Research Center, May 6, 2020, www.pewresearch.org/fact-tank/2020/05/06/share-of-black-white-hispanic-americans-in-prison-2018-vs-2006/. The percentages of Black people in prison come from BJS, *Prisoners in 2000* at 11 (1990 and 2000 percentages); *Prisoners in 2020* at Table 3 (2010 and 2020). The Prisoners series is available at: bjs.ojp.gov/library/publications/list?series_filter=Prisoners

3 Steven Raphael & Michael Stoll, *Why Are So Many Americans in Prison* 15, 17 (2013) & Figure 1.5.

4 Michelle Alexander, *The New Jim Crow* 73 (2020 ed.).

5 BJS, Jail Inmates 2019 (362,900 in jail); BJS, Prisoners in 2019 (394,800 in prison).

6 BJS, Census of State and Federal Adult Correctional Facilities, 2019 – Statistical Tables, Table 3, bjs.ojp.gov/content/pub/pdf/csfacf19st.pdf.

7 BJS, Prevalence of Imprisonment in the U.S. Population, 1974–2001, www.bjs.gov/content/pub/pdf/piusp01.pdf.

8 See, e.g., Incarceration Trends in Idaho, Vera Institute of Justice, www.vera.org/downloads/pdfdownloads/state-incarceration-trends-idaho.pdf. Vera reports that Utah had a 464 percent increase in incarceration while its largest incarcerated minority group (Black) made up 7% of its prison population. Similarly, New Hampshire had a 380% increase in incarceration and 5% of its prisoners were Black; Montana, 355% increase in incarceration and 22% of state prisoners are Native American; Vermont, 297% increase in prison population and 10% of state prisoners are Black; Wyoming, 284% increase in incarceration and 5% of state prisoners are Black.

9 U.S. Sentencing Commission, Annual Report Sourcebook, Table 5 (81.3% of offenders white), www.ussc.gov/sites/default/files/pdf/research-and-publications/annual-reports-and-sourcebooks/2020/Table05.pdf.

10 Alexander, *The New Jim Crow*, at 254 ("white people are collateral damage").

11 BJS, Prisoners in 2010, Table 16B, bjs.ojp.gov/content/pub/pdf/p10.pdf.

12 National Research Council, *The Growth of Incarceration in the United States* at 60 (2014).

13 Michael Tonry & Matthew Melewski, The Malign Effects of Drug and Crime Control Policies on Black Americans, 37 *Crime & Justice* 1, 27 (2008).

14 National Research Council, *The Growth of Incarceration in the United States* at 95, Table 3-3 (2014).

15 Alexander at 234, 233 ("The War on Drugs has given birth to a system of mass incarceration that governs … entire communities of color."), 230 ("This, in brief, is how the system works: the War on Drugs is a vehicle through which extraordinary numbers of black men are forced into the cage.").

16 See, e.g., Marie Gottschalk, *Caught* 5 (2016); James Forman Jr., Racial Critiques of Mass Incarceration: Beyond the New Jim Crow, 87 *New York University Law Review* 21, 49–50 (2012).

17 Alexander, Foreword to 2020 Edition of *The New Jim Crow*, at xxiii.

18 The quote is from BJS, Race and Ethnicity of Violent Crime Offenders and Arrestees, 2018, at 1, bjs.ojp.gov/library/publications/race-and-ethnicity-violent-crime-offenders-and-arrestees-2018; the homicide discussion comes from BJS, Homicide Trends in the United States, 1980–2008, Table 7 (estimating that 52.5 percent of homicides were committed by Black people), bjs.ojp.gov/content/pub/pdf/htus8008.pdf; and BJS, Prisoners in 2010, bjs .ojp.gov/content/pub/pdf/p10.pdf (46 percent of those incarcerated for murder were Black).

19 Sandra G. Mayson, Bias in, Bias Out, 128 *Yale Law Journal* 2218, 2259 (2019).

20 Michael Tonry, *Punishing Race: An American Dilemma Continues* 31 (2011).

21 Alexander, *The New Jim Crow*, at 60 ("backlash"); BJS, Prison Admissions and Releases, 1981, at 2, bjs.ojp.gov/content/pub/pdf/par81.pdf.

22 Randall Kennedy, *Race, Crime and the Law* 48, 69 (1997).

23 Hortense Powdermaker, *After Freedom A Cultural Study in the Deep South* 164, 173 (1939).

24 Gunnar Myrdal, *An American Dilemma: The Negro Problem and Modern Democracy* 542, 551 (1944).

25 Christopher Muller, Northward Migration and the Rise of Racial Disparity in American Incarceration, 1880–1950, 118 (2) *American Journal of Sociology* 281, 310 (2012).

26 Report of the National Advisory Commission on Civil Disorders (Kerner Report) at 1, 161 (1968), belonging.berkeley.edu/sites/default/files/kerner_commission_full_report.pdf. "For most of the twentieth century, the police ignored poor and segregated Black neighborhoods such as 6th Street." Alice Goffman, *On the Run: Fugitive Life in an American City* 2 (2014).

27 Kerner Report at 8.

28 BJS, Criminal Victimization, 2019, 19 ("The largest percentage of violent incidents committed against white, black, and Hispanic victims were committed by someone of the same race or ethnicity"), bjs.ojp.gov/content/pub/pdf/cv19.pdf.

29 BJS, Criminal Victimization and Perceptions of Community Safety in 12 Cities, 1998, at 7, bjs.ojp.gov/content/pub/pdf/cvpcs98.pdf.

30 Richard Frase, What Explains Persistent Racial Disproportionality in Minnesota's Prison and Jail Populations, 38 *Crime & Justice* 201, 224 (2009).

31 Gottschalk, *Caught*, 133.

32 Ben Grunwald, Toward an Optimal Decarceration Strategy, 33 *Stanford Law & Policy Review* 1, 53 (2022).

33 N.J. Courts, Report to the Governor and the Legislature, 21, 2019, www
   .njcourts.gov/courts/assets/criminal/cjrannualreport2019.pdf.

Chapter 10

1 See BJS, Census of State and Local Law Enforcement Agencies, 1992
  (Table 2) (1986 numbers), bjs.ojp.gov/content/pub/pdf/csllea92.pdf; BJS,
  Census of State and Local Law Enforcement Agencies, 2008; BJS, Police
  Departments in Large Cities, 1990–2000, bjs.ojp.gov/content/pub/pdf/
  pdlc00.pdf; Leonard Buder, Number of Police in New York Force Is
  Lowest in Years, *N.Y. Times*, Dec. 6, 1981.
2 GAO, Community Policing Grants, Oct. 2005, www.gao.gov/assets/gao-06-
  104.pdf.
3 BJS, Arrest Data Analysis Tool, www.bjs.gov/index.cfm?ty=datool&surl=/
  arrests/index.cfm.
4 This example comes from Bureau of Justice Statistics, *Felony Sentences in
  State Courts, 2006*, "Crime Definitions" at p. 33, bjs.ojp.gov/content/pub/
  pdf/fssc06st.pdf.
5 David Sklansky, *A Pattern of Violence* 71 (2021).
6 Franklin Zimring describes "the sharp expansion in assault and aggravated
  assault arrests" as the "largest statistical mystery of the last decade" and
  speculates that it resulted from "the willingness of police authorities to give
  greater priority to assaults." Franklin Zimring, *American Youth Violence* 46
  (1998). For a mound charging that did lead to felony assault charges, see
  Frank Litsky, Offerman Charged with Assault after Bat-Wielding Incident in
  Minors, *N.Y. Times*, Aug 16, 2007, www.nytimes.com/2007/08/16/sports/
  baseball/16minors.html.
7 Crime in California, 2001, at 30 (1999 data), oag.ca.gov/sites/all/files/agweb/
  pdfs/cjsc/publications/misc/cinc-full-report.pdf.
8 Reva Siegel, "The Rule of Love": Wife Beating as Prerogative and Privacy,
  105 *Yale Law Journal* 2117, 2170 (1996).
9 ABA, Standards for the Urban Policing Function, 1973 at § 3.3.
10 Del Martin, *Battered Wives* 93–94 (1976). Raymond Parnas, The Police
   Response to the Domestic Disturbance, 1967 *Wisconsin Law Review* 914,
   921 (1967) (Chicago).
11 Aya Gruber, *The Feminist War on Crime* 72–73 (2021).
12 California Office of the Attorney General, Report on Arrests for Domestic
   Violence in California, 1998, oag.ca.gov/sites/all/files/agweb/pdfs/cjsc/publica
   tions/misc/dv98.pdf at 7.
13 Jack Leonard, Homing in on Domestic Violence Crime: O.C. Arrests Surge
   431% in '90s; Felony Filings Even More as Police and Prosecutors Take
   Cases More Seriously, *L.A. Times*, Sept. 5, 1999, at A1.
14 *Botello* v. *State*, 693 S.W.2d 528, 529 (Tex. App. 1985).

15 *Com.* v. *Piole*, 431 Pa. Super. 391, 393 (1994).

16 *State* v. *Powell*, 2009-Ohio-2822, ¶ 3.

17 *State* v. *Ortiz*, No. 59565, 1991 WL 263924, at *4 (Ohio Ct. App. Dec. 12, 1991).

18 *State* v. *White*, 202 Mont. 491, 494 (1983).

19 *Balderson* v. *State*, 2013 WY 107, ¶ 4 (Wyo. Sept. 17, 2013).

20 Arrest Data comes from the BJS Arrest Data Analysis Tool, www.bjs.gov/index.cfm?ty=datool&surl=/arrests/index.cfm#.

21 For an in-depth analysis of the NCVS, see James P. Lynch and Lynn A. Addington, eds., *Understanding Crime Statistics* (2007).

22 BJS, Criminal Victimization, 2019 at 30, bjs.ojp.gov/content/pub/pdf/cv19.pdf.

23 Richard Rosenfeld, Explaining the Divergence between UCR and NCVS Aggravated Assault Trends, in *Understanding Crime Statistics: Revisiting the Divergence of the NCVS and the UCR* 264 (2007).

24 Monitoring the Future, National Survey Results on Drug Use, 1975–2020, vol. 2, at 111 and fig. 5-1, www.monitoringthefuture.org/pubs/monographs/mtf-vol2_2020.pdf; Albany Sourcebook of Criminal Justice Statistics, Table 3.66 www.albany.edu/sourcebook/pdf/t366.pdf (table reflecting Monitoring the Future survey results).

25 Data is available from the BJS Arrest Data Analysis Tool for the Los Angeles Police Dept. www.bjs.gov/index.cfm?ty=datool&surl=/arrests/index.cfm#.

26 Crime in California 1996, 2018 (Table 37). The Crime in California series is available online at oag.ca.gov/cjsc/pubs#crime.

27 See FBI, UCR: Percent of Offenses Cleared by Arrest or Exceptional Means, ucr.fbi.gov/crime-in-the-u.s/2019/crime-in-the-u.s.-2019/tables/table-25 (2019); and Charles Wellford and James Cronin, Clearing Up Homicide Clearance Rates, April 2000, www.ojp.gov/pdffiles1/jr000243b.pdf (offering historical data).

Chapter 11

1 Ronald Wright & Marc Miller, The Screening/Bargaining Tradeoff, 55 *Stanford Law Review* 29 (2002); Marc L. Miller & Ronald F. Wright, The Black Box, 94 *Iowa Law Review* 125, 135 (2008).

2 See BJS, Prosecution of Felony Arrests, 1988, bjs.ojp.gov/content/pub/pdf/pfa88.pdf; BJS, Prosecution of Felony Arrests, 1979, www.bjs.gov/index.cfm/index.cfm?ty=pbdetail&iid=3492.

3 Brian Forst, Prosecution and Sentencing, in James Q. Wilson and Joan Petersilia, eds., *Crime* (1995), p. 364.

4 Crime in California series, table 37 summarizes 1982 to 2020, data-open justice.doj.ca.gov/sites/default/files/2021-06/Crime%20In%20CA%202020.pdf.

5 Forst, Prosecution and Sentencing, at 366.

6 Natalie Neysa Alund et al., Predators Fan Who Threw Catfish on Ice Charged in Pittsburgh, *The Tennessean*, May 30, 2017, www.tennessean .com/story/news/2017/05/30/report-predators-fan-who-threw-catfish-ice-charged-pittsburgh/354356001/; PA Prosecutors Drop Charges against TN Man Who Threw Dead Fish on Ice Rink at Stanley Cup Final, May 31, 2017, www.wtap.com/content/news/PA-prosecutors-drop-charges-against-TN-man-who-threw-dead-fish-on-ice-rink-at-Stanley-Cup-Final-4255102 44.html.

7 Gregory Korte, For a Million U.S. Men, Failing to Register for the Draft Has Serious, Long-Term Consequences, *USA Today*, April 2, 2019, www .usatoday.com/story/news/nation/2019/04/02/failing-register-draft-women-court-consequences-men/3205425002/; DOD Report n. 21, p. 5 ("Annually, the SSS forwards to DoJ a list of roughly 630,000 names and addresses of men aged 19–30, who have either evaded registration or refused to register. In practice, there have been no criminal prosecutions for failure to register since January 1986."), hasbrouck.org/draft/FOIA/DOD-report-17MAR2017.pdf.

8 The BJS, Felony Defendants in Large Urban Counties series reflects that a little over 50 percent of felony cases result in a felony conviction. For example, in 2009 (the last year of the series), 66 percent of felony arrests adjudicated within one year resulted in a conviction: 54 percent resulted in a felony conviction and 12 percent in a misdemeanor conviction:. bjs.ojp.gov/content/pub/pdf/fdluc09.pdf at 22.

9 See BJS, Felony Sentences in State Courts Series, 1986–2006.

10 Crime in California 1996 (Table 37) and 2018 (Table 37), oag.ca.gov/sites/all/files/agweb/pdfs/cjsc/publications/candd/cd96-full-report.pdf.

11 Steven Raphael and Michael Stoll, *Why Are So Many Americans in Prison?* 62 (2013).

12 Memo from Richard Thornburg, Re Plea Bargaining under the Sentencing Reform Act, March 1989, available at 6 Federal Sentencing Reporter 347, 347 (1994).

13 La Follette School of Public Affairs, Public Safety and Assistant District Attorney Staffing in Wisconsin, 2011, lafollette.wisc.edu/outreach-public-service/past-events-initiatives-and-collaborations/public-safety-and-assist ant-district-attorney-staffing-in-wisconsin.

14 BJS, Prosecutors in State Courts, 2005, at 3, bjs.ojp.gov/content/pub/pdf/psc05.pdf.

15 Del Martin, *Battered Wives* 110–11 (1976).

16 William Hart et al., Family Violence, September 1984 (Task Force Report), at 10, files.eric.ed.gov/fulltext/ED251762.pdf; Jack Leonard, Homing in on Domestic Violence Crime: O.C. Arrests Surge 431% in '90s; Felony Filings Even More as Police and Prosecutors Take Cases More Seriously, *L.A. Times*, Sept. 5, 1999, at A1 (Orange County prosecutor statistics).

See also Leigh Goodmark, *Decriminalizing Domestic Violence: A Balanced Policy Approach to Intimate Partner Violence* 2, 15 (2018) (identifying the 1984 report as a turning point in law enforcement's treatment of domestic violence and noting that "[b]y 1996 two-thirds of prosecutors' offices had adopted (primarily soft) no-drop policies [for domestic violence cases].").

17 Using the BJS Arrest Data Analysis Tool, I excluded all offenses unlikely to be prosecuted as felonies, specifically, larceny-theft, nonaggravated assaults, receiving/buying stolen property, vandalism, prostitution, gambling, liquor laws, drunkenness, disorderly conduct, vagrancy, suspicion, curfew/loitering, and runaways. I also exclude the category, "all other offenses" due to the uncertainty about what gets reported in that category.

18 The BJS arrest tool includes all drug possession arrests in one category. The severity of drug possession laws varies by jurisdiction, with some jurisdictions treating some possession offenses as misdemeanors. Since the felony conviction statistics reflect thousands of drug possession convictions, I include drug possession arrests in the "serious arrests" category.

19 BJS, Prosecutors in State Courts, 2005, at 2, bjs.ojp.gov/content/pub/pdf/psc05.pdf.

20 Crime in California, 2001, at 28, oag.ca.gov/sites/all/files/agweb/pdfs/cjsc/publications/misc/cinc-full-report.pdf.

21 See BJS, Felony Sentences in State Court series (1986–2006).

22 BJS, Felony Sentences in State Courts, 2006 – Statistical Tables, at 1, bjs.ojp.gov/content/pub/pdf/fssc06st.pdf.

23 See Carissa Hessick, *Punishment without Trial* 163 (2021).

24 Felony Defendants in Large Urban Counties, 1990, Table 15 and Felony Defendants in Large Urban Counties, 2000, Table 23.

25 D.C. Code § 33–541(a)(1).

26 These totals were derived using the BJS Arrest Data Analysis Tool, available at www.bjs.gov/index.cfm?ty=datool&surl=/arrests/index.cfm – the tool reports 1,089,500 drug arrests in 1990 compared to 1,889,810 in 2006.

27 Data gathered from California Department of Justice, Crime in California Series, and specifically the summary Table 37 in 1996 and 2018 reports. The series is available at: oag.ca.gov/cjsc/pubs#crime

28 Compendium of Federal Justice Statistics, 1984, bjs.ojp.gov/content/pub/pdf/cfjs84.pdf.

29 See BJS, Federal Justice Statistics Series (2009 is at Table 7).

30 These numbers are pulled from the series, BJS, Felony Defendants in Large Urban Counties.

Chapter 12

1 BJS, Felony Sentences in State Courts, 2000, bjs.ojp.gov/content/pub/pdf/fssc00.pdf at 1.

2 Steven Raphael & Michael Stoll, *Why Are So Many Americans in Prison* 41–2 (2013).

3 Franklin Zimring, *The Insidious Momentum of American Mass Incarceration* 47 (2020) Figure 3.1. Estimates like these are complicated by the inclusion or exclusion of federal admissions, jail admissions and probation/parole revocations. For a more direct accounting, Table 1.2.1 in Felony Sentence in State Courts, 2006 shows 141,780 prison and 105,500 jail sentences for State drug offenses, for a total of 247,280 that year, bjs.ojp.gov/redirect-legacy/content/pub/pdf/fssc06st.pdf.

4 These numbers were calculated using data presented by Drug Policy Facts, sourced from the BJS and are available at www.drugpolicyfacts.org/chapter/drug_prison#.

5 Sourcebook of Criminal Justice Statistics 2003, p. 494, www.albany.edu/sourcebook/pdf/t619.pdf.

6 Compare BJS, Prisons and Prisoners, 1982 at 2 (1979 data), bjs.ojp.gov/content/pub/pdf/pp.pdf) with BJS, Prisoners in 2018, at 21, bjs.ojp.gov/content/pub/pdf/p18.pdf (2018 data plus breakdown of breaking down "public order" category).

7 This account can be found in *Oxford Handbook of Prisons and Punishment* 9 (John Wooldredge & Paula Smith, eds.) (2018).

8 Allen J. Beck & Alfred Blumstein, Trends In U.S. Incarceration Rates: 1980–2010 28 (2012). This paper was prepared for the National Research Council's, *The Growth of Incarceration in the United States*.

9 Raphael & Stoll, *Why Are So Many Americans in Prison*, 27, 51.

10 The PEW Center on the States, Time Served, 2012, at 3, www.pewtrusts.org/-/media/assets/2012/06/06/time_served_report.pdf.

11 See PEW, Prison Time Surges for Federal Inmates, Nov. 18. 2015, www.pewtrusts.org/en/research-and-analysis/issue-briefs/2015/11/prison-time-surges-for-federal-inmates.

12 U.S. Sentencing Commission, Supplementary Report on the Initial Sentencing Guidelines and Policy Statements, June 18, 1987, p. 73, Table 5, www.ussc.gov/sites/default/files/pdf/guidelines-manual/1987/manual-pdf/1987_Supplementary_Report_Initial_Sentencing_Guidelines.pdf. For a comprehensive summary of the Federal Sentencing Commission, see Brent E. Newton & Dawinder S. Sidhu, The History of the Original United States Sentencing Commission, 1985–1987, 45 *Hofstra Law Review* 1167 (2017).

13 BJS, Prisoners in 2002 at 2 (Table 1).

14 Zimring, *Insidious Momentum*, at 40.

15 C. Lim et al. Do Judges' Characteristics Matter? 18 *American Law and Economics Review* 302–57 (2016).

16 David Abrams et al., When in Rome … on Local Norms and Sentencing Decisions, *Journal of the European Economic Association*, Sept. 9, 2021, at 9.

17 Susan B. Long and David Burnham, Trac Report: Examining Current Federal Sentencing Practices: A National Study of Differences among Judges, 25 *Federal Sentencing Reporter* 6 (2012).

18 Justin Fenton, In Baltimore's Reception Court, a Behind-the-Scenes Look at How Plea Deals Happen, *Baltimore Sun*, Nov. 3, 2017, www.baltimoresun .com/news/crime/bs-md-ci-baltimore-plea-bargains-peters-20171023-htmlstory .html.

19 Nancy J. King & Ronald F. Wright, The Invisible Revolution in Plea Bargaining: Managerial Judging and Judicial Participation in Negotiations, 95 *Texas Law Review* 325, 326 (2016).

20 For federal rules on plea bargaining, see Federal Rule of Criminal Procedure 11.

21 *United States* v. *Angelos*, 345 F. Supp. 2d 1227, 1230–2 (D. Utah 2004).

22 Sentencing Law and Policy Blog, Breaking News (and SL&P exclusive?): federal Judge Paul Cassell Resigning!, sentencing.typepad.com/sentencing_ law_and_policy/2007/09/breaking-news-a.html.

23 Criticizing Sentencing Rules, U.S. Judge Resigns, *N.Y. Times*, Sept 30, 1990, www.nytimes.com/1990/09/30/us/criticizing-sentencing-rules-us-judge-resigns.html.

24 For the judicial opinion in the case, see *State* v. *Jackson*, 718 So.2d 1001 (La. App. 4 Cir. 1998).

25 James Q. Whitman, *Harsh Justice* 57 (2005).

26 Ram Subramanian & Alison Shames, Sentencing and Prison Practices in Germany and the Netherlands, Oct. 2013, at 10, www.vera.org/downloads/ Publications/sentencing-and-prison-practices-in-germany-and-the-nether lands-implications-for-the-united-states/legacy_downloads/european-ameri can-prison-report-v3.pdf.

Chapter 13

1 For the sports example, see *United States* v. *Dawkins*, 999 F.3d 767, 778 (2d Cir. 2021); for the fish, see *Yates* v. *United States*, 574 U.S. 528, 529 (2015).

2 *People* v. *Valencia*, 28 Cal. 4th 1 (2002).

3 See Shon Hopwood, Restoring the Historical Rule of Lenity as a Canon, 95 *New York University Law Review* 918, 920 (2020).

4 *Pringle* v. *United States*, 825 A.2d 924, 925 (D.C. 2003).

5 *Arthur* v. *United States*, 602 A.2d 174, 175 (D.C. 1992).

6 *Com.* v. *Marrero*, 19 Mass. App. Ct. 921, 921 (1984) (citing Mass. Gen. Laws Ann. ch. 265, § 15A.

7 *Conder* v. *State*, 953 N.E.2d 1197, 1206 (Ind. Ct. App. 2011).

8 *Morgan* v. *State*, 703 S.W.2d 339, 340 (Tex. App. 1985).

9 Monticello, *Sir Walter Raleigh* (Painting), www.monticello.org/site/research-and-collections/sir-walter-raleigh-painting.

10 *People* v. *Taylor*, 83 Cal. Rptr. 2d 919, 920 (Ct. App. 1999).

11 *People* v. *Superior Ct.* (Romero), 37 Cal. Rptr. 2d 364, 382 (Ct. App. 1995).

12 *Ewing* v. *California*, 538 U.S. 11, 17–18 (2003).

13 *United States* v. *Gementera*, 379 F.3d 596, 598 (9th Cir. 2004).

14 See also Antonin Scalia, Originalism: The Lesser Evil, 57 *University of Cincinnati Law Review* 849, 861 (1989) ("I am confident that public flogging and handbranding would not be sustained by our courts.").

15 *Shannon* v. *United States*, 512 U.S. 573, 579 (1994).

16 *Robinson* v. *California*, 370 U.S. 660, 662 (1962).

17 BJS, Felony Sentences in State Courts, 2006 – Statistical Tables, Dec. 2009, bjs.ojp.gov/content/pub/pdf/fssc06st.pdf.

18 434 U.S. 357, 358 & n.1 (1978).

19 *Missouri* v. *Frye*, 566 U.S. 134 (2012).

Chapter 14

1 BJS, Felony Defendants in Large Urban Counties, 2009 – Statistical Tables, Table 7, bjs.ojp.gov/content/pub/pdf/fdluc09.pdf.

2 BJS, Profile of Prison Inmates, 2016, at 1, bjs.ojp.gov/content/pub/pdf/ppi16 .pdf.

3 BJS, Recidivism of Prisoners Released in 24 States in 2008: A 10-Year Follow-Up Period (2008–2018), Sept. 2021, bjs.ojp.gov/library/publica tions/recidivism-prisoners-released-24-states-2008-10-year-follow-period-2008-2018.

4 Sarah Shannon et al., *The Growth, Scope, and Spatial Distribution of People with Felony Records in the United States, 1948–2010*: *Demography* (2017).

5 See BJS, Felony Defendants in Large Urban Counties, 1990 (Table 8), 2000 (Table 10), 2009 (Table 9).

6 S Austin et al., The Impact of Truth-in-Sentencing and Three Strikes Legislation: Prison Populations, State Budgets, and Crime Rates, 11 *Stanford Law & Policy Review* 75, 80, Table 3 (1999).

7 Section 924(e)(1).

8 21 U.S.C. 841(b)(1)(A)(viii).

9 PL 100–690, Nov. 18, 1988, 102 Stat 4181. The 2018 First Step Act slightly reduced these repeat-drug-offender enhancements. Congress reduced the twenty-year mandatory minimum sentence for certain (second) serious drug offenses to fifteen years, and the mandatory life sentence for a third such conviction to twenty-five years. PL 115-391, Dec. 21, 2018, 132 Stat 5194.

10 *People* v. *Superior Ct.* (Romero), 13 Cal. 4th 497, 506 (1996).

11 Dan Morain, Lawmakers Jump on '3 Strikes' Bandwagon, *L.A. Times*, Jan. 31, 1994.

12 Legislative Analyst's Office, A Primer: Three Strikes - The Impact after More than a Decade, Oct. 2005, lao.ca.gov/2005/3_strikes/3_strikes_102005.htm.

13 Eric Slater, Pizza Thief Gets 25 Years to Life; Crime – Judge Cites Five Prior Felony Convictions in Sentencing Jerry DeWayne Williams under "Three Strikes Law," *L.A. Times*, March 3, 1995, at Metro B3

14 Letters to the Editor, *L.A. Times*, Jan. 29, 2021.

15 See *People* v. *Fuhrman*, 16 Cal. 4th 930 (1997).

16 *People* v. *Bealer*, 2007 WL 512524 (Cal. Ct. App. 2007).

Chapter 15

1 Compare Probation and Parole 1981, bjs.ojp.gov/content/pub/pdf/pp81.pdf to Probation and Parole in the United States, 2005, bjs.ojp.gov/content/pub/pdf/ppus05.pdf.

2 Meek Mill, Prisoners Need a New Set of Rights, *N.Y. Times*, Nov. 26, 2018, www.nytimes.com/2018/11/26/opinion/meek-mill-criminal-justice-reform.html. For the procedural history, see *Commonwealth* v. *Williams*, 2017 WL 3934020 (Pa. Super. Ct. Sept. 8, 2017)

3 Compare BJS, Probation and Parole 1981, bjs.ojp.gov/content/pub/pdf/pp81.pdf to BJS, Probation and Parole in the United States, 2019, bjs.ojp.gov/content/pub/pdf/ppus19.pdf.

4 California Department of Corrections, California Prisoners & Parolees 2000, Table 7 (2000) (reporting 39,112 parole violators "WNT," with new term, and 26,359 parole violators "RTC," returned to custody out of a total population of 160,687).

5 BJS, Prisoners in 2017, Table 7 p. 13, www.bjs.gov/content/pub/pdf/p17.pdf and p. 2 (definition of new court commitments); BJS, Prisoners in 2019, Table 8 and p. 11, bjs.ojp.gov/library/publications/prisoners-2019.

6 BJS, Recidivism of Prisoners Released in 24 States in 2008: A 10-Year Follow-Up Period (2008–18), at 2, bjs.ojp.gov/BJS_PUB/rpr24s0810yfup0818/Web%20content/508%20compliant%20PDFs.

7 Crime in California, 2006, at 80, oag.ca.gov/sites/all/files/agweb/pdfs/cjsc/publications/candd/cd06-full-report.pdf (121,849 under supervision in 2006); see also Derek Neal & Armin Rick, The Prison Boom and Sentencing Policy, 45 *Journal of Legal Studies* 1, 31 (2016).

8 Daniel M. Weintraub, Woman Blames Parole Policy in Father's Slaying, *L.A. Times*, Feb. 4, 1994.

9 Sara Mayeux, The Origins of Back-End Sentencing in California: A Dispatch from the Archives, 22 *Stanford Law & Policy Review* 529, 537 (2011).

10 Jeremy Travis, *But They All Come Back* 31–32 (2005).

Chapter 16

1 James Q. Whitman, *Harsh Justice* 182 (2005).

2 For further discussion of this phenomenon, see Margaret Colgate Love, The Twilight of the Pardon Power, 100 *Journal of Criminal Law & Criminology* 1169, 1189 (2010) ("By the end of the 1930s, parole had largely supplanted clemency as a means of releasing prisoners."); and Rachel Barkow, Clemency and Presidential Administration of Criminal Law, 90 *New York University Law Review* 802, 814 (2015) ("Parole essentially replaced clemency as the primary mechanism for reducing sentences.").

3 American Bar Association, Justice Kennedy Commission, Report to the ABA House of Delegates 3, 70–71 (2004).

4 John Gramlich, Trump Used His Clemency Power Sparingly Despite a Raft of Late Pardons and Commutations, PEW Research Center, Jan. 22, 2021, www.pewresearch.org/fact-tank/2021/01/22/trump-used-his-clemency-power-sparingly-despite-a-raft-of-late-pardons-and-commutations/.

5 The George Bush story and some of the Texas pardon numbers come from Jay Root, Once Bitten, Bush Could Be Pardon-Shy President, *Fort Worth Star-Telegram*, March 9, 2001 (reporting numbers from state records). The balance of the table comes from Brandi Grissom, Beg His Pardon? *Texas Tribune*, Dec. 23, 2010, www.texastribune.org/2010/12/23/experts-say-perry-stingy-pardons/ (Mark White's number is described as "nearly 500"); Jessica Hamel & Ryan Murphy, Pardons by Gov. Rick Perry, *Texas Tribune*, Aug. 6. 2014, www.texastribune.org/library/data/search-texas-governor-rick-perry-pardons/; James Barragán, Gov. Greg Abbott Pardons Seven Texans ahead of Christmas, *Dallas Morning News*, Dec. 23, 2020, www.dallasnews.com/news/politics/2020/12/23/gov-greg-abbott-pardons-seven-texans-ahead-of-christmas/ (pardons since 2000).

Chapter 17

1 This data comes from the BJS Jail Inmates series, with the 1978 number coming from Jail Inmates 1984 (Table 5), bjs.ojp.gov/content/pub/pdf/ji84.pdf (see also BJS, Profile of Jail Inmates 1978, bjs.ojp.gov/content/pub/pdf/pji.pdf), and the 2008 and 2019 numbers from Jail Inmates in 2019, bjs.ojp.gov/content/pub/pdf/ji19.pdf.

2 BJS, Jail Inmates in 2019, at 8, bjs.ojp.gov/content/pub/pdf/ji19.pdf.

3 BJS, Profile of Jail Inmates 1978, www.bjs.gov/content/pub/pdf/pji.pdf (Table 3).

4 Ram Subramanian et al. Incarceration's Front Door: The Misuse of Jail in America, Vera Institute of Justice, 2015, at 22, www.vera.org/downloads/publications/incarcerations-front-door-report_02.pdf. The estimates are primarily based on BJS publications.

5 For further discussion of this type of reform, see Adam M. Gershowitz, Justice on the Line: Prosecutorial Screening before Arrest, 2019 *University of Illinois Law Review* 833, 835 (2019). For a comprehensive overview of pretrial incarceration, see Shima Baradaran Baughman, *The Bail Book: A Comprehensive Look at Bail in America's System* (2018).

6 Nebraska Commission on Law Enforcement and Criminal Justice, Nebraska Jail Population Report 1994, 19, bjs.ojp.gov/content/pub/pdf/njpr94.pdf.

7 *Vermont* v. *Brillon*, 556 U.S. 81, 89–90 (2009).

8 *Barker* v. *Wingo*, 407 U.S. 514, 536 (1972).

9 *Stack* v. *Boyle*, 342 U.S. 1, 5 (1951) (quote and ruling re: excessive bail).

10 Pretrial Services Agency for the District of Columbia, www.psa.gov/.

11 Pretrial Justice Institute, The State of Pretrial Justice in America, 2017, at 3, www.ncsc.org/__data/assets/pdf_file/0023/16718/the-state-of-pretrial-in-america-pji-2017.pdf.

12 BJS, Impact of COVID-19 on the Local Jail Population, January–June 2020, bjs.ojp.gov/content/pub/pdf/icljpjj20.pdf.

Chapter 18

1 Gabriella Paiella, How Would Prison Abolition Actually Work? *GQ*, June 11, 2020, www.gq.com/story/what-is-prison-abolition.

2 See California Department of Corrections and Rehabilitation, Fall 2020 Population Projections, at 3, www.cdcr.ca.gov/research/wp-content/uploads/sites/174/2021/03/Fall-2020-Population-Projections.pdf; Keaton Ross, Oklahoma's Prison Population Is Dropping amid the Pandemic. Will the Trend Continue? Oklahoma Watch, Aug. 2020, oklahomawatch.org/2020/07/15/oklahomas-prison-population-is-dropping-amid-the-pandemic-will-the-trend-continue/.

3 See Congressional Research Service, Base Closure and Realignment, April 25 2019 at 7, sgp.fas.org/crs/natsec/R45705.pdf.

4 Connecticut Department of Corrections, Monthly Statistics, portal.ct.gov/DOC/Report/Monthly-Statistics; Lisa Backus, CT Prison Population Drops to Lowest in 25 Years, *CT Post*, May 15, 2019, .www.ctpost.com/local/article/CT-prison-inmate-population-drops-to-lowest-in-25-13848350.php.

5 Connecticut Board of Pardons and Paroles, Statistical Information, portal.ct.gov/BOPP/Research-and-Development-Division/Statistics/Historical (showing previous ten years).

6 Connecticut Summary Statistics, 2010, www.dpsdata.ct.gov/dps/ucr/data/2010/Connecticut%20Summary%20Statistics%202010.pdf.

7 Connecticut Department of Corrections, Incarcerated Population and Authorized Positions, portal.ct.gov/DOC/Report/Number-of-Authorized-Positions.

8 Benjamin Levin, The Consensus Myth in Criminal Justice Reform, 117 *Michigan Law Review* 259 (2018).

Chapter 19

1 BJS, Prisoners 1979, bjs.ojp.gov/content/pub/pdf/psfi79-fr.pdf.
2 BJS, Prisoners in 2019 (Table 1), bjs.ojp.gov/content/pub/pdf/p19.pdf; Prisoners in 2020 – Statistical Tables (Table 1), bjs.ojp.gov/content/pub/pdf/p20st.pdf.
3 BJS, Prisoners in 1980 at 1, www.bjs.gov/content/pub/pdf/p80.pdf.
4 BJS, Federal Justice Statistics, 2019, Table 2 (Arrests) & 6 (Prosecutions), bjs.ojp.gov/content/pub/pdf/fjs19.pdf.
5 bjs.ojp.gov/content/pub/pdf/dlv80–86.pdf Table 5.
6 BJS, Federal Offenses and Offenders, Drug Law Violations 1980–6 (Table 7), bjs.ojp.gov/content/pub/pdf/fdo99.pdf.
7 BJS, Federal Sentencing in Transition, 1986–90 at 3, bjs.ojp.gov/library/publications/federal-sentencing-transition-1986-90
8 Federal Sentencing in Transition, Table 3 (76 percent to 76 percent).
9 BJS, Compendium of Federal Justice Statistics, 1990, Table 5.8, bjs.ojp.gov/content/pub/pdf/cfjs90.pdf.
10 BJS, Compendium of Federal Justice Statistics, 2000, Table 7.9, bjs.ojp.gov/content/pub/pdf/cfjs00.pdf.
11 BJS, Federal Justice Statistics 2010 – Statistical Tables, Table 7.9, bjs.ojp.gov/content/pub/pdf/fjs10st.pdf.
12 University at Albany, Sourcebook of Criminal Justice Statistics 2003, p. 519, www.albany.edu/sourcebook/pdf/t657.pdf,
13 U.S. Sentencing Commission, Quick Facts, www.ussc.gov/sites/default/files/pdf/research-and-publications/quick-facts/Felon_In_Possession_FY18.pdf.
14 U.S. Sentencing Commission, Illegal Reentry Offenses, April 2015, www.ussc.gov/sites/default/files/pdf/research-and-publications/research-projects-and-surveys/immigration/2015_Illegal-Reentry-Report.pdf
15 Compare BJS, Prisoners 1994, Table 13, bjs.ojp.gov/content/pub/pdf/Pi94.pdf with BJS, Prisoners 2010, Appendix Table 18, bjs.ojp.gov/content/pub/pdf/p10.pdf.

Chapter 20

1 Plea Bargaining and Prohibition in the Federal Courts, 1908–34, 24 *Law & Society Review* 413, 420 (1990).
2 Gregory Korte, For a Million U.S. Men, Failing to Register for the Draft Has Serious, Long-Term Consequences, *USA Today*, April 2, 2019, www.usatoday.com/story/news/nation/2019/04/02/failing-register-draft-women-court-consequences-men/3205425002/.

3 Charles Hanson Towne, *The Rise and Fall of Prohibition: The Human Side of What the Eighteenth Amendment Has Done to the United States* 129–30, 156–62 (1923) (discussing increase in crime during Prohibition).

4 Drug Enforcement Agency, National Heroin Threat Assessment Summary, June 2016, www.dea.gov/sites/default/files/2018-07/hq062716_attach.pdf.

5 PEW Charitable Trusts, More Imprisonment Does Not Reduce State Drug Problems, March 2018, www.pewtrusts.org/-/media/assets/2018/03/pspp_more_imprisonment_does_not_reduce_state_drug_problems.pdf.

6 BJS, Drug Use and Crime, June 1, 2021, https://bjs.ojp.gov/drugs-and-crime-facts/drug-use-and-crime.

7 NHTSA, National Statistics, www-fars.nhtsa.dot.gov/Main/index.aspx.

8 Selective Service System, FAQ, www.sss.gov/faq/.

9 Korte, Failing to Register for the Draft.

10 Susan J. Hoppea, Yan Zhanga, Brittany E. Hayes, Matthew A. Bills, Mandatory Arrest for Domestic Violence and Repeat Offending: A Metaanalysis, 53 *Aggression and Violent Behavior* 7 (2020).

11 See Leigh Goodmark, *Decriminalizing Domestic Violence: A Balanced Policy Approach to Intimate Partner Violence* (2018).

12 For an overview, see Mario Salas and Angela Ciolfi, Driven by Dollars, 2017, www.justice4all.org/wp-content/uploads/2017/09/Driven-by-Dollars.pdf ("Forty-three states and the District of Columbia use driver's license suspension to enforce court debt. Three other states have laws that prevent renewals for expired driver's licenses in some cases of unpaid court debt. Only four states – California, Kentucky, Georgia, and Wyoming – do not suspend for unpaid court debt at all."). For Kansas data, see Alexis Padilla, Over 227,000 Kansans Have a Suspended Driver's License, KSN.com, Oct. 2021, www.ksn.com/news/local/kansas-non-profit-hosting-free-clinic-to-help-drivers-with-suspended-license/. For the North Carolina study, see William E. Crozier & Brandon L. Garrett, *Driven to Failure: An Empirical Analysis of Driver's License Suspension in North Carolina*, 69 *Duke Law Journal* 1585, 1590 (2020).

Chapter 21

1 See John Gramlich, What the Data Says (and Doesn't Say) about Crime in the United States, PEW Research Center, Nov. 20, 2020, www.pewresearch.org/fact-tank/2020/11/20/facts-about-crime-in-the-u-s/.

2 See Council on Criminal Justice, Update: Pandemic, Social Unrest, and Crime in U.S. Cities, June 2021, counciloncj.org/impact-report-1/.

3 For clearance rate data, see FBI, UCR: Percent of Offenses Cleared by Arrest or Exceptional Means, ucr.fbi.gov/crime-in-the-u.s/2019/crime-in-the-u.s.-2019/tables/table-25 (2019); and Charles Wellford and James Cronin,

Clearing Up Homicide Clearance Rates, April 2000, www.ojp.gov/pdffiles1/
jr000243b.pdf (offering historical data).

4 For insights into this phenomenon see, Jill Leovy, *Ghettoside: A True Story of
Murder in America* (2015); and Monica C. Bell, Police Reform and the
Dismantling of Legal Estrangement, 126 *Yale Law Journal* 2054, 2116 (2017).

5 Aaron Chalfin et al., Police Force Size and Civilian Race, National Bureau of
Economic Research, Dec. 2020, www.nber.org/system/files/working_papers/
w28202/w28202.pdf.

6 Thomas Abt, *Bleeding Out* 84, 88 (2019).

7 Graham Farrell, Nick Tilley, Andromachi Tseloni, Why the Crime Drop? 43
Crime & Just. 421, 458 (2014).

8 Sarah Maslin Nir, Here's Why Car Thefts Are Soaring, *N.Y. Times*, Jan. 6,
2021, www.nytimes.com/2021/01/06/nyregion/car-thefts-nyc.html.

9 A. B. Chafin, et al., Reducing Crime through Environmental Design, *Journal
of Quantitative Crime* 1–31 (2021); Anne Sofie Tegner Anker et al., The
Effects of DNA Databases on the Deterrence and Detection of Offenders, 13
(4) *American Economic Journal: Applied Economics* (Oct. 2021), www.aeaweb
.org/articles?id=10.1257/app.20190207.

10 E. L. Piza, B. C. Welsh, D. P. Farrington, & A. L. Thomas, CCTV
Surveillance for Crime Prevention: A 40-year Systematic Review with
Meta-analysis, 18(1) *Criminology & Public Policy* 135–59 at 148 (2019).

11 David Mitre-Becerril et al., *Can Deterrence Persist? Long-Term Evidence from
a Randomized Experiment in Street Lighting* (2022).

12 For a related argument that one way to achieve "a reduction of hard surveillance of people of color" is to "require an increase in soft surveillance
of everyone"; see I. Bennett Capers, Race, Policing, and Technology,
95 *North Carolina Law Review* 1241 (2017).

13 *Utah* v. *Strieff*, 579 U.S. 232 (2016).

14 See Brice Cooke et al., Using Behavioral Science to Improve Criminal Justice
Outcomes, Ideas 42, Jan. 2018 www.ideas42.org/wp-content/uploads/2018/
03/Using-Behavioral-Science-to-Improve-Criminal-Justice-Outcomes.pdf.

Chapter 22

1 BJS, Prisoners 1925–81, bjs.ojp.gov/content/pub/pdf/p2581.pdf at Table 1.
This historical rate does not capture all of the era's jail population. See
pp. 2–3.

2 kingcounty.gov/depts/community-human-services/mental-health-substance-
abuse/diversion-reentry-services/lead.aspx.

3 Michael Rempel et al., *Center for Court Innovation, The New York State
Adult Drug Court Evaluation: Policies, Participants and Impacts*, at 270
(2003) (Table 18.2). For further discussion, see Josh Bowers,
Contraindicated Drug Courts, 55 *UCLA Law Review* 783 (2008).

4 See Prison Policy Initiative, March 24, 2020, www.prisonpolicy.org/reports/
   pie2020.html.
5 Anna Roberts, Dismissals as Justice, 69 *Alabama Law Review* 327, 330
   (2017); Minn. Stat. Ann. § 631.21 (West 2009).
6 BJS, Prisoners 1978 at 6, https://bjs.ojp.gov/content/pub/pdf/psfi78.pdf.
7 Information on this reform can be found in New Jersey Courts, Report to the
   Governor and the Legislature, in 2019 and 2018, www.njcourts.gov/courts/
   assets/criminal/cjrannualreport2019.pdf;   www.njcourts.gov/courts/assets/
   criminal/2018cjrannual.pdf; and the MDRC Center for Criminal Justice
   Research, Evaluation of Pretrial Justice System Reforms That Use the
   Public Safety Assessment, 2019, www.mdrc.org/sites/default/files/PSA_
   New_Jersey_Report_%231.pdf.
8 Emily Bazelon, *Charged* 290 (2019).
9 For arguments along these lines, see John Pfaff, *Locked In* (2017), and
   Rachel Barkow, *Prisoners of Politics* (2021). For the California study, see
   Aurélie Ouss, Misaligned Incentives and the Scale of Incarceration in
   the United States, *Journal of Public Economics* 191, 2020; for Missouri and
   Philadelphia examples, see Heather Ratcliffe, Missouri Judges Get Penalty
   Cost before Sentencing, *St. Louis Dispatch*, Sept. 14, 2010, www.stltoday
   .com/news/local/crime-and-courts/article_924097a5-9f4d-54bb-80ca-
   4cc4160dde7c.html; Philadelphia's New DA Wants Prosecutors to Talk
   Cost of Incarceration While in Court, NPR, March 31, 2018, www.npr.org/
   2018/03/31/598318897/philadephias-new-da-wants-prosecutors-to-talk-cost-
   of-incarceration-while-in-cou.
10 For a description of Minnesota's unique process, see Dale G. Parent, What
    Did the United States Sentencing Commission Miss? 101 *Yale Law
    Journal* 1773, 1784 (1992).
11 Ashley Nellis, No End in Sight: America's Enduring Reliance on Life
    Imprisonment, The Sentencing Project, Feb. 20, 2020, sentencingproject.
    org/publications/no-end-in-sight-americas-enduring-reliance-on-life-impris-
    onment/.
12 For a summary of judicial appointment and election rules, see www
    .brennancenter.org/our-work/research-reports/judicial-selection-significant-
    figures.
13 See Matt McKillop & Alex Boucher, Aging Prison Populations Drive Up
    Costs, PEW Charitable Trusts, Feb. 20, 2018 www.pewtrusts.org/en/
    research-and-analysis/articles/2018/02/20/aging-prison-populations-drive-
    up-costs.
14 Michael Rocque, Chad Posick, and Justin Hoyle, Age and Crime, in
    The Encyclopedia of Crime and Punishment, 2016 onlinelibrary.wiley.com/
    doi/pdf/10.1002/9781118519639.wbecpx275#:~:text=This%20relationship
    %20shows%20that%20crime,not%20questioned%20by%20schol%2D%20ars.
15 BJS, Prisoners 1925–81 at 1, bjs.ojp.gov/content/pub/pdf/p2581.pdf.

16 For RDAP, see Federal Bureau of Prisons, www.bop.gov/inmates/custody_
and_care/substance_abuse_treatment.jsp. For effectiveness, see B. Pelissier
et al., Federal Prison Residential Drug Treatment Reduces Substance Use
and Arrests after Release, 27(2) *American Journal of Drug and Alcohol Abuse,*
315–37 May 2001; and Federal Bureau of Prisons, TRIAD Drug Treatment
Evaluation Project, www.bop.gov/resources/TRIAD.jsp.

INDEX

CPSIA information can be obtained
at www.ICGtesting.com
Printed in the USA
LVHW081057150123
737198LV00006B/598